BPEC	Appliance Specific G

Course Structure

Appliance Specific Gas Safety Modules

- Module 17 Domestic Central Heating and Water Heaters (CENWAT)
- Module 18 Domestic Cookers (CKR1)
- Module 19 Domestic Space Heaters, Gas Fires and Wall Heaters (HTR1)
- Module 20 Domestic Warm Air (DAH1)

Introduction

All operatives are required to prove their competence in Gas Safety, Installation, Service and Maintenance.

Since 1st August 1998 that proof of competence has been carried out through the Nationally Accredited Certification Scheme (ACS) for Individual Gas Fitting Operatives. Each operative is required to have successfully completed the assessment requirements laid down by an accredited UKAS certification body and then be re-assessed at periods of no more than five years.

The BPEC Services Ltd – CCN1 Initial/Re-assessment Domestic Gas course is intended to provide the training required to support proving competence in this area of work.

Training Objectives

The aim of this open learning/tutor taught training package is to furnish you with the information to enable the **Nationally Accredited Certification Scheme (ACS)** assessments for appropriate appliances to be completed.

Method of Study

You can undertake the study by either self learning:

In which case you are required to study through the manuals at your own time and pace undertaking the questions highlighted in the knowledge question manual when prompted at the end of each module. You will then attend an approved assessment centre to undertake assessment.

NOTE: To undertake assessment you must:

    a) Feel that you can completely meet all the knowledge objective requirements, and

    b) Feel that you can competently carry out practical tasks covering the full range of modules discussed.

Or alternatively you can attend a training course at a BPEC training centre. You will progress through the course manuals in a structured learning environment. In addition, you will also work through a course practical task manual which links directly to the practical performance requirements identified previously.

If in doubt about completing the practical or knowledge requirements, it is always advisable to go for the BPEC training course option.

| BPEC | Module 17 |

Contents

	Page
Introduction	2
Section 1 – Types of Appliances and their Operating Principles	3
Part 1 – Wet Central Heating/Hot Water Boilers	3
Part 2 – Circulators	12
Section 2 – Installation and Commissioning of Central Heating Boilers and Circulators	14
Part 1 – Permitted Installation Locations for Appliances	14
Part 2 – Appliances Installed in Cupboards/Compartments	15
Part 3 – Roof Space Installations	18
Part 4 – Fireback Installations	19
Part 5 – Flue Requirements for Central Heating Boilers and Circulators	21
Part 6 – Commissioning of Central Heating Boilers and Circulators	23
Section 3 – Service, Maintenance and Repair of Central Heating Boilers and Circulators	29
Part 1 – Unsafe Situations – Case Seals	29
Part 2 – Service and Maintenance of Central Heating Boilers and Circulators	29
Part 3 – Typical Gas Components Faults on Central Heating Boilers and Circulators	34
Section 4 – Types of Appliances and their Operating Principles	40
Part 1 – Small Instantaneous Hot Water Heaters	41
Part 2 – Large Instantaneous Hot Water Heaters	44
Section 5 – Installation and Commissioning of Instantaneous Hot Water Heaters	50
Part 1 – Permitted Installation Locations for Appliances	50
Part 2 – Commissioning of Instantaneous Hot Water Heaters	51
Section 6 – Service, Maintenance and Repair of Instantaneous Hot Water Heaters	54
Part 1 – Unsafe Situations	54
Part 2 – Service and Maintenance of Instantaneous Hot Water Heaters	54
Part 3 – Typical Gas Component Faults on Instantaneous Hot Water Heaters	57
Practical Tasks	61
Knowledge Questions	74
Model Answers	79

Introduction

The objective of this module is to enable you to successfully complete assessment across the following range of gas fired central heating boilers and instantaneous water heaters:
- Open flued.
- Room sealed (natural and fanned draught).
- Condensing.
- Back boiler units.
- Combination boilers.
- Combination units.
- Flueless – single point (under 12kW heat input).
- Large multipoint heaters – open flued, room sealed natural draught and fan assisted.

You will be required to prove that you can install, disconnect, service, repair, breakdown and commission domestic gas fired central heating/hot water boilers and circulators up to 70kW and domestic gas fired instantaneous water heaters.

Practically, you should be able to ensure the following:
- The appliance assembly is complete and is fit for purpose.
- The gas supply is isolated prior to work commencing.
- The appliance is correctly sealed to the balanced flue set.
- The appliance is correctly sealed to the open flue set.
- The gas supply is re-established.
- The work carried out is gas tight.
- The appliance is correctly located, level and stable.
- The appliance operational gas safety components are dismantled and cleaned, using appropriate cleaning methods and agents (e.g. burners, primary air ports, combustion chambers, ignition devices, thermostat, limit stats, pressure switches and flame supervision).
- The appliance is commissioned as follows:
  - The appliance is purged of air.
  - The working pressure at the appliance is correct.
  - The burner flame pictures, stability and ignition are correct.
  - The user controls are operating correctly.
  - The safety control devices are operating correctly.
  - The temperature controls are operating correctly.
- The flue connections are sound and flues are operating correctly.
- Defects on gas safety components are identified.
- The safe operation and use of the appliance is explained.

Additionally, you should know the following:
- Identification of unsafe conditions.
- Diagnosis of gas safety faults.
- The effects of unsatisfactory appliance case seals.
- Recognition of suitable and unsuitable appliance room/space locations.
- Clearance requirements (proximity of combustible materials) and fire proofing of compartments.
- The operation of mechanical and electrical controls.

Section 1 – Types of Appliances and their Operating Principles

Introduction

In sections 1 to 3 you shall be taking a look at the various types of appliances and the key operating principles of:

- Wet central heating/hot water boilers.
- Circulators.

Part 1 – Wet Central Heating/Hot Water Boilers

For the purposes of this module wet central heating/hot water boilers shall be defined as gas appliances designed to provide heat to wet space heating systems or combined wet space heating and hot water systems.

What types of appliance are available?

Boilers generally fall into one of three categories, related to possible positions where they may be sited:

- Floor standing.
- Wall mounted.
- Back boilers (behind a fire) GFBB (gas fired back boilers).

These categories can be manufactured as open flued room sealed or fanned draught models with the exception of back boilers, which are only available as open flued appliances.

Boilers can, however, be categorised further:

- Open flued or fanned draught.
- Room sealed – natural draught or fanned draught.
- System boilers.
- Combination boilers.
- Combination units.
- Condensing boilers.

By understanding the operating principles of these six appliance types, you should be able to describe how the mechanical and electrical controls operate within the majority of appliances which you may have to install or maintain.

| BPEC | Domestic Central Heating and Water Heaters (CENWAT) |

Natural draught room sealed

Figure 1 is an exploded diagram of a typical room sealed natural draught gas boiler. The casing and control panel (including the boiler thermostat) have been omitted from the diagram for the purposes of clarity.

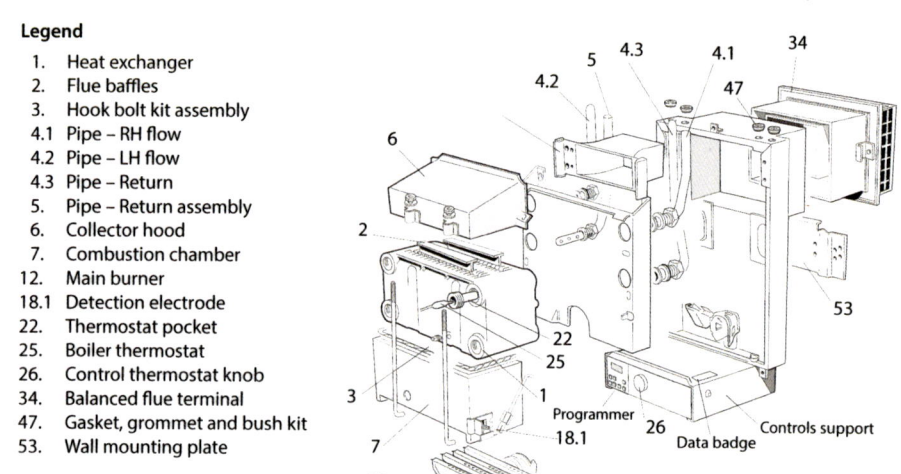

Legend
1. Heat exchanger
2. Flue baffles
3. Hook bolt kit assembly
4.1 Pipe – RH flow
4.2 Pipe – LH flow
4.3 Pipe – Return
5. Pipe – Return assembly
6. Collector hood
7. Combustion chamber
12. Main burner
18.1 Detection electrode
22. Thermostat pocket
25. Boiler thermostat
26. Control thermostat knob
34. Balanced flue terminal
47. Gasket, grommet and bush kit
53. Wall mounting plate

Figure 1: Typical room sealed natural draught floor standing boiler

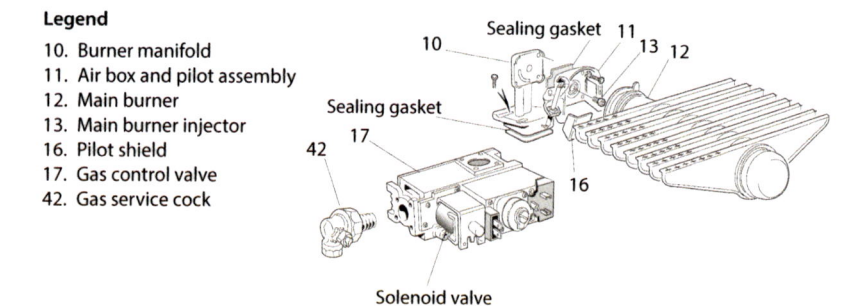

Legend
10. Burner manifold
11. Air box and pilot assembly
12. Main burner
13. Main burner injector
16. Pilot shield
17. Gas control valve
42. Gas service cock

Figure 2: Burner and controls

© BPEC   April 2017

How does the appliance work?

The boiler shown incorporates a combination of both mechanical and electrical gas control devices. It uses a permanent pilot as its source of main burner ignition.

Gas is supplied via the service cock (the main point of appliance gas isolation) to the inlet of the multifunctional control valve, which incorporates:

- Constant pressure governor.
- Flame supervision device (in this case working on the thermo-electric principle, using a thermocouple).
- Solenoid valve.

A pilot pipe and thermocouple lead connect the multifunctional control valve to the pilot assembly, which is situated adjacent to the main burner. The function of the pilot is to light the main burner. The pilot assembly incorporates:

- Pilot burner (incorporating pilot injector).
- Thermocouple.
- Spark electrode.

The spark electrode is connected via a lead to the piezo unit; its function is to light the pilot burner.

The purpose of the flame supervision section of the multifunctional control valve and its associated thermocouple is to only permit a flow of gas to the main burner when the presence of a pilot flame has been detected. The gas governor section of the control valve allows for adjustment of gas flow through to the main burner. The electric solenoid valve section provides for on/off operation of the main burner.

A boiler (control) thermostat, which can usually be adjusted in terms of water temperature, is electrically connected to the solenoid section of the multifunctional valve. The thermostat, includes a thermostat phial and lead. The phial is placed inside the thermostat pocket, which projects into the heat exchanger waterways. The thermostat electrically activates the solenoid valve in response to water temperature fluctuations.

The outlet of the multifunctional control valve connects directly to the main burner via connecting pipework. The gas itself is discharged into the main burner through an injector.

In the case of room sealed appliances, the air supply is entrained from the outside of the building via the air duct assembly directly into the combustion chamber of the appliance.

Flue gases are discharged through the heat exchanger (which may include a series of flue baffles) into the collector hood, discharging to outside air via the flue duct assembly.

Natural draught open flued

The appliance in Figure 3 is a natural draught flued back boiler. Its gas controls operate on the same principle as those previously for the room sealed model, with the exception of the atmosphere (vitiation) sensing device (ASD). Its purpose is to extinguish the pilot and eliminate gas flow through to the burner in the event of incorrect combustion taking place. The appliance shown above incorporates a combined thermocouple/atmosphere sensing device. Also shown in Figure 3 is the sensing pipe, which is connected to the pilot aeration tube.

The open flued appliance's primary air supply for combustion is drawn from the space in which it is located. Figure 3 shows the lint arrestor, which prevents lint from entering into the main burner. The flue gases are discharged via the flue outlet to a traditional open flue. In this appliance the down draught diverter, which is required on open flued boilers, is built into the flue hood connection. In this case a gas fire also discharges into the flue hood.

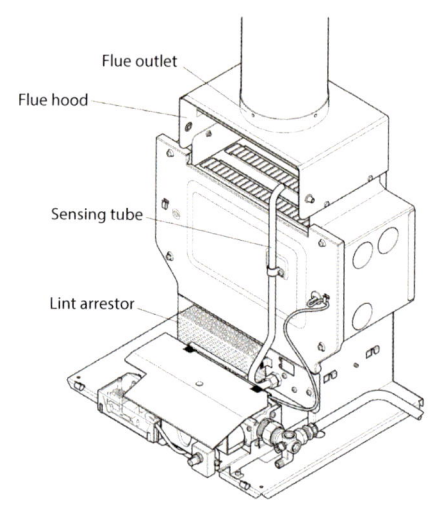

Figure 3: Natural draught open flued back boiler

Open flued fanned draught

Certain manufacturers produce open flued appliances that incorporate a fan in the flue system. This helps increase the appliance's efficiency and makes them compliant with the requirements of SEDBUK (Seasonal efficiency of domestic boilers in the UK). All new boilers installed should now have a SEDBUK rating of A.

An open flued fanned draught system is not reliant on the motive force created by buoyancy – or in simple terms, density difference between the hot flue gases and the colder air surrounding the flue. Motive force is created by the fan in the appliance.

Open flued fanned draught appliances have greater siting options, with more flexibility on flue routes than that of an open flued natural draught type.

Open flued fanned draught systems incorporate:
- A primary flue.
- A draught diverter.
- A secondary flue.
- A terminal.

Because the flue system is reliant on the fan to clear the products of combustion, the current Gas Safety (Installation and Use) Regulations 1998 require that the system must incorporate a fan sensing device to prevent the burner lighting, should the fan fail.

Forced draught burner

Forced draught burners are not a new concept as they have been used within the non-domestic gas sector for many years, however with continued demands being placed on manufacturers to develop more energy efficient gas-fired appliances there has been a marked rise in their use within the domestic market.

Whereas a natural draught burner uses the gas to induce a portion of its combustion air with any additional air required for complete combustion taken from the combustion chamber, a forced draught burner uses a fan to "force" all the air required for complete combustion to the burner head. Being 100% pre-mix means that there is no requirement for additional air to be present within the combustion chamber ultimately increasing the combustion efficiency of the appliance.

With these types of burner the fan can be located either upstream or downstream of the heat exchanger. A fan upstream will push air into the burner resulting in the combustion chamber being at a positive pressure whereas a fan downstream will induce (suck) air into the burner resulting in the combustion chamber being at a negative pressure. The method used is dependent on application and manufacturers preference of design. In most cases domestic appliances have the fan upstream. Since the operation of the fan is imperative for the safe operation of the appliance a pressure switch is used to ensure the fan is running before gas is introduced into the burner.

To ensure the burner operates safely throughout its operational range, the air/gas mixture was, and in some cases still is, adjusted manually, however with advancements in burner design to suit the smaller burner application methods have now been introduced where, once set by the manufacturer, the burner will adjust automatically over the appliance operational range.

One such development is the air/gas ratio control valve that uses the suction generated by the combustion fan to induce the correct amount of gas required for complete combustion. Increasing and decreasing the speed of the fan can vary the amount of suction placed on the air/gas ratio control valve in turn automatically varying the amount of gas induced into the burner relative to the available air. This type of control sometimes uses a zero governor which allows gas to flow at a positive pressure equal and opposite to that generated by the fan, therefore the burner pressure would read zero on a gauge no matter the throughput of the control. Since the combustion fan induces the gas, if the fan were to fail no gas would be present at burner, therefore removing the requirement for an air pressure switch.

The fan speed, and in turn the heat input of the appliance, is controlled by means of a pcb linked to a thermistor which senses the temperature in the appliance waterways. This optimum control ensures the correct amount of heat is transferred into the water depending on its temperature greatly increasing the efficiency of the appliance.

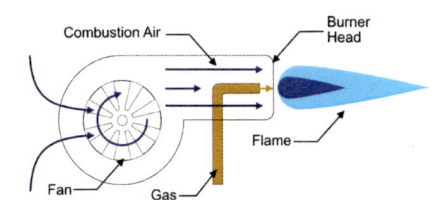

Figure 4a: Normal forced draught burner

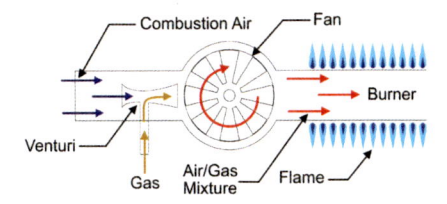

Figure 4b: Forced draught burner with air/gas ratio

Additional features of natural draught appliances

In addition, natural draught boilers may have an overheat (limit) device. This may be fitted as standard on low water content appliances or could be an optional extra on other models. Overheat devices can be either a direct acting, which are wired in line with the temperature control thermostat and the gas valve on the appliance, or indirect acting, which form part of the flame supervision device and shuts down the gas supply from the gas valve via a thermocouple interrupter. The purpose of the device is to provide added protection to the appliance in the event of thermostat failure.

An overheat thermostat must always be incorporated in the boiler controls where sealed water heating systems are used.

The electrical controls on the appliance, dependent on the model type, may be either 240 volts or alternatively they may be low voltage, usually 24 volts, supplied via a transformer.

Fanned draught

Gas fired fanned draught boilers may be open or room sealed appliances, incorporating either of the following main burner lighting arrangements:

- Permanent pilot.
- Intermittent pilot.

The fan

A fan is used to assist with removal of the products of combustion and to supply combustion air. The principal additional safety feature is the air pressure switch, which must be fitted to all fan assisted appliances. The pressure switch prevents the boiler's lighting sequence taking place in the event of the fan not operating.

A different multifunctional control valve is used in fanned draught appliances to that which is used in natural draught appliances. For natural draught appliances, flame supervision is carried out using electronic circuitry built into the printed circuit board (PCB).

The multifunctional valve in fanned draught appliances uses a solenoid as a means of allowing gas flow to the pilot (which operates on an intermittent basis). The presence of a flame at the pilot light is relayed back to the PCB via the combined ignition/detection electrode. The PCB also provides automatic spark generation to light the pilot.

The following shows the boiler's sequence of operation:

Step 1

- Thermostat – calls for heat.
- Fan starts.
- Air pressure switch detects fan operation.

Step 2

- PCB activates pilot spark ignition.
- Spark occurs at pilot assembly.
- Pilot solenoid is activated – allows gas flow through to pilot burner.
- Pilot ignites.

Step 3

- Ignition/detection electrode senses the presence of a flame.
- Spark ignition stops.
- Main solenoid allows gas flow to main burner.
- Main burner lights.

Figure 5 illustrates the electrics in a fanned draught appliance.

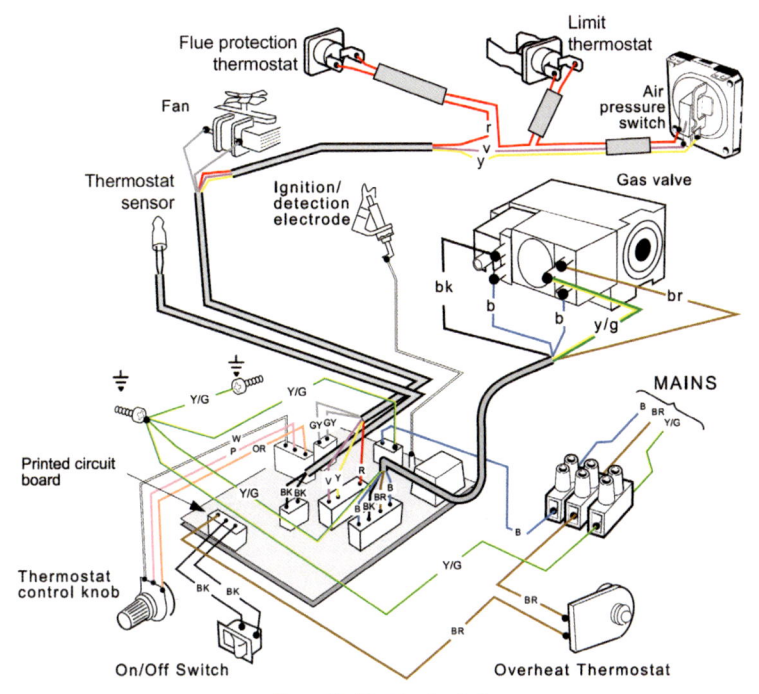

Figure 5: Electric circuit diagram

Figure 5 shows the electrical components, including the overheat thermostat, which provides for over-heat protection of the appliance. There are two types of overheat thermostat:
- Manual reset.
- Automatic reset.

Figure 5 also shows the manual reset version with its associated push button. Manual reset is regarded as the safest option, as the boiler will not re-fire again until the reset button is pressed, and the possible cause of fault investigated.

Fanned draught appliances may be incorporated in open flue systems, again employing an air pressure switch to protect against fan failure.

Fanned draught appliances may also operate using a permanent pilot light arrangement. The permanent pilot version incorporates a combination of gas/electrical controls including:
- Air pressure switch.
- Fan.
- Multifunctional control valve – utilising the thermo-electric flame supervision principle.
- Thermostat(s).

| BPEC | Domestic Central Heating and Water Heaters (CENWAT) |

The fan itself usually incorporates a two speed motor. Low speed (when the boiler main burner is not firing) is to clear the products of combustion of the pilot burner. High speed fan operation is for when the boiler calls for heat. If the fan fails, the air pressure switch will not activate and therefore the main burner cannot light. Eventually, the pilot light becomes starved of oxygen and extinguishes itself, causing the multifunctional control valve to activate and the gas supply to be cut.

System boilers

A system boiler is a boiler which incorporates the main central heating system safety devices, control components, pumps etc. either within the boiler casing or alternatively, as shown in Figure 11, in an add-on kit linked to a standard boiler model. System boilers are available usually in fan flued or open flued options, incorporating permanent or intermittent pilot lighting arrangements.

The gas/electric controls within the boiler operate on the same principles as those already highlighted for natural and fan assisted appliances. For boilers specifically designed for sealed systems, they may also include a low water pressure cut-off, which prevents the boiler from operating if the system pressure is too low.

Combination boilers

By a combination boiler we mean a boiler which gives us the advantage of central heating and domestic hot water combined within the one unit. In other words there is no requirement for a traditional hot water storage system, as the domestic hot water is delivered instantaneously from the boiler via the mains water supply.

The combination boiler works as illustrated in Figure 6.

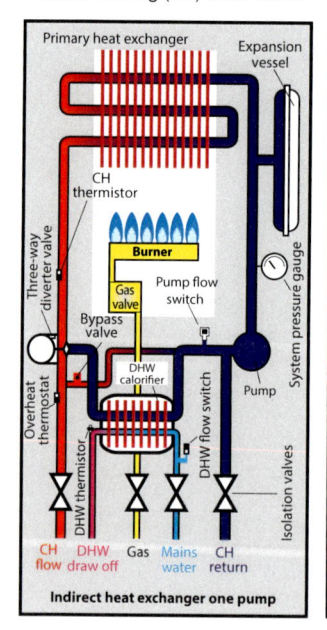

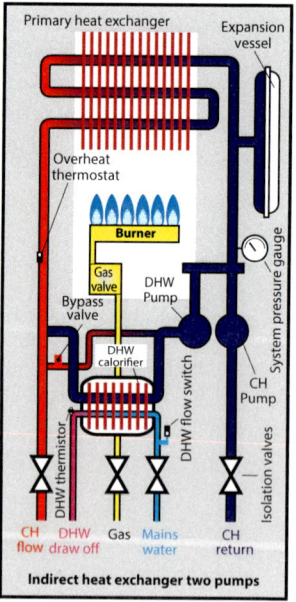

Figure 6: Combination boiler operation

© BPEC

April 2017

With no call for CH, the boiler fires only when DHW is drawn off. When there is a call for CH, the heating system is supplied at the selected temperature until DHW is drawn off. The full output from the boiler is then directed via the diverter valve to the calorifier, to supply a maximum DHW draw off (e.g. hot water taking priority over central heating).

Combination boilers may be open flued, room sealed or fan assisted appliances, incorporating either permanent or intermittent pilots.

The central heating circuit works on the same principle as the system boiler.

The word condensing describes the way that the boiler achieves its high efficiency (approx 94% efficient during condensing mode).

The actual principle is quite simple. At the centre of all boilers is a heat exchanger through which water flows. The water is heated by a gas burner.

This process does not always use all of the energy that the gas burner releases; in fact the flue gas temperature from an ordinary gas boiler is in the region of 170°C to 250°C.

The condensing boiler uses this normally wasted flue gas temperature to heat the extra tubes of its heat exchanger. Because of this, the flue gas temperature exiting the boiler is less than 75°C. By utilising this normally wasted heat, the condensing boiler is able to heat a central heating system with less fuel than a conventional boiler.

With the flue gases being at a low temperature, the products of combustion contains a higher content of water vapour (condense), hence the name condensing boiler.

To handle the water vapour, which is in the form of a weak acid, condensing boiler components, such as heat exchangers, need to be manufactured of different materials to their traditional counterparts to minimise corrosion. The boiler contains a sump, in which the waste collects prior to being discharged via a siphon to an appropriate drainage point. The boiler may also incorporate a sump blockage detector, shown in Figure 7.

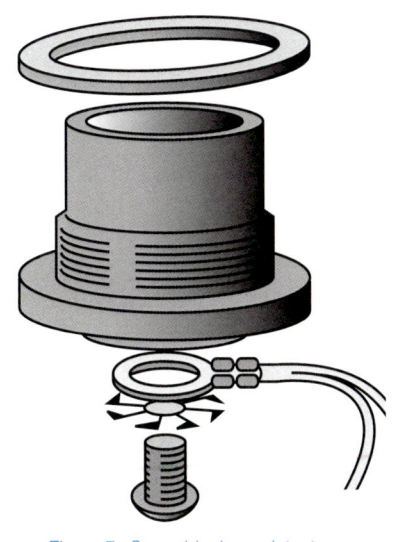

Figure 7: Sump blockage detector

This device detects blockages in the discharge pipework, preventing the boiler from operating.

BPEC   Domestic Central Heating and Water Heaters (CENWAT)

Part 2 – Circulators

British Standard – BS 5546: 2010 for gas-fired water heating appliances defines a circulator as a water heating appliance with a heat input not exceeding 6kW (net) designed for the production of sanitary hot water by gravity circulation. They are available as:

- Fireback models (back circulator unit).
- Wall mounted models.

Flueing options can be:

- Open flued.
- Room sealed.

Modern room sealed circulators incorporate gas/electrical controls which are common with their central heating boiler counterparts. We shall therefore not consider the operating principles of these appliances further.

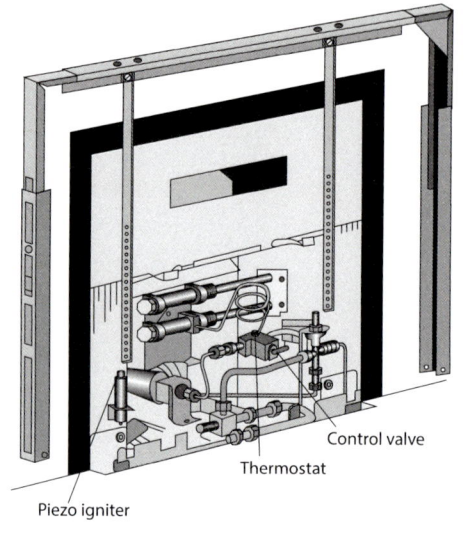

Figure 8: Gas fired back circulator

Traditional circulators do, however, differ from central heating boilers in that they use mechanically operated gas controls. Figure 8 is an exploded diagram of a gas fired back circulator (the gas fire section omitted for the purposes of clarity).

The gas controls are shown in Figure 9.

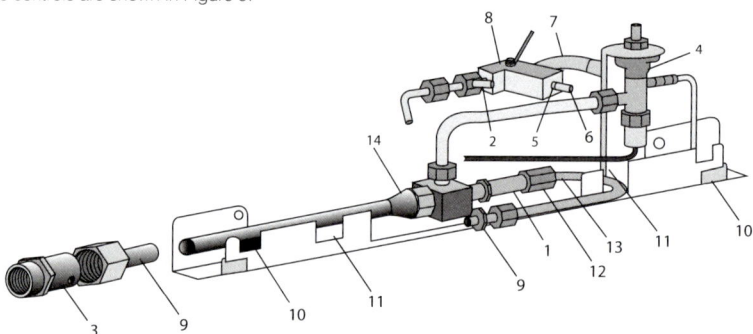

Legend

1. Gas fire service cock
2. Pressure test point
3. Main service cock
4. Control valve
5. Releasing screw
6. Spindle
7. Locking plate
8. Thermal housing
9. Gas fire adaptor
10. Tube clip
11. Thermocouple
12. Union nut
13. Connection pipe
14. Connector

Figure 9: Gas controls

© BPEC   12   April 2017

The flame supervision device works on the thermo-electric principle (some circulators employ bi-metallic strips) and is connected to a manual control valve providing the following functions:

- Flame supervision.
- Gas supply to the pilot light.
- Gas supply to the main burner via the thermostat.

The thermocouple and pilot tube from the control valve connect to a burner assembly, situated adjacent to the main burner. The pilot lighting procedure is via a piezo igniter. The pilot light is established using the same principles as those identified for natural draught central heating boilers.

Once the pilot light has been successfully established, the control valve is manually turned to the main burner position.

The thermostat directly controls the amount of gas supplied to the burner, based on the demand for heat.

The thermostat in this case modulates the gas rate down as water temperature increases, until a bypass rate is reached, which keeps the water at the correct temperature and prevents cycling of the appliance.

The control valve can be moved to pilot only, during periods when heat is not required.

Section 2 – Installation and Commissioning of Central Heating Boilers and Circulators

Introduction

In this section we shall focus on the key installation and commissioning aspects of wet central heating/hot water boilers and circulators by looking at:

- Permitted installation locations for appliances installed in cupboards/compartments.
- Roof space installations.
- Fireplace installations.
- Flue requirements for central heating boilers and circulators.
- Installation of central heating boilers and circulators.
- Commissioning of central heating boilers and circulators.

Some of the information contained in Parts 1 to 4 may seem familiar from other modules, but have been mentioned again in the context of central heating boilers.

Part 1 – Permitted Installation Locations for Appliances

Central heating boilers and circulators cannot be installed in any room. It is usually the appliance flue type which affects the rooms in which central heating boilers and circulators may be installed.

Remember that wherever possible, it is preferable to install a room sealed appliance as the safest option.

Bathrooms/shower room

Open flued appliances may not be installed in bathrooms or shower rooms.

Room sealed appliances may be installed, but there are restrictions placed on the actual appliance location (for appliances incorporating electric's) by the IET Wiring Regulations 17th Edition.

Toilets/cloakrooms

It is strongly recommended that **only** room sealed appliances are installed in these rooms.

Where open flued appliances are installed, air supply for combustion (where required) should be provided direct from the outside air.

Private garages

Up until 31st October 1994, the installation of open flued appliances in private garages was not permitted. A relaxation brought about by the revised Gas Safety (Installation and Use) Regulations 1998 now permits open flued installations in this location.

Sleeping accommodation

Appliances over 14kW heat input gross must be room sealed.

As of 1st January 1996, opened flued appliances rated at under 14kW, input gross may be installed. However, the appliance must have a safety device (atmosphere sensing device) for automatic shutdown of the appliance in the event of a build-up of products of combustion.

Where a combined appliance is used (a back boiler and gas fire), the 14kW limit applies to the total heat input gross of both appliances, i.e. the input (gross) for the gas fire should be added to the back boiler input, so to determine whether the appliance may be installed.

For water heating appliances, where the room volume is less than 20m^3, the appliance must be room sealed.

Note: Installation of appliances in a bedroom or bed-sitting room should only be considered where no other practicable alternative location is available.

Other siting issues

There are further limitations placed on the siting of boilers and circulators, namely:

- The provision of adequate space, in accordance with the manufacturer's installation instructions:
  - To ensure sufficient air circulation for draught diverter operation.
  - To ensure sufficient air for combustion and cooling purposes.
  - To allow for maintenance and servicing, e.g. removal of the burner tray.
- Protection of the floor or wall on which the appliance is mounted, in line with the manufacturer's installation instructions.

Part 2 – Appliances Installed in Cupboards/Compartments

British Standards – BS 6798: 2014: *Specification for selection, installation, inspection, commissioning, servicing and maintenance of gas-fired boilers of rated input not exceeding 70kW net, and BS 5546: 2010: Specification for installation and maintenance of gas-fired water heating appliances of rated input not exceeding 70kW net*, place restrictions on the installation of boilers and circulators in the following situations:

- Compartments.
- Airing cupboards.
- Under stairs cupboards.

What is a compartment?

A compartment is an enclosure specifically designed or adapted to house a gas appliance.

Open flued appliances should not be installed in cupboards and compartments located in sleeping accommodation, unless the appliance is under 14kW heat input (gross) and incorporate an atmosphere (vitiation) sensing device (ASD).

Open-flue boilers and circulators must not be installed in a cupboard or compartment where access to the appliance is gained from, or any openings intrude into, a bathroom or shower room.

Compartment installations

Figure 10 illustrates an installation in a compartment.

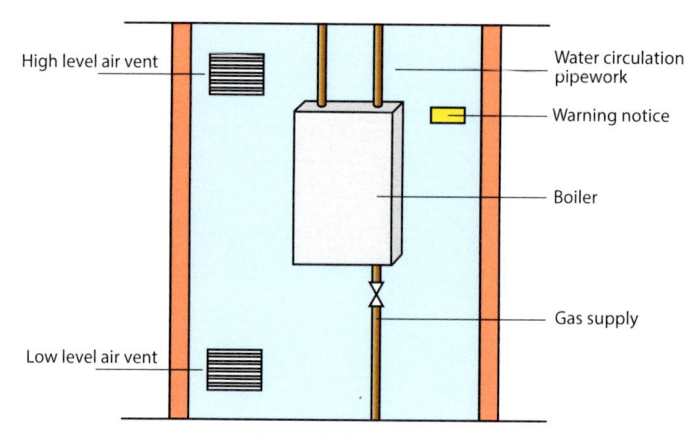

Figure 10: Installation in compartment

Compartments housing central heating boilers and circulators must:

- Be fixed, rigid structures with internal surfaces that comply with any special requirements of the appliance manufacturer. If these are not known, combustible materials should be at least 75mm from the boiler, or where this is not possible, a non-combustible shield of at least 25mm thickness should be provided.
- Allow access for inspection.
- Allow access for maintenance.
- Utilise a warning notice advising against:
  – It being used for the purposes of storage.
  – Blocking or restricting of any air vents or grilles into the compartment.
- Be ventilated in accordance with the requirements of BS 5440-2: 2009: *Flueing and ventilation for gas appliances of rated input not exceeding 70kW net* – (some room sealed appliances do not require compartments to be ventilated).

Compartment ventilation for an open-flue boiler or circulator must not communicate, either directly or indirectly, with a room containing a bath or shower, a bedroom or a bed-sitting room.

Additional requirements for compartments opening into bedrooms

Installing an open flued appliance in a compartment which opens into a bedroom should only be considered as an absolute last resort, where there are no other location options the compartment should include the following additional features:

- A draught proofed self-closing door.
- Label to indicate the door must be closed at all times, except for the re-setting of controls.
- The compartment must not be used as an airing cupboard, or for storage purposes.
- Additional warning notices should state that the compartment should not be used for purposes other than housing the boiler, and that the door must be kept closed at all times.
- The appliance must have a heat input rating below 12.7kW (net) or 14kW (gross) and must incorporate an atmosphere sensing device (ASD), to shut down the appliance before there is high build-up of dangerous combustion products into the room concerned.

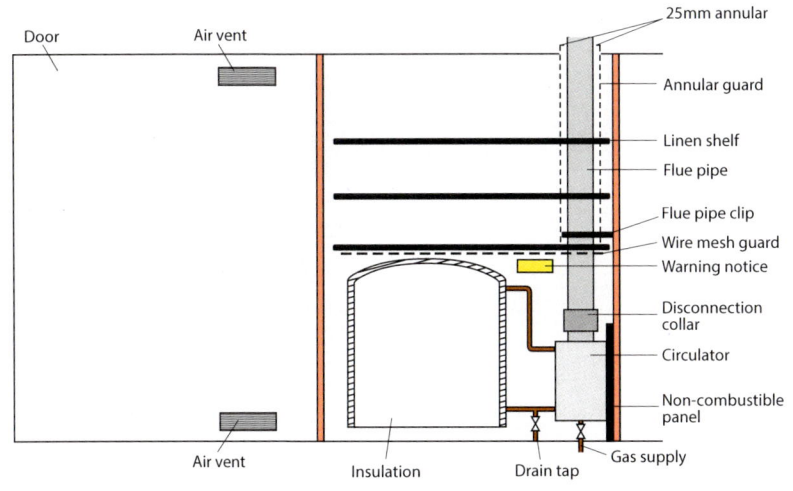

Figure 11: Compartment as airing cupboard

If a compartment is to be used as an airing cupboard, as shown in Figure 11, it must comply with the compartment details shown in the previous pages, and also the following:

- The airing space must be separated from the boiler by a partition, wire mesh or be in a frame.

Any perforations in the mesh or frame should be no larger than 13mm.

- If the boiler or circulator is of the open flued type, the flue will also need to be protected with at least a 25mm air gap between the flue and protecting material. Where twin walled flue pipe is to be used, the air gap between the two walls may be considered to be adequate protection.
- The compartment should have a warning label fitted, highlighting that any ventilation grills or louvres should not be blocked or restricted.

There is potential fire hard risk from storing, airing or drying outside the purpose provided storage area.

Understairs cupboard installations

Where the understairs cupboard housing the boiler or circulator is in a property with no more than two stories, the general compartment requirements are as follows:

In buildings of more than two stories, all the internal surfaces of the compartment must be non-combustible or be lined with a material providing 30 minutes fire resistance, in accordance with BS 476-22. Additionally, all air vents must communicate directly with the outside air.

Installation in an understairs cupboard should only be considered if there is no other alternative suitable location. Wherever possible, the boiler in an understairs cupboard should be of the room sealed type.

Part 3 – Roof Space Installations

Boilers and circulators installed in roof space situations are required to meet specific British Standard requirements.

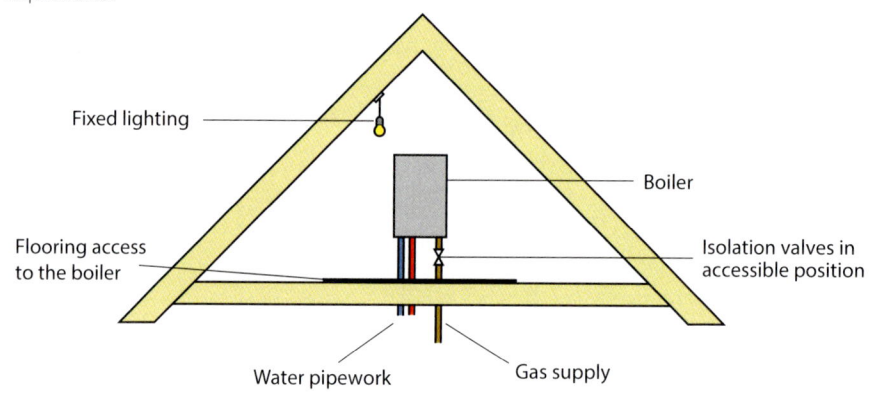

Figure 12: Room sealed boiler installed in a roof space

Room sealed and open flued boilers and circulators may be installed in roof spaces, provided that the following requirements are met (see Figure 12):

- Flooring area is provided – sufficient for access and servicing of the appliance.
- For wall mounted appliances, mounting arrangements are capable of supporting the weight of the filled boiler and associated equipment.
- For floor standing appliances, the base must be of non-combustible materials, of at least 12mm thickness.
- Permanent access is required to the roof space, for instance with a fixed retractable loft ladder.
- The roof space exit must be protected with a guard rail, to protect against falls.
- Adequate fixed lighting should be provided.
- Stored articles should be separated from the appliance (where required) by means of a guard.
- Gas, water and electrical isolation points should be provided outside the roof space, so the boiler can be isolated without having to gain access to the space.
- Ventilation requirements may also need to be considered.

BPEC   Module 17

Part 4 – Fireback Installations

Existing boilers or circulators installed in fireplace openings tend to be combined units incorporating gas fires. However, new units incorporating condensing type boilers only incorporate electric fires.

Gas fire mounting arrangements may be either:
- Hearth mounted.
- Wall mounted.

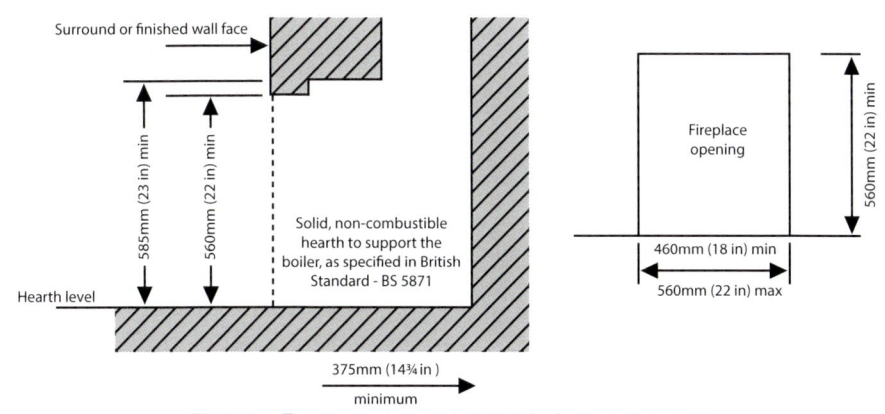

Figure 13: Typical spacing requirements for fireplace openings

General requirements

As seen in Figure 13, the boiler or fireplace location should:
- Be provided with sufficient space to allow for air circulation to give correct draught diverter performance and an adequate supply of combustion air. Space should be provided for adequate maintenance and servicing to be undertaken. Figure 14 shows typical detail provided in manufacturer's installation instructions.
- The boiler should be provided with a non-combustible solid hearth of not less than 25mm thickness, located on non-combustible supports of not less than 25mm thickness.
- The boiler hearth should extend not less than 150mm from the sides and back of the appliance, unless there is a wall within 150mm of the boiler, in which case the hearth should extend to that wall.
- The boiler enclosure itself should have no openings other than any internal air inlet(s) from the room and an outlet via the flue. Openings made for pipework and any under-grate air ducts etc. must be sealed.

Hearth mounted fires

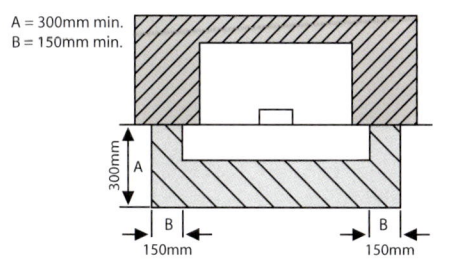

Figure 14: Gas fire hearth requirements

| BPEC | Domestic Central Heating and Water Heaters (CENWAT) |

Before installing a hearth mounted gas fire associated with a back boiler or circulator, unless the manufacturer's installation instructions specify otherwise, the following criteria should be adopted (see Figure 15):

- The hearth should have a minimum depth back to front of 300mm.
- The hearth should be at least 50mm above the finished floor level, of which the top surface should be comprised of non-combustible maternal at least 12mm thick.
- The hearth should project at least 150mm beyond each edge of the naked flame or incandescent material.
- The boiler base hearth should be level with the fire hearth.

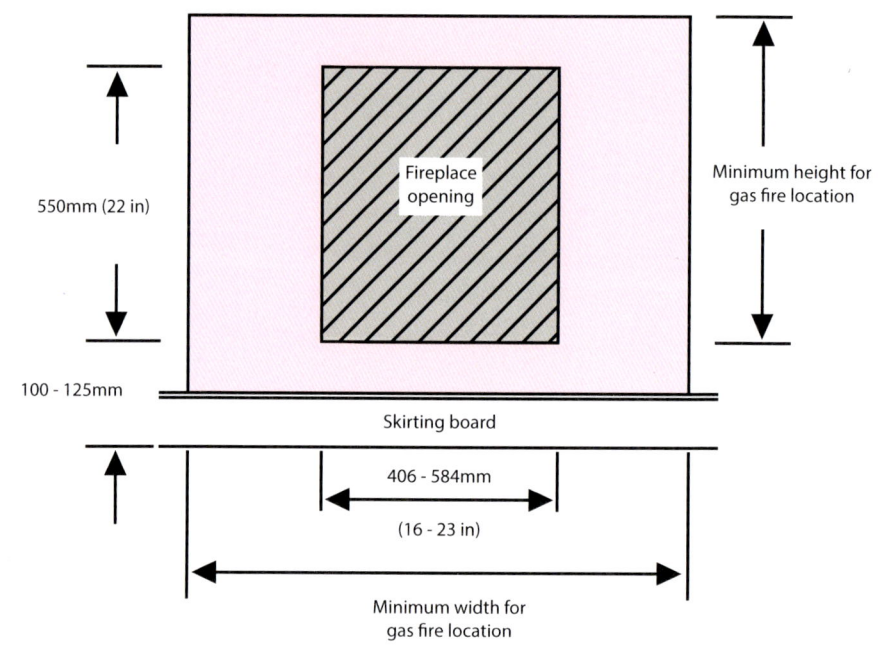

Figure 15: Typical wall mounted fire clearance requirements

With wall mounted fires:

- Where the floor is of fixed combustible material, no part of the gas fire flame or incandescent material should be within 225mm of the finished floor level.
- Where the floor will permit the fitting of a carpet, no part of the flame or incandescent material should be within 300mm of the finished floor level.

Figure 15 shows typical dimensions provided by manufacturer's instructions. In this case the minimum dimensions are inbuilt into the gas fire design. All the installer has to ensure is that the boiler hearth is 100-125mm above finished floor level.

BPEC   Module 17

Part 5: Flue Requirements for Central Heating Boilers and Circulators

Now that we have looked at restrictions on siting the different types of boilers and circulators, it is time to look at the flue system, which can impact on where boilers or circulators can be located.

The flue system

Remember that central heating boilers and circulators are appliances, which must have a flue. The flue system can have a considerable impact on where the appliance can be located.

You should have already covered, in previous modules, the key features of the following flue systems. Here is how they apply to boilers and circulators:

- Room sealed flue systems.
- Open flued boilers and circulators with independent flue systems (not built into the building).
- Open flued boilers discharging into traditional flue systems (built into the building).
- Open flued fire back circulators discharging into traditional flue systems.

Note: Flue systems must comply with the requirements of BS 5440-1: 2008 Flueing and ventilation for gas appliances of rated input not exceeding 70kW net (1st, 2nd and 3rd family gases).

Room sealed flue systems

Room sealed flue systems must:

- Terminate in an acceptable position (as per BS 5440-1: 2008 Flueing and ventilation).
- Be suitable for the wall thickness through which they are to discharge.

Additionally for fanned draught flues:

- The flue must be adequately supported.
- The flue system and installation must comply with manufacturer's instructions in terms of length of run and number of bends used.

Open flued boilers and circulators with independent flue systems

Open flued boilers and circulators with independent flue systems must:

- Effectively discharge and terminate in an acceptable position, as required by BS 5440-1: 2008 which is not affected by down draught.
- Be of adequate size. The cross sectional area of the flue should not be less than that of the boiler flue outlet.
- Be correctly terminated, i.e. with an approved cowl.
- Be adequately supported.
- Where run externally or through unheated spaces, the flue should be twin wall design.
- Where external runs exceed three metres in length, double walled insulated flue pipe should be used.
- Be of sufficient height (refer to appliance manufacturer's instructions).
- Incorporate a down-draught diverter, normally at the appliance.

April 2017   © BPEC

Open flued boilers discharging into traditional flues

There tend to be two types of traditional flue system:

- Unlined.
- Existing lined (house built after 1965).

Unlined flues

These must:

- Be lined, usually with a stainless steel flexible flue liner to BS EN 1856-2 and be in one continuous length, forming no angle greater than 45° from the vertical.
- The liner should be adequately sealed at the top and bottom.
- The flue system should be adequately terminated, with an approved terminal.
- The liner and associated connecting flue pipework cross sectional area should be at least equal to the cross sectional area of the boiler flue outlet.
- The liner should be adequately connected to either the boiler or flue pipework using manufacturer's proprietary materials.
- Be of sufficient height (refer to appliance manufacturer's instructions).
- Incorporate a down-draught diverter, normally at the appliance.

Note: Any chimney that has previously been used by an appliance burning any fuel other than gas should be thoroughly swept before installing a flue liner or appliance.

Existing stainless steel liners

Existing stainless steel liners should preferably be replaced when installing a new appliance. However, providing that the existing liner is in good condition consideration can be given to reusing the liner, providing the gas operative is confident that it will continue to function safely throughout the life time of the new appliance, which is normally 10 to 15 years.

Existing lined flues

These are usually of 175mm (7 in) diameter, manufactured from clay. They must:

- Be of sound construction and pass a satisfactory flue flow test.
- Be adequately terminated, with approved pot or terminal.
- Enable a flue pipe (same diameter as the appliance outlet) to project at least 150mm into the flue.
- Be adequately sealed between flue pipe and clay liner.
- Be of sufficient height (refer to appliance manufacturer's instructions).
- Incorporate a down-draught diverter, normally at the appliance.

Additional note

Where the appliance is discharging into an existing liner of considerable length, re-lining the flue with a liner of the same size as the boiler flue outlet should be considered, in order to avoid excessive cooling of the flue gases and production of water vapour. Again, any chimney that has previously been used by an appliance burning any fuel other than gas, should be thoroughly swept before installing a flue liner or appliance.

Open flued fire back circulators discharging into traditional flue systems

Fireback circulators can usually be connected to un-lined traditional flue systems. The flue system must:

- Be unaffected by downdraught.
- Be of sufficient height (refer to manufacturer's installation instructions).
- Be of suitable size (usually a minimum circular diameter of 125mm (5 in).
- Be of sound construction and pass a satisfactory flue flow test.
- Be appropriately terminated.

Where the flue length is excessive, usually above 10 m, it may be necessary to line the flue.

We have now covered the main points relating to the siting and positioning of boilers and circulators.

Part 6 – Commissioning of Central Heating Boilers and Circulators

The commissioning of gas fired appliances tends to be slightly different for each appliance manufactured. However, by taking a look at the commissioning procedures associated with the following appliance types, we should have an overview of the commissioning procedures for all types of boilers and circulators:

- Open flued natural draught appliances.
- Additional requirements of fanned draught appliances.
- Additional requirements of boilers incorporating modulating gas controls.
- Additional requirements of fireback circulators.

Upon completion of commissioning new appliances you must leave the installation and user instruction with the appliance (normally adjacent to the gas meter). S/he should also complete the Benchmark Log Book and give this to the customer.

Before we look at appliance commissioning in detail, remember that if you have not installed the appliance, you need to go through all the relevant checks first to ensure that the installation meets both legislative and manufacturer requirements.

Open flued natural draught appliances

The following identifies a common procedure for commissioning an open flued natural draught boiler:

- Ensure all preliminary checks have been carried out, including compliance with legislation, gas tightness test, check for adequate ventilation, flue flow etc.

Legend
a   Gas control knob
b   Burner pressure test point
c   Main burner pressure adjuster
d   Inlet pressure test point
e   Gas service cock
f   Sight glass
g   Piezo ignition button
h   Boiler thermostat knob

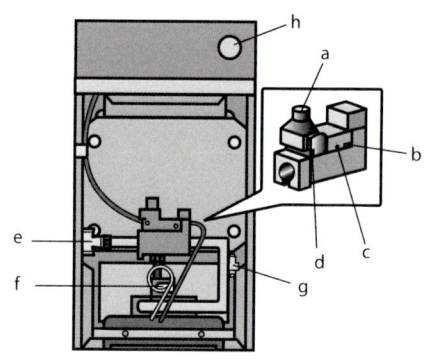

Figure 16: Internal components

Referring to Figure 16:

- Check that the gas service cock (e) is on and the boiler thermostat knob (h) is off.
- Loosen the screw in the burner pressure test point (b) and connect a gas pressure gauge via a flexible tube.
- Turn the gas control knob (a) **clockwise** until resistance is felt and then release it.
- Push in and retain fully depressed the gas knob (a). Press and release piezo ignition button (g) repeatedly until the pilot lights.
- Hold the gas control knob (a) depressed for 15 seconds after the pilot has ignited. If the pilot burner fails to remain alight at this stage, repeat the procedure detailed above, but wait longer than 15 seconds before releasing the gas control knob (a).
- Check the appearance of the pilot flame to ensure that it envelopes the tip of the thermocouple and is approximately 25mm. Check that the thermocouple is between 10 – 15 mv closed circuit.
- Switch the boiler thermostat knob (h) to maximum and check that the burners cross-light smoothly.
- Test for gas tightness around the pilot burner connection, using leak detection fluid.
- Test for gas tightness around the remaining boiler components, using leak detection fluid.
- Operate the boiler for 10 minutes to stabilise the burner temperature. Boilers tend to be pre-set at the factory to their maximum nominal rating, but can be range rated to suit the system design requirements.

If the burner pressure setting requires adjustment, turn the pressure adjusting screw to increase and decrease the pressure.

- If the boiler output is set to mid or minimum, affix the appropriate indicator label, supplied with the appliance Data Plate.
- Immediately check that there is no spillage of combustion products from the draught diverter outlet by, carrying out a spillage test as detailed in BS 5440-1: 2008. Remember, where the room contains an extractor fan, carry out the test with the fan operating at maximum and all the doors and windows closed. Where the fan is in an adjacent room, the test should be carried out with the connecting door open. Directional fans must be tested in both directions.
- Turn the boiler thermostat knob (h) to off.
- Remove the pressure gauge and tube. Retighten the screw in the pressure test nipple, ensuring that a gas-tight seal is made. Check with leak detection fluid.
- Check the operation of the flame supervision device (FSD):

Additional requirements of fanned draught appliances

The commissioning procedures are similar to those for natural draught appliances. Particular attention, however, needs to be given to the appliance case seals. In some cases, fans are installed on the combustion air flow side of the appliance, which makes the appliance chamber operate under positive air pressure. If the case seals fail the products of combustion can discharge into the room in which the appliance is located. This can be dangerous.

Remember that checking the case seals and sight glass seals is extremely important on all types of boilers, particularly those using fans.

Conversely, boilers that incorporate fans on the flue side of the appliance make the appliance operate under negative pressure. If the case seals leak, air will be drawn into the chamber from the room, possibly causing the pressure switch to activate and the boiler not to operate.

These types of appliance usually include an overheat thermostat which may be in the trip position on initial lighting. The thermostat may therefore require re-setting.

Additional requirements of boilers incorporating modulating gas controls

With some appliances there will be no need to adjust the modulating gas controls. However, other manufacturer's types may require a degree of manual adjustment. A typical procedure follows:

- Check the minimum burner pressure by disconnecting one of the modulating valve electrical connections and take a gas pressure reading, referring to manufacturer's instructions.
- Re-connect and check maximum burner pressure against requirements.

If adjustment to minimum or maximum settings is necessary the following needs to be carried out:

Adjustment of the modulating valve

Pressures are measured by connecting the positive connection of a pressure gauge to the gas outlet and the negative connection to the base of the inner casing of the boiler. Set the pressures to the values identified by the manufacturer by adjusting the gas valve as illustrated in Figure 17 and explained below.

Remember, it is important to note the order in which the maximum and minimum pressures are set.

The maximum pressure must always be set before adjustment of the minimum pressure.

a) Adjust screw for minimum pressure setting
b) Adjust nut for maximum pressure setting

Adjusting the maximum pressure:

- Cut off tie retaining modulator cover.
- Remove cover by twisting it anticlockwise 90° and levering off with a small screwdriver.
- With a 10mm spanner, turn nut (B) clockwise to increase pressure.
- Adjust to the value for a maximum pressure.

Adjusting the minimum pressure:

This adjustment is only to be made after the maximum setting has been completed:

- Disconnect one of the electrical connections of the modulating coil and tape.
- Using a 10mm spanner, hold nut (B) and adjust screw (A) with a screwdriver. Set to the value for minimum pressure.
- Reconnect the electrical connection to the modulator.
- Check maximum and minimum settings. Repeat adjustment if required.
- Refit cover, snap into place and turn.

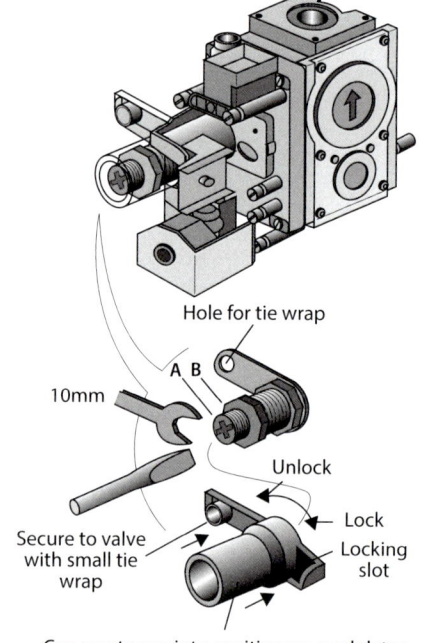

Hole for tie wrap
10mm
A B
Secure to valve with small tie wrap
Unlock
Lock
Locking slot
Cap must snap into position on modulator

A Adjust screw for minimum pressure setting
B Adjust nut for maximum pressure setting

Figure 17: Modulating multifunctional control valve

After the setting operation, remove the pressure gauge tubes from gas valve body and inner casing. Refit the pressure test point screws and test with a suitable leak detection fluid.

Remember that other types of modulating controls will employ different setting up procedures.

- The mechanical thermostat is pre-set at 60°C. This can be manually adjusted by referring to manufacturer's instructions.
- As the appliance heats and reaches circulating temperature, in this type of appliance the bypass rate through the thermostat should be checked using the pressure gauge. At the bypass rate, the appliance should be turned off and on to check for adequate cross-lighting.

- The operation of the flame supervision device should be checked to ensure that it will shut off the gas supply to the main burner within manufacturer's tolerances. A tightness test should be carried out between the FSD and the service cock, to ensure that the multifunctional control valve is not passing gas, or alternatively pass a lit taper over the main burner.
- The gas fire should be installed as per manufacturer's requirements; connecting pipework should be tightness tested.
- A spillage test should be carried out on the gas fire with the boiler operating at full gas rate.
- The appliance should be handed over to the user, including providing an instruction of its operation.

All instruction user manuals should be left on site and the customer advised on annual servicing requirements.

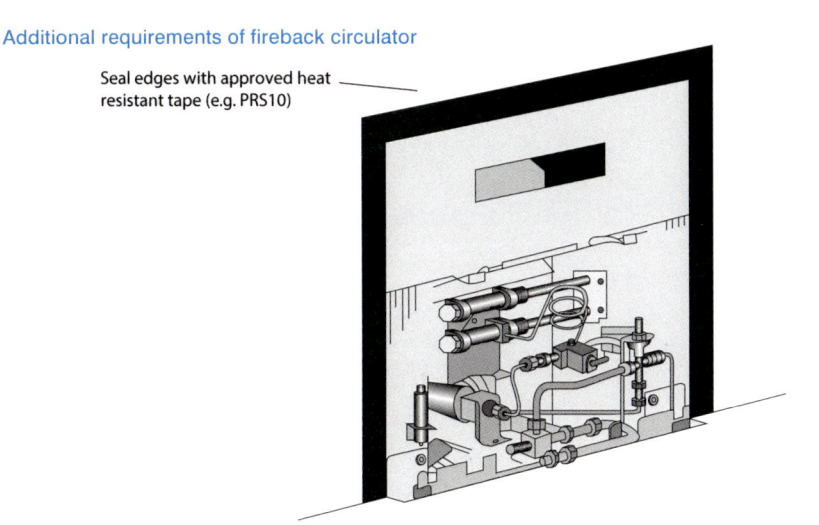

Additional requirements of fireback circulator

Seal edges with approved heat resistant tape (e.g. PRS10)

Figure 18: Fireback circulator with sealed closure plate

The commissioning procedures are relatively similar to those for natural draught appliances. There are, however, several differing types of components installed in this type of appliance, and we will look at the commissioning procedure in more detail:

- Check the appliance installation to ensure that it conforms with legislative and manufacturer's requirements (this may include having to seal the closure plate as shown in Figure 18).
- Light the pilot using the procedure shown in the installation instructions.
- Connect the pressure gauge to the burner test point and light the main burner. The reading taken should come within manufacturer's tolerances. The appliance is fixed gas rated, so if outside manufacturer's limits, check the meter pressure governor and pipework size to the appliance.
- Check that the pilot flame envelopes the thermocouple tip.
- Test all gas components for tightness with a suitable leak detection fluid.
- Carry out a spillage test on the back boiler.

Adjustment of appliances with zero governor or air/gas ratio valves

In some cases, where adjustment of the air/gas ratio control may be necessary, the procedure for doing so must be carried out strictly in accordance with the specific manufacturer's instructions and will involve the use of an electronic hand held flue gas analyser.

Most appliance manufacturers use one of several different control valves currently available from manufacturers such as Dungs, Honeywell, SIT and Siemens, but the method of use of the valve system may vary from appliance to appliance. To assist operatives in recognising the particular air/gas ratio valves and the method of use Gas Safe Register have issued Technical Bulletin No. 013 – Air/Gas ratio valves.

On each air/gas ratio valve there is usually a throttle, this is a needle screw which intrudes into the gas or airway to the burner, thereby altering the gas/air mix when adjusted. A flue gas analyser is then used to check products of combustion to ensure the CO_2 figure achieved after adjustment is in line with that specified by the appliance manufacturers.

In many cases the manufacturer has sealed the zero governor itself with red sealing wax so as to ensure nobody attempts to adjust it, to do so will seriously affect the safety of the appliance.

Section 3 – Service, Maintenance and Repair of Central Heating Boilers and Circulators

Part 1 – Unsafe Situations – Case Seals

A further serious problem which can occur, particularly with wall mounted appliances, is fume leakage associated with defective case seals.

Fumes can leak to a larger or lesser extent from appliance case seals which are intended to prevent flue gases entering the room. Wall mounted appliances tend to be those in which defective case seals may be the greatest problem, as usually there will be an inner case which incorporates a seal surrounding the heat exchanger/burner etc. This seal, if care is not taken, may not be made correctly on initial installation or the sealing material may break on removing the inner case when undertaking servicing.

The result of leaking case seals and sight glass seals can be serious, particularly on fan assisted appliances working under positive pressure in the combustion chamber, as the appliance is effectively pressurised.

Dependent on the degree of fume leakage, it may be appropriate in certain instances to categorise fume leakage from defective case seals as Immediately Dangerous (ID).

Remember, always check to ensure that an effective case seal has been made. Always repair defective seals with the materials prescribed by the appliance manufacturer.

Having established whether an appliance may fall into the unsafe category, we will take a look at service and maintenance.

Part 2 – Service and Maintenance of Central Heating Boilers and Circulators

The following identifies a general procedure for carrying out service/maintenance of central heating boilers and circulators:

Step 1 – Carry out preliminary checks

- Light the appliance and put into full operation; check flame picture by checking the function of the appliance components.
- Check the general condition of the installation and its conformity with the Gas Safety (Installation and Use) Regulations 1998 and British Standard requirements.
- For open flued installations, check to ensure that sufficient free area of ventilation has been provided and conforms to current regulations.
- Check compartment ventilation requirements and provision of appropriate warning notices.
- Check that the flue is free from obvious defects.
- Check that the flue terminal is suitable and that the termination location is acceptable, in accordance with BS 5440-1: 2008.
- Check that the appliance includes an atmosphere sensing device (ASD) where required.
- Check for signs of spillage or scorching on the appliance and adjacent decoration.

Note any defects and advise the customer prior to the service taking place.

Step 2 – Servicing procedures

- Isolate the gas and electrical supplies to the appliance; check fuse rating.
- Remove the casing and any control panel, electrical connections and thermostat phials to permit the burner and controls assembly to be removed (see Figure 19).

Figure 19: Front casing removal

Step 3 – Remove burner tray

Remove the main burner and controls assembly from the combustion chamber (see Figure 20).

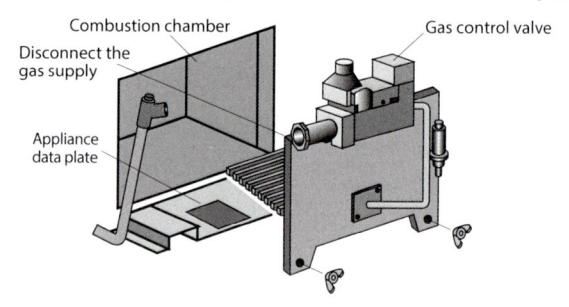

Figure 20: Burner tray removal

Step 4 – Clean burner components

Clean the lint arrestor. Lint gauze arrestors may be included within the burner, mounted on the burner or included within the appliance casing (see Figure 21).

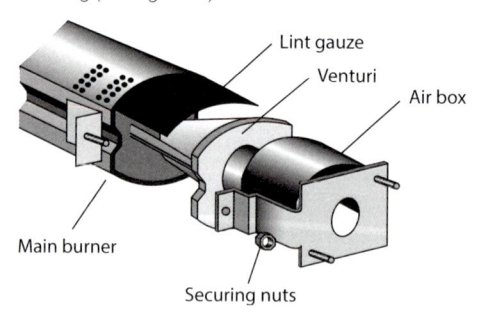

Figure 21: Burner components

BPEC   Module 17

Step 5 – Cleaning the burner assembly

- Brush off any deposits that may have fallen onto the burner head, ensuring that the flame ports are unobstructed. Remove any debris that may have collected on the assembly components. Brushes with metallic bristles should not usually be used for this purpose.
- Remove the burner injector(s). Ensure that there is no blockage or damage. Clean or renew as necessary.
- Refit the injector(s) using an approved jointing compound.
- Inspect the pilot, thermocouple and spark electrode; ensure that they are clean and in good condition.

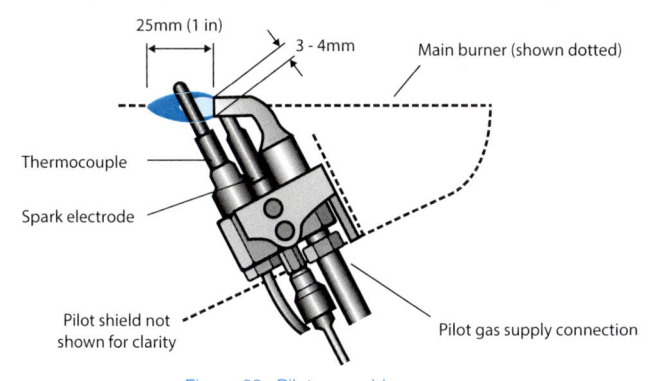

Figure 22: Pilot assembly

In particular check that:

- The pilot burner is clean and unobstructed. Clean the pilot injector if necessary.
- The spark electrode is clean and undamaged. The piezo igniter works.
- The spark lead is in good condition and securely connected.
- The spark gap is correct.
- The thermocouple tip is not burned or cracked.
- The position of the thermocouple relative to the pilot burner is correct as shown in Figure 22.
- The thermocouple terminal at the gas valve is clean and tight.
- Clean or renew components as necessary.

Step 6 – Clean the flueways

Remove the flue hood cover and check seals; replace if necessary (see Figure 23). Brush out any deposits on the top of the heat exchanger. Brush through the fins of the heat exchanger with an appropriate flue brush, removing all deposits. Remove all debris from the combustion chamber base and check that the flue outlet is unobstructed.

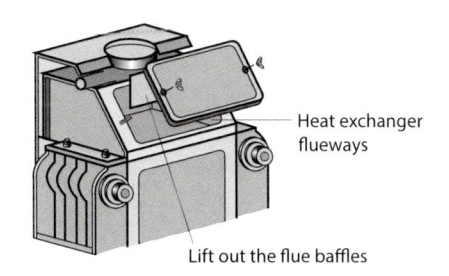

Figure 23: Flue baffles

April 2017   © BPEC

Step 7 – Re-assemble
Re-assemble the appliance, checking that the sight glass is unbroken and that the seals are in good condition.

Step 8 – Check connections
Check the appliance gas connections for gas tightness including multi-functional valve connections, main burner connections, pilot burner connections and connections to gas service cocks, test points etc.

Step 9 – Check seals and joints
Check all the appliance seals and joints and replace as necessary. Carry out flue-flow test.

Step 10 – Check electrical continuity
Check that there is no obvious damage to the electrical wiring; carry out polarity and earth continuity electrical checks.

Final checks
- Light the appliance pilot.
- Check to ensure that the pilot flame correctly envelopes the thermocouple/FSD.
- Light the main burner and check/re-set the operating pressure to meet system requirements (confirm satisfactory flame picture).
- Carry out a spillage test on open flued appliances.
- Check the operation of the flame supervision device and air pressure switch (if fitted), following manufacturer's procedures.
- Check the operation of the thermostat(s).
- Leave the site in a clean and tidy condition; ensure that the customer understands the safe and efficient operation of the appliance.

Other appliance types
The servicing procedure tends to be common for most appliance types. There are, however, additional requirements for condensing appliances and combined boilers/circulators and gas fires.

Condensing appliances
These may include stripping down of the heat exchanger and cleaning of the condense sump outlet.

Combined boilers/circulators and gas fires
This type of appliance will require the fire to be serviced also. The following highlights a combined gas fire servicing procedure.

Servicing procedures

- Remove and strip down the fire.
- Clean the burner and its injectors.
- Clean the lint arrestor(s).
- Clean the pilot and injector(s) where fitted; check spark electrode and ignition system.
- Clean and examine the flueways, heat exchanger and flue and pilot assembly.
- Clean or replace the flame supervision device (if fitted).
- Clean radiants, coals etc. and rest of appliance; check operation of controls.
- Re-assemble appliance and connect to gas supply, ensuring that all connections are gas tight.
- Check that all appliance seals are correctly made; renew if necessary.

Final checks

- Light appliance.
- Test fire for spillage with boiler/circulator main burner operating at maximum.
- Confirm satisfactory flame picture.
- Re-check flame supervision device (FSD) operation.
- Clean and tidy up.

Positive Pressure Combustion Chamber Appliances

These type of appliances use a fan to draw fresh air from the outside into the unit for combustion, and then expel the products of combustion back out to the outside. Great care should be taken with Positive pressure combustion chamber appliances regarding the case seals. During the 1980s a mixture of both Positive and Negative pressure fanned balanced flue appliances were installed, Positive pressure appliances having defective seals or where the case has not been located correctly in certain circumstances can induce a dramatic increase in spillage of Carbon Monoxide, the positive pressure within the combustion chamber spilling products into the room containing the appliance.

Due to this potential problem manufacturers ceased production of positive pressure appliances in favour of negative pressure appliances, however, since the development of condensing appliances forced draught combustion appliances are now being manufactured again, but are predominantly negative pressure combustion chambers.

For any fanned balanced flued appliance, you will need to ensure that the case/combustion seal is carefully checked, any appliance where the case/combustion seals are found to be faulty must be made safe until remedial action has been made.

The manufacturer's instructions must always be followed when installing, servicing or fault finding on positive pressure appliances, the following checks are the typical for these type of appliances:

- The seals around sight glasses, backplates and entry points for ignition leads or weep tubes are correctly fitted and sealed.
- The seals around air intakes and flue ducts are correctly fitted and sealed.
- Ensure that all flue ducts have been cut square and are adequately sealed.
- Check that flue joints, bends and terminals are of the correct manufacture and adequately sealed.

Symptoms of possible products of combustion spillage from a positive pressure appliance may be:

- Flame picture disturbance.
- Discoloration around the appliance (soot/heat marks).
- Customer complaint (smell/headaches).

Rectification of faulty case seals on positive pressure appliances:

- A physical inspection of case/combustion seals, replacing as necessary.
- Ensure the case/combustion covers are correctly located and secured.
- Once re-assembled the working appliance case seal can be checked with an approved Carbon Monoxide detector around the seals, and in additon,
- The case/combustion seals checked with a lighted taper or match – observing any movement of the flame or smoke plume.

Part 3 – Typical Gas Component Faults on Central Heating Boilers and Circulators

Due to the increasing complexity of modern central heating boilers fault finding has become increasingly difficult unless you have the manufacturer's instructions. You will also be required to use a multimeter and follow approved electrical isolation and testing procedures. However, basic faults associated with specific components can be rectified by following the guidance provided in Module 11.

Unsatisfactory ignition of burners

Let us take a look at the faults which may occur with the unsatisfactory ignition of burners.

The pilot ignition

The manufacturer will usually include a flow chart identifying possible faults on appliances. Remember to use this as it can make life much easier. This is how the flow chart could apply to pilot ignition.

BPEC Module 17

Pilot will not light

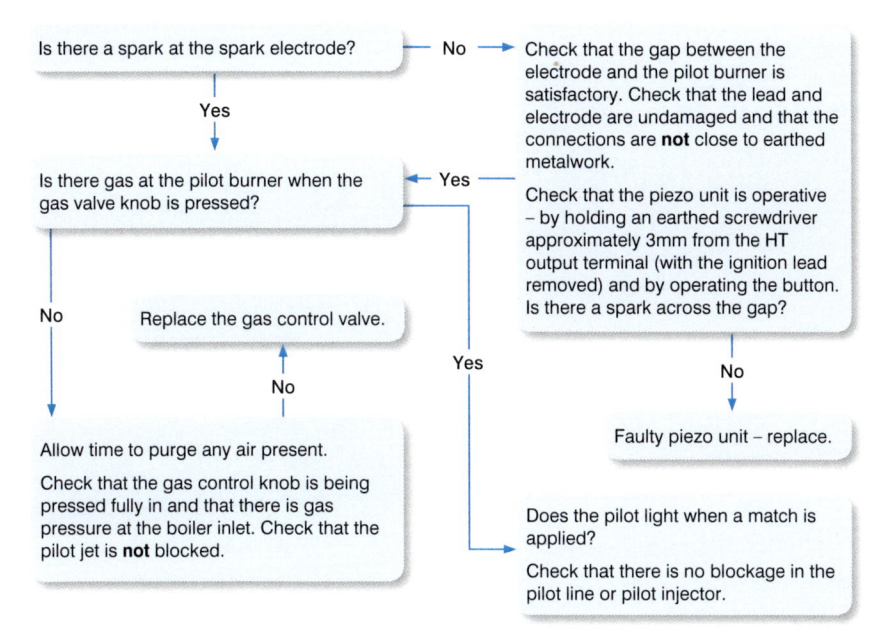

Is there a spark at the spark electrode? — **No** → Check that the gap between the electrode and the pilot burner is satisfactory. Check that the lead and electrode are undamaged and that the connections are **not** close to earthed metalwork.

↓ Yes

Is there gas at the pilot burner when the gas valve knob is pressed? ← **Yes** — Check that the piezo unit is operative – by holding an earthed screwdriver approximately 3mm from the HT output terminal (with the ignition lead removed) and by operating the button. Is there a spark across the gap?

↓ No → Replace the gas control valve.
         ↑ No
↓   ↑ Yes   ↓ No

Allow time to purge any air present.   Faulty piezo unit – replace.

Check that the gas control knob is being pressed fully in and that there is gas pressure at the boiler inlet. Check that the pilot jet is **not** blocked.

→ Does the pilot light when a match is applied?

Check that there is no blockage in the pilot line or pilot injector.

Pilot will not stay lit when the gas control valve knob is released

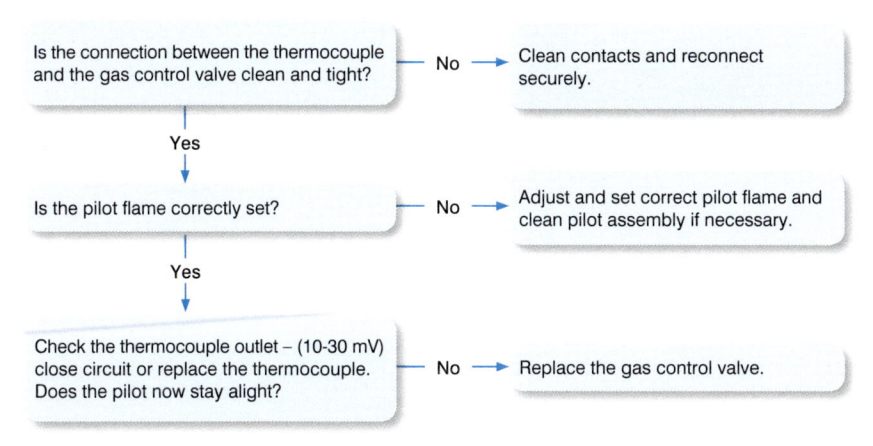

Is the connection between the thermocouple and the gas control valve clean and tight? — **No** → Clean contacts and reconnect securely.

↓ Yes

Is the pilot flame correctly set? — **No** → Adjust and set correct pilot flame and clean pilot assembly if necessary.

↓ Yes

Check the thermocouple outlet – (10-30 mV) close circuit or replace the thermocouple. Does the pilot now stay alight? — **No** → Replace the gas control valve.

The test procedure will differ slightly with fan assisted appliances, incorporating flame conduction and rectification flame supervision devices. You should, however, follow the manufacturer's diagnostic flow chart. In this case, the printed circuit board could be at fault.

April 2017 © BPEC

Main burner ignition

Main burner ignition may be affected by a problem associated with the electrical components incorporated within the appliance (remember some appliance controls operate at low voltage). The flow chart below is usually of assistance.

Pilot lit, but no mains gas

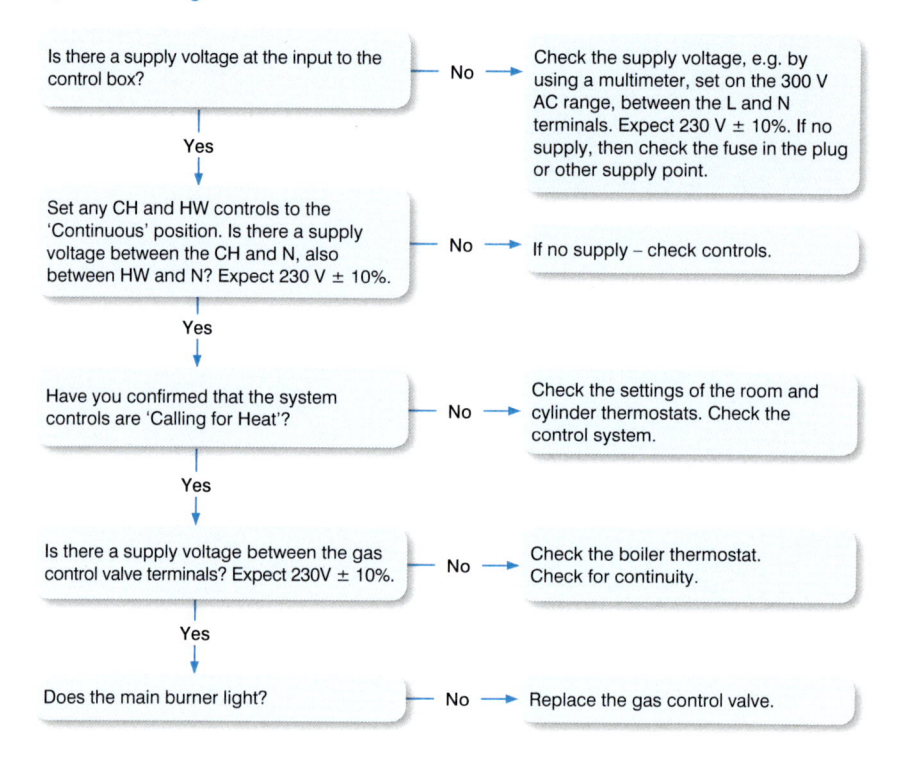

Is there a supply voltage at the input to the control box? → **No** → Check the supply voltage, e.g. by using a multimeter, set on the 300 V AC range, between the L and N terminals. Expect 230 V ± 10%. If no supply, then check the fuse in the plug or other supply point.

↓ **Yes**

Set any CH and HW controls to the 'Continuous' position. Is there a supply voltage between the CH and N, also between HW and N? Expect 230 V ± 10%. → **No** → If no supply – check controls.

↓ **Yes**

Have you confirmed that the system controls are 'Calling for Heat'? → **No** → Check the settings of the room and cylinder thermostats. Check the control system.

↓ **Yes**

Is there a supply voltage between the gas control valve terminals? Expect 230V ± 10%. → **No** → Check the boiler thermostat. Check for continuity.

↓ **Yes**

Does the main burner light? → **No** → Replace the gas control valve.

There may also be problems with the actual main burner lighting procedure, where the main burner does not light smoothly or lights with a bang.

This can be associated with this possible fault:

- The pilot assembly is partially blocked or incorrectly positioned, resulting in the pilot flame not adequately playing on to the main burner. In terms of this fault, the pilot burner assembly should be cleaned and/or re-positioned.

Unstable flame picture

With central heating boilers or circulators, an unstable flame picture is usually caused by:

a) **An inadequate supply of combustion air.** Air inlets which are choked with lint or a blocked heat exchanger or flueways will result in an unstable flame picture.

The symptoms of this problem are flames which have long or non existent cones with soft yellow tipped flames. The solution to this problem is to:

- Ensure that adequate permanent ventilation is provided.
- Clean any choked lint arrestors, burners or boiler flueways.

b) **Incorrectly set gas rate.** The main problem here tends to be with over gassing of the appliance. This can be caused by installation of the wrong sized injectors or incorrect setting of the gas rate.

The symptoms of over-gassing are similar to a lack of air supply, where the flames become longer and softer.

The solution in this case could be to check the injectors, if these are believed to be of the wrong size, or to correctly set the appliance gas consumption rate.

Signs of spillage

Flue spillage is a particular concern with open flued appliances and will result in the products of combustion being discharged into the room in which the appliance is situated.

Typically, where spillage occurs, appliance surfaces (above pilot windows) and wall surfaces around draught diverter inlets will show signs of discolouration.

Spillage on open flued appliances will usually be caused by either or a combination of the following:

- Incorrect flue system/incorrect ventilation.
- Incorrect gas rate at the appliance.
- Appliance requiring cleaning/servicing.

A sooted (blocked) heat exchanger will result in the products of combustion being discharged through openings in the combustion chamber, such as primary air ports. Spillage/discolouration at the draught diverter will indicate signs of either a blocked/partially blocked secondary flue, an inadequate flue terminal or an incorrectly positioned flue terminal.

Remember that flue spillage is a serious defect and requires immediate attention.

Note: Spillage can be caused by the use of extract/paddle fans having a adverse effect on flue performance.

Inoperative control and high limit thermostats (mechanical/electrical control components)

Always make sure that the phial is correctly housed in the phial pocket before going any further.

Control thermostat

This component may:

- Fail to supply electricity through to the multifunctional control valve (usually associated with a failure of the mechanism).
- Cease to correctly read temperature, in which case it will turn the multifunctional control valve off at insufficient appliance operating temperature, or it will cause the appliance to overheat and it may begin to boil.

Electrical supply through to the multifunctional valve can be tested by checking the thermostat for continuity:

- Remove the connections from the thermostat.
- Carry out a continuity check with a multi meter (zero resistance should be present on the test dial).

When the boiler overheats, it is most likely that the thermostat has failed and requires replacement. Beware however, this fault can also occur due to sludge formation within the boiler waterways. Similarly, failure of the pump may cause the boiler to short cycle, and with cast iron heat exchangers, latent heat within the boiler casting may increase the water temperature to boiling point. Where overheating is occurring the pump operation should be checked before replacing thermostats.

A thermostat believed to be under-heating the appliance can be diagnosed by taking a temperature reading of the flow pipework adjacent to the appliance.

Control thermostats cannot usually be adjusted and therefore replacement is normally necessary.

Overheat (limit) thermostat

The thermostat usually trips out when either the control thermostat on the appliance has failed or when the high limit device itself is faulty. The test procedure for checking overheat (limit) thermostats is to utilise the same procedures as for control thermostats.

Careful attention needs to be given to ensuring that it is the overheat thermostat which has failed, and not the control thermostat. Tripping of overheat thermostats may be caused by insufficient boiler flow rate and not a failing of the control or overheat thermostat.

Modern boilers can also utilise thermistors as a device for measuring temperature. The thermistor acts as a resistor; its correct operation can be confirmed by taking resistance readings with a multimeter and confirming these with manufacturer's requirements.

Inoperative mechanical thermostat (circulator)

These thermostats are invariably of the vapour pressure type. They can be checked by heating up on a high setting and turning down to a low one. If the gas supply fails to be controlled by the thermostat, it will need replacing. If the gas rate begins to fluctuate, it may need re-calibrating. This can be carried out by following manufacturer's guidance.

For circulators incorporating thermostats which operate on a by-pass rate principle, the minimum gas by-pass rate can be checked by measuring the by-pass gas rate against manufacturer's requirements.

If the thermostat is damaged or cannot be re-calibrated, it must be replaced.

Inoperative air pressure switches

An air pressure switch is usually installed in an appliance which may have relatively complex electronic circuitry. The manufacturer's fault flow chart should be referred to at all times.

The symptom of air pressure switch failure is usually that the boiler fan fails to start resulting in the boiler failing to commence its ignition sequence.

The air pressure switch can be checked (if possible) by pulling off one of the input pipes. Fit a suitable input tube to the input port, blow gently into the valve and listen for clicking of the micro-switch. Its operation can also be checked using a multimeter continuity test, which should show a zero reading.

Remember that the air pressure switch may be affected by defective case seals and by splits, kinks or loose connections associated with air supply tubes. The printed circuit board could also be the cause of any problem associated with an air pressure switch.

Inoperable multifunctional control valves

The procedure for checking the FSD section of a multifunctional control valve has already been covered. The valve will usually, however, contain one or more solenoids. It is usually possible to replace the defective solenoid sections of the valve.

To determine if a fault on the solenoid has occurred, the valve should be checked to ensure that 240V is available at the connections (or lower voltage with low voltage components). Many newer appliances now operate on 24V low voltage supply. If the voltage reading is correct and either of the solenoids has not operated, it has more than likely failed and the valve will need replacing.

Remember that boilers with intermittent pilots have two solenoids.

If the resistance values of the solenoids are known, it is possible to confirm solenoid valve failure by carrying out a resistance check.

Section 4 – Types of Appliances and their Operating Principles

Introduction

In sections 4 to 6 we shall be looking at the various types of appliances and the key operating principles of:

- Small instantaneous water heaters.
- Large instantaneous water heaters.

What is an instantaneous hot water heater?

An instantaneous water heater is an appliance which has been designed to produce instant hot water. That is, it heats the incoming water to a required temperature as it passes through it.

Nowadays these appliances are usually designed to raise the water temperature by no more than approximately 55°C. Since the average incoming cold water temperature is 10°C, then the typical maximum temperature of the hot water being delivered will be no more than approximately 65°C.

This delivery temperature should be suitable to deal with the day to day hot water requirements in a household, as we can see by the list of typical temperatures and uses shown below:

Washing and bathing   33-43°C
Washing-up   60-70°C
Household cleaning   30-70°C

Before we move on, let us look at the definitions of the two types of appliances we shall be looking at:

- **Small instantaneous water heater (single point)** – A water heater with a heat input not exceeding 12kW intended to supply hot water to a sink or basin.

- **Large instantaneous water heater (multipoint)** – A water heater with a heat input exceeding 12kW intended to supply hot water to a bath or a comprehensive supply to a number of draw-off points.

Whilst small instantaneous heaters are usually flueless, large instantaneous heaters may be:

- Open flued.
- Room sealed, natural draught.
- Room sealed, fanned draft.

We will take a look at the operating principles of these appliances.

BPEC Module 17

Part 1 – Small Instantaneous Hot Water Heaters

This type of water heater is no longer generally manufactured except for applications in Leisure Accommodation Vehicles and most replacement parts are unavailable, however, operatives will still find them in use and serviceable.

This is a type of instantaneous hot water heater which delivers hot water usually from a spout which is part of the appliance. Because of this type of delivery, the appliance is commonly known as a single point water heater (see Figure 24).

Its heat input should not exceed 12kW gross (10.8kW net) and it is normally flueless, unless:

- It serves more than one outlet.
- The outlet is not in the same room.
- It is likely to be used for periods greater than five minutes. *Note: there should be a notice clearly displayed on the unit to the effect that the appliance should not be used for periods in excess of five minutes.*
- The room or compartment in which it is installed must have a volume of not less than 5m^3.
- It is located in a room containing a shower or bath, in which case the flue system must be room sealed only.
- It is to be installed in sleeping accommodation, and it is without an atmosphere (vitiation) sensing device.

Figure 24:
Small instantaneous hot water heater

The component parts of a small instantaneous hot water heater

We can see the components in Figure 25(a) and (b), which is a diagram of a small instantaneous water heater.

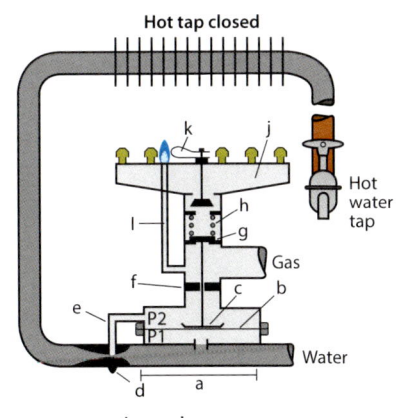

Legend

a. Diaphragm housing
b. Rubber diaphragm
c. Bearing plate
d. Venturi
e. Low pressure duct
f. Stuffing box or gland
g. Gas valve
h. Gas valve spring
j. Burner
k. Bi-metallic cut-off
l. Pilot

Figure 25(a): Hot tap closed

Figure 25(b) – Hot tap open

April 2017 © BPEC

The purpose of the components

Rubber diaphragm (see Figure 25(a) and (b))

The rubber diaphragm is found within the water section of the heater and is designed to flex upwards when water is drawn through the heater. As it flexes upwards, it pushes the bearing plate (c), which in turn lifts the gas valve (g), allowing gas into the gas section of the heater (as shown in Figure 25(b)).

If the pilot (l) is lit and the flame supervision device (FSD) (k) is in the open position, the gas will flow to the burner, usually via an injector, where it will be ignited by the pilot and heat the water.

Why does the diaphragm flex upwards?

If you look at Figure 25(a) you can see that there is no water flow from the heater. When this is so, the pressure on P1 and P2 is equal, thus the diaphragm is in the rest position.

However, when we examine Figure 25(b) we can see that there is water flowing from the heater.

When this is so, the water flowing through the venturi (d causes a reduction in pressure at its throat, as the velocity of flow increases. This causes a reduction in pressure at P2 via the low pressure duct (e), thus the greater pressure at P1 pushes the diaphragm upwards.

The FSD illustrated uses the bi-metallic strip principle to hold the gas valve open. Generally, on newer appliances this has been replaced by a thermocouple operating on the thermo-electric principle.

The pilot is lit by means of a Piezo igniter which is connected via a spark electrode to a pilot assembly arrangement as shown in Figure 26.

The pilot assembly, containing the flame supervision device, igniter and pilot burner fed via an injector, is positioned adjacent to the main burner to permit lighting of the burner, as shown in Figure 27.

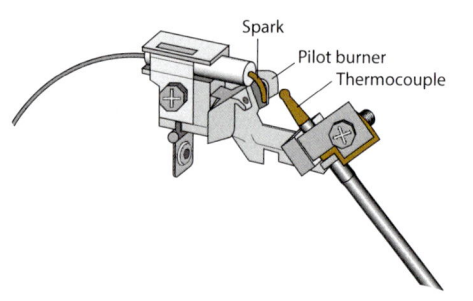

Figure 26: Pilot assembly – FSD

If the pilot light fails, a thermo-electric valve or bi-metallic strip will close the gas supply to the main burner.

Figure 27: Burner and pilot assembly

On new appliances, an atmosphere sensing device (ASD) will usually be incorporated within the appliance design, as shown in Figure 28.

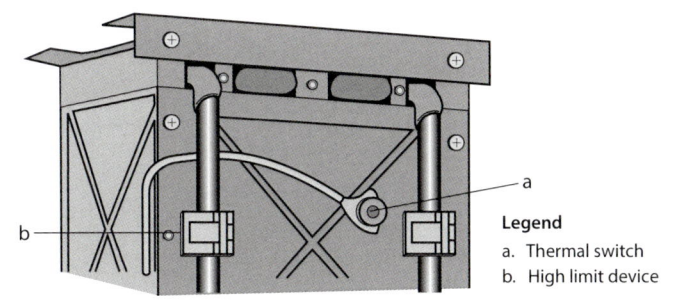

Legend
a. Thermal switch
b. High limit device

Figure 28: Atmosphere sensing device

This appliance incorporates an atmosphere (vitiation) sensing device (ASD), where the thermocouple circuit is fitted with a thermal switch located on the front of the combustion chamber of the heater. Should the oxygen in the atmosphere in the locality of the heater become diminished and unable to support safe combustion, the products of combustion pass through an orifice in the front panel, and the increase in temperature is detected by the thermal switch. When the switch is activated, it interrupts the thermo-electric valve and the pilot and main burner are extinguished.

Note: Appliances produced by other manufacturers may use atmosphere sensing devices operating on different principles.

The appliance may also include a slow ignition device. For further details see Part 2 on large instantaneous water heaters.

How does the water heat instantaneously?

The heat from the flames is transferred to the water via the finned heat exchanger. The design of the appliance ensures that the flow rate of water through the heater is such that the heat transfer rate is capable of raising the water temperature to the designed standard.

The heat exchanger

Figure 29 illustrates a heat exchanger for an instantaneous hot water heater.

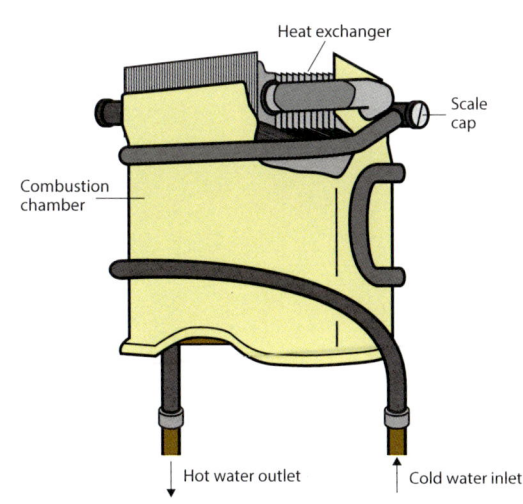

Figure 29: Heat exchanger

This appliance may also include a scale reducer to minimise the effects of hard water on the heat exchanger.

BPEC   Domestic Central Heating and Water Heaters (CENWAT)

Part 2 – Large Instantaneous Hot Water Heaters
In understanding the operating principles of these appliances (multipoints) we shall focus on:
- Room sealed natural draught heaters.
- Room sealed fanned draught heaters.

Note: Open flued and natural draft room sealed models operate on the same principles as their room sealed counterparts. The majority of the models which have been installed tend to be of the room sealed variety.

What is a large instantaneous water heater?
This is a type of instantaneous hot water heater which delivers hot water to draw-off points throughout the property in which it is installed. Because of this type of delivery the appliance is commonly known as a multipoint water heater.

Its heat input is greater than 12kW and therefore must be flued. Here we will take a look at the natural draught room sealed model (see Figure 30).

Figure 31 shows a diagram of the internal components of a large instantaneous water heater.

Figure 30: Room sealed natural draught instantaneous water heater

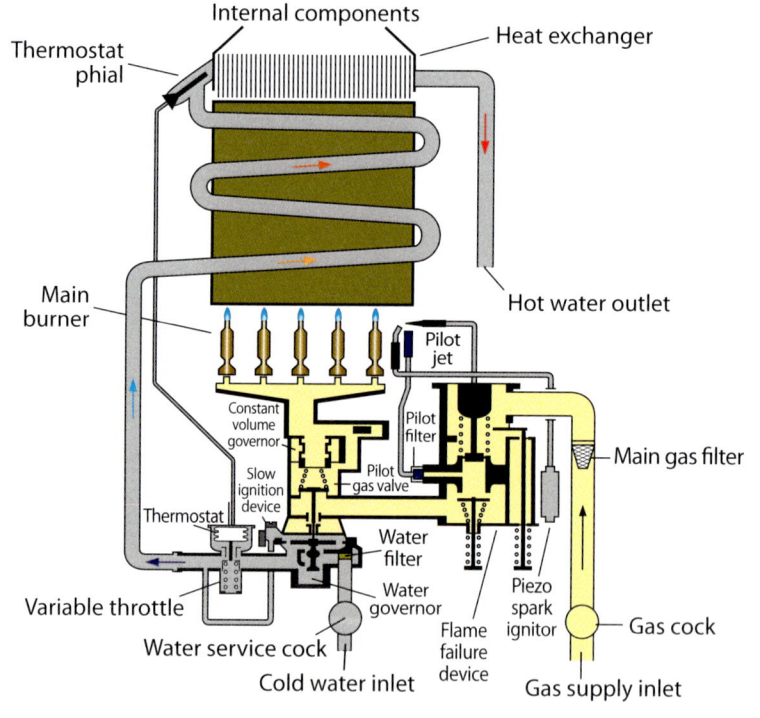

Figure 31: Internal components

© BPEC   44   April 2017

Further description of these components

Thermostat

A multipoint water heater will include a device to control the temperature of the water leaving the appliance.

Figure 32 shows a multipoint heater using a vapour pressure thermostat device, which modulates the water flow rate through the heater and controls the outlet water temperature.

A cylindrical throttle (water throttle) forms a restriction in the waterway of the heater. When the restriction, which is governed by the movement of the bellows, becomes greater, then less flow rate will pass through the heater and in turn the outlet water temperature will increase.

However, in order to prevent damage to the heat exchanger due to overheating, the throttle assembly is connected to the automatic valve of the water section via a small pipe. The throttle therefore also acts in a similar way to a Venturi, and if the flow rate passing through the heater becomes too low, the differential pressure within the water section's automatic valve will equalise and shut off the flow of gas to the burner.

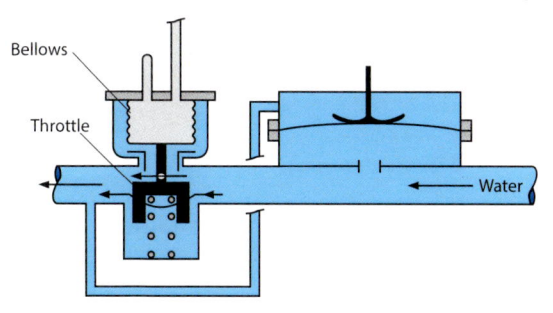

Figure 32: Multipoint heater with vapour pressure thermostat

Water heater models that are now available are fitted with screw-in throttle devices that reduce or increase the flow rate of water, adjusting the water temperature accordingly (see Figure 33).

Note: The throttle can be set during commissioning to give a desired temperature (consult the manufacturer's instructions).

Temperature selector (not fitted to all models)

A simpler method of temperature selection is shown in Figure 33. The temperature selection is controlled by means of a screw-in throttle, which will in turn alter the water flow rate passing through the heater, thus altering the temperature.

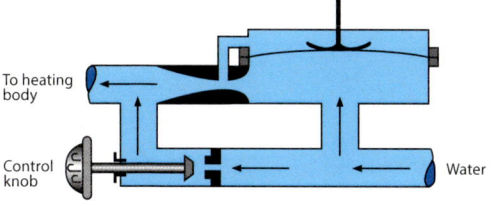

Figure 33: Temperature selector control

Water governor

Water heaters fitted to the cold water mains supply can be subject to varying water inlet pressures, therefore a water governor will be required. The governor can be a separate unit or an integral component of the heater. Figure 34 shows it within the water section of the device.

This type of water governor works in a similar fashion to that of a gas constant pressure governor. When incorporated with an in-line Venturi, a constant water flow rate is achieved.

Slow ignition device (SID)

This is a desirable component which regulates the graduation of gas flow to the burner, in order to minimise noisy ignition of the gas.

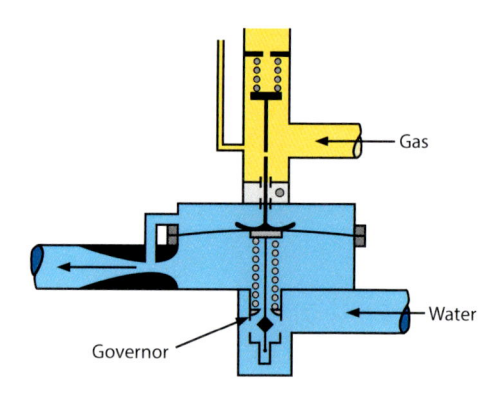

Figure 34: Water governor

From Figure 35 we can see that the device can be adjusted by altering the position of the screw in the low pressure duct connected to the Venturi.

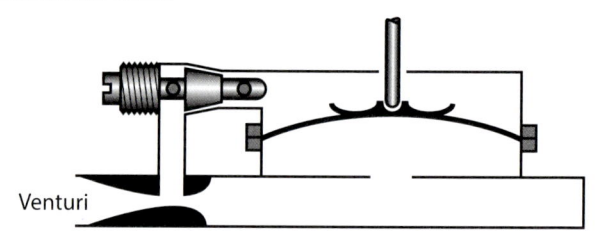

Figure 35: SID internal components

However, in Figure 36 we can see how the slow ignition device operates.

When the valve is opening as shown in 36(a), the loose ball blocks the central orifice, reducing the flow from the upper side of the valve's diaphragm. The gas valve will therefore be opened slowly, graduating the flow of gas to the burner. When the valve is closing as shown in 36(b), the loose ball frees the orifice, increasing the flow to the upper side of the valve's diaphragm. Therefore the gas valve will close quickly.

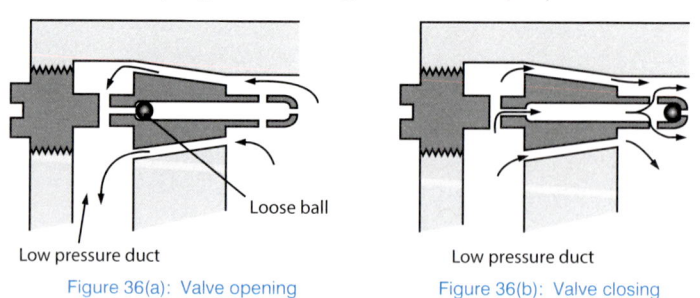

Figure 36(a): Valve opening

Figure 36(b): Valve closing

Constant volume gas governor

A constant volume gas governor (see Figure 37) will deliver a constant volume of gas to the burner. Instantaneous water heaters alter their hot water outlet temperature by increasing or decreasing the water flow rate, i.e. less water flow rate and constant volume of gas = higher temperature.

Therefore greater water flow and constant volume of gas = lower temperature.

The governor consists of an aluminium disc float, which slides freely over a vertical tube. The tube has a number of gas ports, which are closed or opened depending on the position of the float. If the gas pressure is increased, the rate of flow increases and so does the pressure differential across the float at P1 and P2 in Figure 25(a) and (b). The float therefore rises to close the gas ports until the flow rate is restored to the required volume.

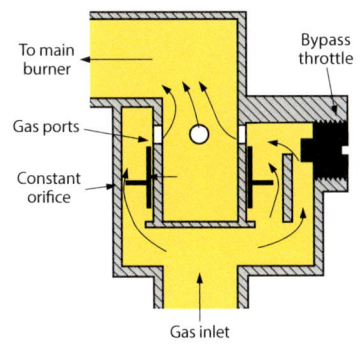

Figure 37: Constant volume gas governor

Room sealed fanned draught instantaneous water heater

Figure 38 shows a typical room sealed fanned draught water heater.

Here is how it works

A fan is used to assist with removal of the products of combustion and the supply of combustion air. The principal additional safety feature is the air pressure switch, shown in Figure 39, which must be fitted to all fanned draught appliances. The pressure switch prevents the boiler lighting sequence taking place in the event of the fan not operating, e.g. power cut or fan failure.

Figure 38: Room sealed fanned draught instantaneous water heater

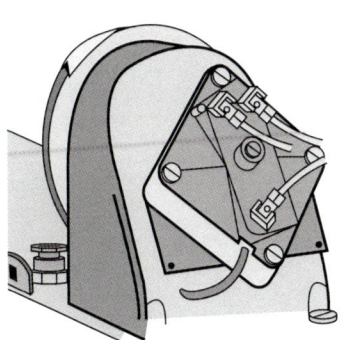

Figure 39: Air pressure switch

April 2017 © BPEC

Instantaneous water heater controls

For lighting purposes, the main burner ignition employs a permanent pilot arrangement, similar to that for the natural draught model. The gas/water control devices are also relatively similar.

The controls on this appliance comprise a range of thermal, electric and electronic switches. Broadly speaking, the thermal controls are for the pilot flame supervision, the electric controls are for functional switching and the electronic controls (printed circuit board) act as a fail safe (security) measure for the functional controls. Figure 40 shows the appliance operating sequence.

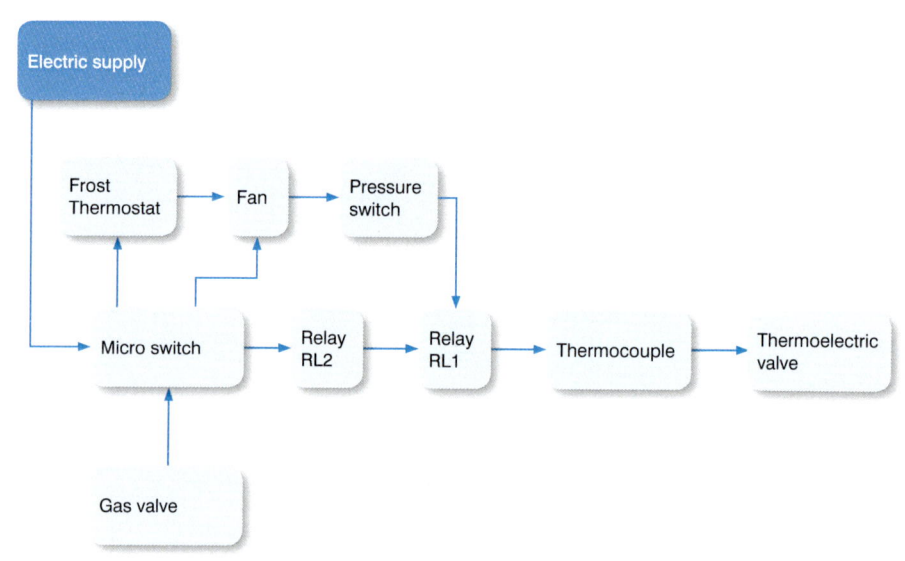

Figure 40: Appliance operating sequence

The circuit is designed so that, under normal conditions, the fan runs continuously at low speed and changes to high speed when the gas valve opens. If however, the incoming air temperature approaches 0°C an integral frost protection thermostat (optional) interrupts the low fan speed signal. Under this condition, if there is a demand for hot water, then the fan re-commences at high speed. There is an in-built delay circuit to prevent the supply devices operating prematurely.

The pilot can only be established under the control of the thermocouple flame failure circuit. After the mains electricity connection is made, it is dependent on the energising of relay – RL1. If the air flow is not proved on high speed, the flame supervision device will operate by interrupting the thermocouple as a result of the de-energising relay – RL1. Figure 41 shows a typical appliance operational wiring diagram.

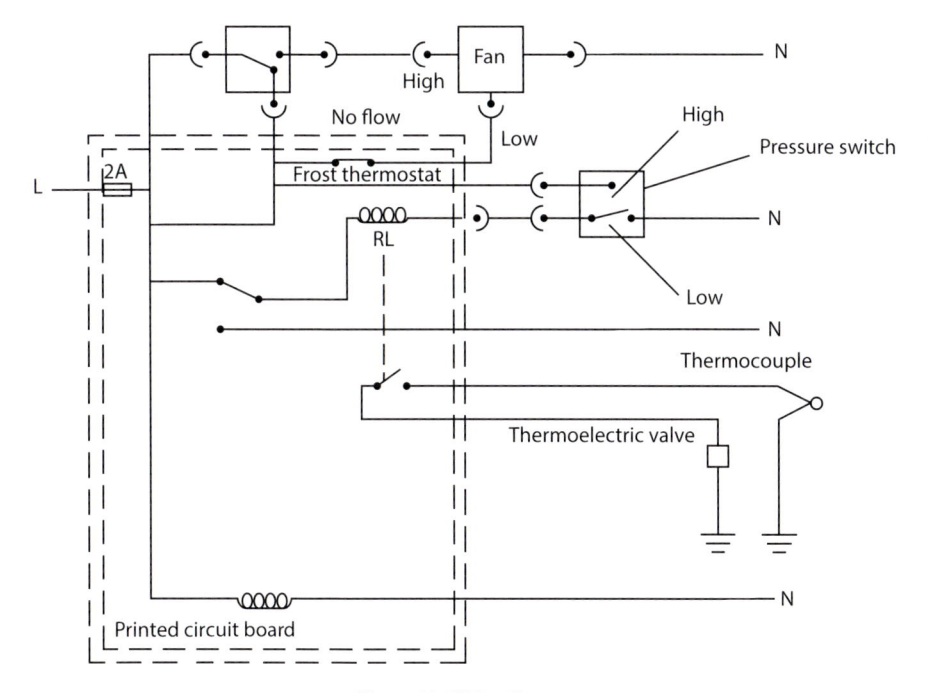

Figure 41: Wiring diagram

We have now covered the various types of instantaneous hot water heaters and their operating principles in some detail. This provides important preliminary learning before progressing into the installation/commissioning and service/maintenance.

# Section 5 – Installation and Commissioning of Instantaneous Hot Water Heaters

Introduction

In this section we will focus on the key installation and commissioning aspects of instantaneous hot water heaters by looking at:

- Permitted installation locations for appliances.
- Appliances installed in cupboards/compartments.
- Roof space installations.
- Flue requirements of instantaneous hot water heaters.
- Installation of instantaneous hot water heaters.
- Commissioning of instantaneous hot water heaters.

Part 1 – Permitted Installation Locations for Appliances

Rooms in which instantaneous hot water heaters can be installed are governed by the appliance flue type, which effects the rooms in which they may be installed.

Specific attention needs to be given to flueless heaters. They should:

- Not be installed in rooms with a volume of $5m^3$ or less. They should be fitted into rooms with openable windows and permanent free area of ventilation should be provided as follows:
  - Room size between $5m^3$ to $10m^3$ requires $100cm^2$ of ventilation.
  - Room size between $11m^3$ to $20m^3$ requires $50cm^2$ of ventilation.
  - Room size above $20m^3$ requires no ventilation.
- Not be operated for periods of five minutes or more.
- Not be used to supply a draw-off tap outside the room or space in which it is situated.
- Not be used to feed a shower and should only be used to feed basins and sinks.

The majority of multi-point appliances installed are of the room sealed type, although older appliances tend to be open flued.

Remember that wherever possible it is preferable to install a room sealed appliance as the safest option!

Bathrooms/shower rooms

Open flued/flueless appliances may not be installed in bathrooms or shower rooms.

Room sealed appliances may be installed; there are, however, restrictions placed on the actual appliance location (for appliances incorporating electrics) by the IET Wiring Regulations, 17th Edition.

Toilets/cloakroom

It is strongly recommended that only room sealed appliances are installed in these rooms.

Flueless appliances are not allowed in toilets or cloakrooms having a volume less than $5m^3$. Where open flued/flueless appliances are installed, air supply for combustion (where required) should be provided directly from the outside air.

Bed sit and bedrooms (sleeping accommodation)

Appliances installed over 14kW gross heat input must be room sealed.

As of 1st January 1996 open flued appliances rated at under 14kW gross heat input may be installed. However, the appliance(s) must also have an atmosphere sensing device for automatic shut down of the appliance in the event of a build up of products of combustion.

Other siting issues

There are further limitations placed on the sitting of water heaters, namely:

- The provision of adequate space, in accordance with the manufacturer's installation instructions:
  - To ensure sufficient air for combustion and cooling purposes.
  - To allow for maintenance and servicing, e.g. removal of the burner tray.
- Protection of the floor or wall on which the appliance is mounted, in line with the manufacturer's installation instructions.
- Any water heater located in a compartment should have at least 75mm clearance from combustible materials or be suitably protected with non-combustible material.

Part 2 – Commissioning of Instantaneous Hot Water Heaters

The commissioning of gas fired appliances tends to be slightly different for each appliance manufactured. However, by taking a look at the commissioning procedures associated with the following appliance types, we should have an overview of the commissioning procedures for all types of boilers and circulators:

- Flueless single point heaters.
- Additional requirements of natural draught multipoint appliances.
- Additional requirements of fanned draught multipoint appliances.

Before we look at appliance commissioning in detail, remember that if you have not installed the appliance, then you need to go through all the relevant checks first to ensure that the installation meets both legislative and manufacturer's requirements. Here are the checks for each type.

Flueless single point heaters – Checks

- Open the gas and water service taps.
- Ensure that the pilot assembly and its components are correctly positioned.
- Fit the gas and water control knobs, purge and flush the appliance where necessary; light the pilot.
- When the pilot is alight, wait 10 seconds then turn the gas control fully anti-clockwise to the main gas position.
- Turn on the hot tap; the main burner will now light.
- Check for gas tightness on appliance gas carrying components. Turn off the gas control knob.
- Check the burner pressure by removing the screw from the pressure test point (A) in Figure 42 on the end of the burner manifold. Attach a suitable pressure gauge. Light the appliance and check the working gas pressure. If the gas pressure is not correct, check the pressure at the meter. The gas installation should be examined for any possible blockage if the pressure is not correct. The heat input is pre-set and non-adjustable.

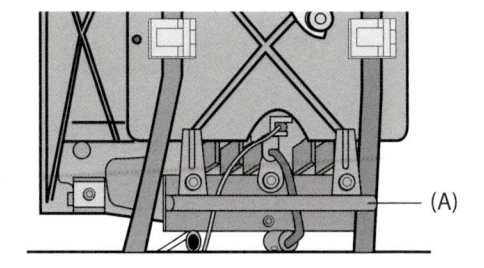

Figure 42: Burner pressure test point

- Ensure that the main burner lights smoothly. The slow ignition device may require adjustment in the event of explosive lighting of the main burner.
- Turn off at the gas control knob, remove pressure gauge, replace the test point screw, re-light and check for gas tightness around the screw, with leak detection fluid or soft soap solution.
- Check the safe operation of the flame supervision device:
  - By blowing out the pilot. The flow of gas to the pilot will cease and the thermo-electric valve should drop out with an audible click, within a maximum period specified by the manufacturer. Carry out a tightness test between the multifunctional control valve and gas cock to ensure that the FSD is not passing gas.
  - Ensure that the room is well ventilated and the heater is cold (having been off for a minimum of usually 15 minutes).
  - Light the pilot, then turn the gas control knob to the main gas position.
  - Place a plate, as shown in Figure 43, over the deflector and then open the hot water tap.
  - The atmosphere sensing device should turn off the pilot and main gas valve within a time period prescribed by the appliance manufacturer.
- The water temperature rise across the appliance should be measured together with the appliance flow rate to determine whether these meet manufacturer requirements:
  - Temperature rise is measured by comparing the cold water (incoming mains) temperature reading at a suitable tap, then taking a hot water reading at the hot water outlet.
  - Water flow rate is measured using a flow meter, or weir gauge.
  - Where flow rate is not meeting manufacturer's requirements, some appliances may be adjusted.
- If all checks are completed successfully, the casing should be replaced.

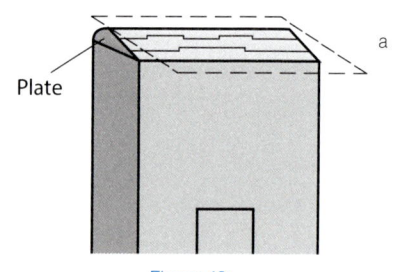

Figure 43: Testing atmospheric sensing device

And remember, before leaving the site you should:
- Demonstrate the application of the appliance and controls to the user.
- Leave all relevant appliance instructions on site and advise the customer about the appliance servicing requirements.

Additional requirements of natural draught multipoint appliances

The commissioning procedures are similar to those for the flueless single point heater. Additional checks include:
- Checking the burner pressure and adjusting the gas rate where necessary.
- On open flued appliances check that there is no spillage of combustion products from the draught diverter outlet by carrying out a spillage test as detailed in BS 5440-1: 2008.

Note: Where the room contains an extractor fan, carry out the test with the fan operating at maximum speed and all the doors and windows closed. When the fan is in an adjacent room, the test should be carried out with the connecting door open.

Additional requirements of fanned draught multipoint appliances

Additionally, the following should be carried out:

Microswitch

Whilst the microswitch is usually factory set (Figure 44) it may require adjustment. When the appliance is at rest, the fan runs continuously at low speed.

Check operation as follow: Set temperature selector to high – then open draw-off. The fan should now come to high speed before the burner ignites. On closing draw-off, the burner should extinguish before the fan resumes at low speed. If fan burner operational sequence is **not** as described, the micro-switch can usually be adjusted by referring to manufacturer's guidance.

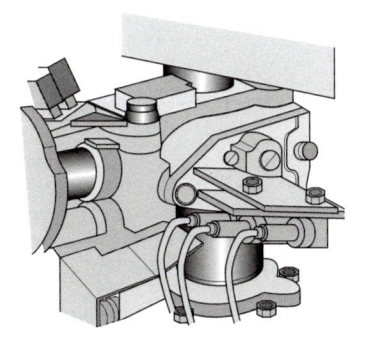

Figure 44: Micro switch assembly

Air pressure switch

Check the operation of the air pressure switch in Figure 45 as follows: Open draw-off, fan comes to high speed and the burner ignites. Close draw-off, burner extinguishes and when fan resumes at low speed listen for the click as the relay changes over. This should be followed within 15 seconds by a lighter click as the pressure switch changes over.

If the time separation is greater than 15 seconds or if the pilot extinguishes, it suggests that the pressure switch is incorrectly set. This can usually be adjusted by referring to manufacturer's instructions.

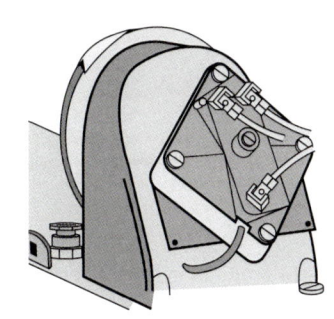

Figure 45: Air pressure switch

Thermo-electric circuit

The thermo-electric circuit is fitted with an interrupter, so that if the air flow is not proved on high speed the circuit is incomplete and the flame supervision device will operate. In the case of intermittent pilot failure or permanent pilot failure, the thermocouple circuit can be checked with a multimeter or suitable millivolt meter to determine if the pilot failure is due to poor thermocouple output, high resistance through Relay-1 contact or faulty thermo-electric valve.

The thermocouple output measured at the printed circuit board terminals will usually be specified by the manufacturer.

With fan assisted appliances, particular attention needs to be given to the appliance case seals. In some cases fans are installed on the combustion air flow side of the appliance, which makes the appliance chamber operate under positive air pressure. If the case seals leak, the products of combustion can discharge into the room in which the appliance is located. This can be dangerous.

Remember that checking the case seals is extremely important on all types of heaters, particularly those using fans.

Conversely, heaters that incorporate fans on the flue side of the appliance make the appliance operate under negative pressure. If the case seals leak, air will be drawn into the chamber from the room, possibly causing the pressure switch to activate and the heater not to operate.

Section 6 – Service, Maintenance and Repair of Instantaneous Hot Water Heaters

Part 1 – Unsafe Situations

A serious problem which can occur with appliances is fume leakage associated with defective case seals.

Fumes can leak to a greater or lesser extent from appliance case seals which are intended to prevent flue gases entering the room. Wall mounted appliances tend to be those in which defective case seals may be the greatest problem, as usually there will be an inner case which incorporates a seal surrounding the heat exchanger/burner etc. This seal, if care is not taken, may not be made correctly on initial installation or the sealing material may break on removing the inner case when undertaking servicing.

The result of leaking case seals can be serious, particularly on fan assisted appliances working under positive pressure in the combustion chamber, as the appliance is effectively pressurised. Dependent on the degree of fume leakage, it may be appropriate in certain instances to categorise fume leakage from defective case seals as Immediately Dangerous (ID).

Remember to always check to ensure that an effective case seal has been made. Always repair defective seals with the materials recommended by the appliance manufacturer.

Having established whether an appliance may fall into the unsafe category, let us take a look at service and maintenance.

Part 2 – Service and Maintenance of Instantaneous Hot Water Heaters

The following identifies a general procedure for carrying out service/maintenance of instantaneous hot water heaters:

Step 1 – Carry out preliminary checks

- Light the appliance and put into full operation, checking the function of the appliance components.
- Check the general condition of the installation and its conformity with the Gas Safety (Installation and Use) Regulations 1998 and British Standard requirements.
- For open flued/flueless installations, check to ensure that sufficient free area of ventilation has been provided, and check for any fan systems that may be fitted, e.g. mechanical extraction.
- Check compartment ventilation requirements and provision of appropriate warning notices.
- Check the flue – it should be free from obvious defects.
- Check the flue terminal is suitable and that the termination location is acceptable.
- Check that the appliance includes an atmosphere (vitiation) sensing device (ASD) where required.
- Check for signs of spillage on the appliance and adjacent decoration.

Note any defects and advise the customer prior to the service taking place.

BPEC Module 17

Step 2 – Servicing procedures

- Isolate the gas, water and any electrical supplies to the appliance, checking the correct rated fuse is fitted, carry out electrical check, e.g. earth continuity, short circuit and polarity where applicable.
- Remove the appliance front casing (see Figure 46).

Step 3 – Burner

Remove the combustion chamber front panel:

- Remove the burner from the appliance and clean following manufacturer's procedures.
- Replace the burner, making sure that the seal between the gas tube and main burner is gas tight (see Figure 47).

Figure 46: Appliance casing

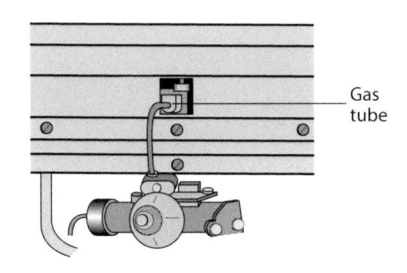

Figure 47: Gas tube assembly

Step 4 – Pilot

- Clean the pilot burner following manufacturer's procedures.
- Re-assemble the pilot burner and check the position of the pilot assembly components (see Figure 48).

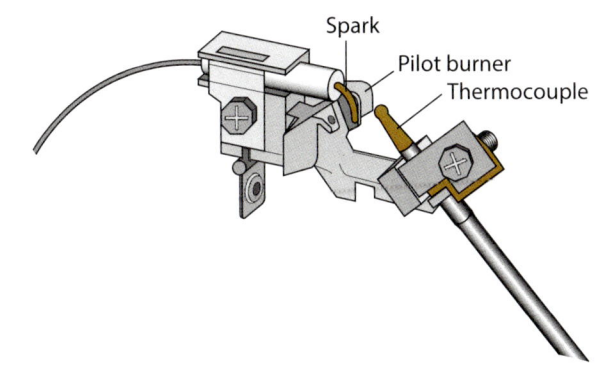

Figure 48: Pilot assembly components

April 2017 © BPEC

Step 5 – Heat exchanger

- Ensure the combustion chamber panel is removed, then clean the flueways. If extensive cleaning is necessary, the heat exchanger may need to be removed from the appliance.
- Periodically it may be necessary to remove scale deposits from the waterways of the appliance to ensure continued and efficient operation. The frequency will depend largely on the hardness of the water in each specific area (see Figure 49).

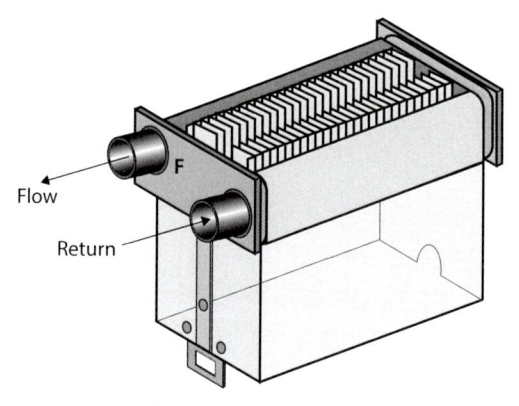

Figure 49: Heat exchanger

Step 6 – Main gas valve

- Strip down the main gas valve following manufacturer's procedures.
- Remove the hexagonal spring.
- Grease spindle with approved grease.
- Renew sealing washers as necessary and assemble components.

Step 7 – Water governor

- Drain the appliance.
- Remove the governor situated in the base of the water section.
- Clean the components with water and grease (as necessary).
- Check that the spring loaded piston moves freely.
- Replace in reverse order.

Step 8 – Gas and water filters

- Remove and clean out the appliance gas and water filters.

Step 9 – Appliance seals
- Check all the appliance seals, joints (including casing seals) and components.
- Check the effectiveness and continuity of the flue. Re-assemble appliance, replace components as necessary and fit panels and case etc.

Step 10 – Technical checks
- Check that there is no obvious damage to the electrical wiring, and carry out electrical checks where necessary.

Final checks
- Turn on gas, water, electric supplies, purge gas, check for water and gas leaks.
- Light the appliance pilot.
- Check to ensure that the pilot flame correctly envelopes the thermocouple/FSD.
- Light the main burner and check/re-set the operating pressure to meet system requirements (confirm satisfactory flame picture and smooth lighting).
- Carry out a spillage test on open flued appliances; where fans are fitted, with and without fan operating (maximum speed).
- Check the operation of the flame supervision device, atmosphere sensing device (if fitted) and air pressure switch (if fitted) following manufacturer's procedures.
- Check the appliance's water flow rate and water temperature rise.
- Check the operation of the thermostat and the operation of any safety devices.
- Check working pressure and gas rates are correct and determine that the gas pipe is correctly sized for the appliance.
- Leave the site in a clean and tidy condition.

Part 3 – Typical Gas Component Faults on Instantaneous Hot Water Heaters

This section focuses on the diagnosis of faults associated with the key gas safety components which are installed in instantaneous hot water heaters. The section will focus on:

- Unsatisfactory ignition of burners/defective flame supervision devices.
- Unstable flame picture.
- Signs of flue spillage.
- Scaled heat exchanger.
- Inoperable air pressure switches.
- Defective gas valve assembly.

Before undertaking this section you should understand how a multimeter is used. Remember to always work safely – a safe electrical isolation procedure is included in that section. Only use test equipment that has been regularly safety checked and calibrated.

| BPEC | Domestic Central Heating and Water Heaters (CENWAT) |

Unsatisfactory ignition of burners

Let us take a look at the faults which may occur with the unsatisfactory ignition of burners.

The pilot ignition

The manufacturer will usually include either a fault diagnostic flow chart or a simple chart listing the possible faults. Table 1 shows typical faults associated with pilot ignition:

Table 1: Pilot fault chart

Pilot does not light.	i) Gas service cock closed.	Open service cock.
	ii) Air in pipe.	Purge line.
	iii) Pilot injector blocked.	Clean or change.
	iv) No ignition spark.	Check electrode, lead and ignitor.
Poor pilot flame.	i) Pilot injector dirty.	Clean or change.
	ii) Wrong injector.	Change for correct diameter.
	iii) Pilot head blocked.	Clean.
	iv) Faulty pilot tube.	Clean or replace.
	v) Pilot injector loose.	Tighten.
Pilot will not stay alight.	i) Pilot flame poor.	(See above checks).
	ii) Faulty flue.	(See above checks).
	iii) Thermocouple (FSD) not working.	a) Check connection is clean and tighten if necessary not working.
		b) Replace if output less than 8mv.
	iv) Thermoelectric valve faulty.	Replace if drop out greater than 5mv.
	v) Gas pressure low/variable.	Check at inlet to appliance.
	vi) Terminal wrongly positioned.	Re-position.
	vii) Badly assembled flue.	Refit check seal and check appliance operation.
	viii) Pressure switch faulty.	Replace.
	ix) Plug loose on PCB.	Secure.
	x) PCB faulty.	Replace.

Main burner ignition

Main burner ignition may be affected by a number of possible faults, as indicated in Table 2.

Table 2: Burner fault flow chart

Main burner does not light correctly.	i) Gas service cock not open fully.	Open fully.
	ii) Gas pressure low.	Check at manifold and at inlet with the appliance running.
	iii) Water flow rate low.	Check if water rate sufficient.
	iv) Gas valve not opening.	Check v) and vi).
	v) Diaphragm punctured.	Change diaphragm.
	vi) Venturi blocked or loose.	Check Venturi.
	vii) Gas control tap faulty.	Check operation of user's gas control tap.
	viii) Slow ignition device screwed fully home.	Adjust.
	ix) PCB failure.	Replace PCB.

© BPEC   April 2017

There may be problems with the actual main burner lighting procedure where the main burner does not light smoothly or lights with a bang. This can be associated with two possible faults:

- The pilot assembly is partially blocked or incorrectly positioned, resulting in the pilot flame not adequately playing on the main burner. In terms of this fault the pilot burner assembly should be cleaned and/or re-positioned.
- The slow ignition device may need adjusting in accordance with manufacturer's requirements.

Unstable flame picture

With instantaneous hot water heaters an unstable flame picture is usually caused by:

a) **An inadequate supply of combustion air.** Air inlets which are choked with lint or a blocked heat exchanger or flueways will result in an unstable flame picture. The symptoms of this problem are flames which have long or non existent cones with soft yellow tips. The solution to this problem is to:

- Ensure that adequate permanent ventilation is provided.
- Clean any choked lint arrestors, burners or heater flueways.

b) **Incorrectly set gas rate.** The main problem here tends to be with over-gassing of the appliance. This can be caused by installation of the wrong sized injectors or incorrect control of the gas burner pressure.

The symptoms of over-gassing are similar to a lack of air supply, where the flames become longer and softer. The solution in this case could be to check the injectors if these are believed to be of the wrong size, or correctly set the appliance gas burner pressure.

Signs of flue spillage

Flue spillage on open flued appliances will result in the products of combustion being discharged into the room in which the appliance is situated. Typically, where spillage occurs, appliance surfaces (above pilot windows) and wall surfaces around draught diverter inlets and the outlet of flueless heaters will show signs of discolouration.

Spillage on open flued appliances will usually be caused by either one or a combination of the following:

- Incorrect flue system.
- Lack of permanent ventilation.
- Appliance requiring cleaning/servicing.

A sooted (blocked) heat exchanger will result in the products of combustion being discharged through openings in the combustion chamber such as primary air ports/pilot windows. Spillage/discolouration at the draught diverter will indicate signs of either a blocked/partially blocked secondary flue, an inadequate flue terminal or an incorrectly positioned flue terminal.

Excessive levels of products of combustion into the room from a flueless appliance can be caused by one or a combination of the following:

- Appliance in operation for too long a period of time.
- Lack of permanent ventilation.
- Appliance requiring cleaning/servicing.

Where spillage occurs, immediate remedial action should be taken.

Scaled heat exchanger

A scaled heat exchanger usually results in the heaters heat exchanger transmitting a noise due to a reduction in the water flow rate. As the problem persists, the scale deposited on the inner surfaces of the heat exchanger will cause the appliance to overheat and ultimately to cease to operate.

The water temperature at the outlet will be hotter than usual, and the water may have a milky appearance.

The appliance can usually be de-scaled in accordance with manufacturer's procedures. In cases where a high degree of scaling has occurred, the heat exchanger may have to be replaced.

In hard water areas it is always advisable to install a scale reducer to minimise problems.

Inoperative air pressure switches

An air pressure switch is usually installed in an appliance which may have relatively complex electronic circuitry. Therefore, the manufacturer's flow chart should be referred to at all times.

The symptom of air pressure switch failure is usually that the fan will start but the heater does not commence its lighting sequence.

The manufacturer may have a procedure developed for checking the operation of the air pressure switch, or alternatively the switch can be checked (if possible) by pulling off one of the input pipes. Fit a suitable input tube to the input port, blow gently into the valve and listen for clicking of the micro-switch. Its operation can also be checked using a multimeter continuity test, which should show a zero reading.

Remember that the air pressure switch may be affected by defective case seals and by splits, kinks or loose connections associated with air supply tubes.

Defective gas valve assembly

A defective gas valve assembly will usually result in the main burner failing to light. Preliminary checks should be carried out to ensure that the flame supervision device, air pressure switch, fan, etc. are operating correctly. Failure will usually be caused by:

- Defective diaphragm.
- Failure of the valve mechanism itself.

On simpler models the failure of the burner to light could also be caused by:

- Bent or sticking gas valve push rod.
- Blocked low pressure duct.
- Incorrectly adjusted slow ignition device.

A bent or sticking push rod could also cause the reverse problem with the gas valve. If the valve spring cannot force the push rod down to allow the gas valve to close correctly, a flame may remain on the burner without water flowing through the heat exchanger. The result will be overheated water that expands rapidly and may cause the heat exchanger water ways to split explosively. It is for this reason that many manufacturers recommend greasing the gas valve push rod at every annual service.

The solution will be to replace or lubricate/grease components as deemed necessary.

Practical Tasks

The practical activities link directly with the performance criteria of the Nationally Accredited Certification assessments (ACS) for Domestic Central Heating and Water Heaters (CENWAT).

Your tutor will assess your practical training requirements before undertaking the practical tasks and may require you to:

- Complete all the tasks identified, or
- Complete some of the tasks identified (based on previous experience).

You should have access to the appliance manufacturer's instructions. You may also use the knowledge manuals associated with the course.

You will be given the following activities to be carried out:

- Installation (or exchange) of either a room sealed, natural draught boiler or an open flued natural draught boiler. The flue systems will be pre-installed for either of these two appliances. Specific installation tasks on other appliances may also be required.
- Commissioning a natural draught boiler.
- Servicing a natural draught boiler.
- Diagnosing typical faults on a range of gas central heating boilers.
- Installation (or exchange) of a room sealed instantaneous multi-point water heater.
- Commissioning an instantaneous multi-point water heater.
- Servicing an instantaneous multi-point water heater.
- Diagnosing typical faults on a range of instantaneous hot water heaters.

To assist you in the process of carrying out the work, you should complete the information required in the following pro-forma.

Note – To complete all the tasks you will be required to work on more than one appliance.

| BPEC | Domestic Central Heating and Water Heaters (CENWAT) |

Pre-installation checks

Task 1

Is the proposed appliance location in a permissible position?   Yes   No

If no, identify the problem:

Task 2

Visually check the existing pipework system and note any defects below, including any remedial actions necessary, e.g. pipework fixings, pipe size materials etc.

Task 3

Check to ensure that the gas supply has been effectively isolated prior to the work commencing.
Has the gas supply been effectively isolated?   Yes   No

If no, what remedial action is necessary?

Task 4

Carry out a gas tightness test of the existing pipework installation prior to the work commencing.
Does the tightness test indicate that the pipework system is leak free?   Yes   No

If no, what remedial actions are necessary?

Task 5

Visually check the flue system to confirm that it conforms with manufacturer/British Standard requirements.
Is the flue system acceptable?   Yes   No

If no, what remedial actions are necessary?

Task 6

Visually check the appliance to be installed and identify whether there are any obvious defects.
Is the appliance in a suitable condition?   Yes   No

If no, what defects have you identified?

Installation (or exchange) of the appliance

Task 7
Connect the appliance to the flue system following manufacturer's installation procedures.

Task 8
Connect the gas pipework to the appliance.

Task 9
Carry out a gas tightness test on the installation.
Is the reading acceptable?   Yes   No

Task 10
On a room sealed boiler check that the flue connection has been made satisfactorily.
Are the boiler/flue seals adequate?   Yes   No
Are the casing seals adequate?   Yes   No

If no, what remedial actions are necessary?

Task 11
On an open flued boiler check that the flue connection has been made satisfactorily. Carry out a flue flow test on the appliance.
Is the flue system satisfactory?   Yes   No

If no, what remedial actions are necessary?

Commissioning the appliance

Task 12
Is the appliance/installation purged of air? Yes No

Task 13
Is the working pressure at the appliance correct? Yes No

Task 14
Are the burner flame picture, stability and ignition correct? Yes No

Task 15
Does spillage test on an open flued appliance confirm that the flue system is operating correctly? Yes No

Task 16
Are the user controls operating correctly? Yes No

Task 17
Are the safety (flame supervision) devices operating correctly? Yes No

Task 18
Are the temperature controls operating correctly? Yes No

Tasks 12-18 – Note any deficiencies identified during the commissioning procedure in this box:

Task 19
Subject to the installation being satisfactorily commissioned, explain the safe operation of the appliance to the customer/user of gas, leaving the manufacturers' installation and user instructions with them.

| BPEC | Domestic Central Heating and Water Heaters (CENWAT) |

Servicing an appliance

Task 20

Carry out a full service on a gas boiler. The following table is included for your use. Note any components in the box below which may need replacement.

Component	Serviced/Cleaned Yes/No	Not fitted to Appliance
Burner(s)/injector(s)		
Primary air port		
Combustion chamber		
Heat exchanger		
Ignition device		
Control thermostat		
Overheat thermostat		
Air pressure switch		
Flame supervision device		

Note defects identified here:

Fault diagnosis

Task 21

You will be given a number of appliances with specific gas safety faults. Your tutor will advise on the number of faults per appliance. You should list the faults associated with each appliance below.

Appliance 1 – Faults identified:

Appliance 2 – Faults identified:

Appliance 3 – Faults identified:

Appliance 4 – Faults identified:

Appliance 5 – Faults identified:

Water Heaters Pre-installed checks

Task 22
Is the proposed appliance located in a permissible position?   Yes   No

If no, identify the problem(s).

Task 23
Visually check the existing pipework system and note any defects below, and any remedial actions necessary, e.g. pipework fixings, pipe size, cross bonding etc.

Task 24
Check to ensure that the gas supply has been effectively isolated prior to the work commencing.
Has the gas supply been effectively isolated?   Yes   No

If no, what remedial action is necessary?

Task 25
Carry out a gas tightness test of the existing pipework installation prior to the work commencing.
After satisfactory let-by, does the tightness test indicate that the pipework system is leak free?   Yes   No

If no, identify the problem(s).

Task 26
Visually check the flue system and ventilation requirements to confirm that it conforms with manufacturer/British Standard requirements. Note BS715 recommends that where a replacement appliance is to be installed into an existing satisfactory flue, the flue must last the lifetime of the appliance, normally 10-15 years.
Is the flue system acceptable?   Yes   No

If no, what remedial action is necessary?

Task 27
Visually check the appliance to be installed and identify whether there are any obvious defects. Check also for safety identification marks etc and that the appliance is suitable for the gas being used.
Is the appliance in suitable condition?   Yes   No

If no, what remedial action is necessary?

| BPEC | Domestic Central Heating and Water Heaters (CENWAT) |

Installation (or exchange) of the appliance

Task 28
Connect the appliance to the flue system in accordance with manufacturer's installation procedures.
Check the ventilation requirements of the replacement appliance, where applicable.

Task 29
Connect the gas pipework to the appliance.

Task 30
Carry out a gas tightness test on the installation.
Is the installation gas tight?   Yes   No

Task 31
On a room sealed, natural draught multipoint heater, check that the flue connection has been made satisfactorily.

Are the heater/flue seals adequate?   Yes   No

Are the casing seals adequate?   Yes   No

If no, what remedial action is necessary?

Commissioning the appliance
Is the ventilation, where appropriate, adequate for the appliance?   Yes   No

Are all the joints sound?   Yes   No

Has the appliance been completely flushed to remove debris and   Yes   No
jointing compounds, flux etc.?

Has a test for gas tightness been carried out?   Yes   No

BPEC   Module 17

Task 32
Has the appliance/installation been purged of air?   Yes   No

Light the appliance in accordance with manufacturer's instructions.

Task 33
Is the working pressure at the appliance correct?   Yes   No

Is the gas rate correct?   Yes   No

Task 34
Has the ignition and stability of burners been checked?   Yes   No

Have all the water joints been re-checked after running hot for water leaks?   Yes   No

Have checks for spillage, and in the case of room sealed appliances,   Yes   No
flue and case seal checks been carried out?

Task 35
Are the user controls operating correctly?   Yes   No

Task 36
Are the safety and FSD control devices operating correctly?   Yes   No

Task 37
Are the temperature controls operating correctly?   Yes   No

Task 38
Is the appliance adjusted to give correct temperature rise and   Yes   No
water flow rate?

Task 32 – 38 Note any deficiencies in the commissioning procedure in this box:

Task 39
Subject to the installation being satisfactorily commissioned, explain the safe operation of the appliance. Ensure that the customer is left with the manufacturer's and user's instructions demonstrating the use of controls and efficient operation on final completion.

Servicing an appliance

Task 40
Carry out a full service on a gas water heater. The following table is included for your use. Note any components which may need replacement.

Component	Serviced/Cleaned Yes/No	Requiring replacement Yes/No	Not fitted to appliance
Burner(s)/injector(s)			
Primary air ports			
Combustion chamber			
Heat exchanger			
Ignition device			
Thermista-stat(s)			
Slow ignition device			
Water controls/filters			
Flame supervision device			

Note further details here:

Fault diagnosis

Task 41

You will be given a number of appliances with specific gas safety faults. Your tutor will advise the number of faults per appliance. You should list the faults associated with each appliance below.

Appliance 1 – Faults identified:

Appliance 2 – Faults identified:

Appliance 3 – Faults identified:

Appliance 4 – Faults identified:

Appliance 5 – Faults identified:

Knowledge Questions

Domestic Central Heating and Water Heaters (CENWAT)

Section 1 – Types of Appliances and their Operating Principles

1. What is the purpose of an atmosphere (vitiation) sensing device (ASD) fitted to an open flued appliance?

2. What are the three separate control devices incorporated into a standard multifunctional control valve fitted to a gas boiler?
   a)
   b)
   c)

3. What is the purpose of the following components which may be fitted to gas boilers?
   a) Control thermostats
   b) Overheat thermostats

4. What is the name of the component fitted to a fan assisted boiler which prevents the boiler from operating if the fan fails?

5. What is the purpose of a lint arrestor fitted to a boiler burner?

6. Why does a condensing boiler require condensate water to be drained away from the appliance?

7. Do traditional fire back circulators use fully mechanical thermostats?

8. What are the two components of the pilot assembly in a fan assisted appliance using a flame supervision device working on the flame conduction and rectification principle?
   a)
   b)

Section 2 – Installation and Commissioning of Central Heating Boilers and Circulators

1. Can an open flued circulator be installed in a bathroom?

2. What added safety device should be fitted to an open flued boiler of 10kW heat input to be installed in a bed-sitting room?

3. What are the four key requirements which must be met when installing a boiler in a compartment?
    a)
    b)
    c)
    d)

4. When siting a circulator in an understairs cupboard in a four storey property, the cupboard must incorporate two additional features to those you have described in question 3. What are these?
    a)
    b)

5. What is the minimum thickness of hearth for a fire-back boiler?

6. When siting a combined fire back boiler and gas fire, what is the minimum distance that is specified between the gas fire flame and the floor?

7. Which seven requirements must be met for a boiler to be installed in a roof space?
    a)
    b)
    c)
    d)
    e)
    f)
    g)

8. Can a room sealed boiler be installed in a private garage?

Section 3 – Service, Maintenance and Repair of Central Heating Boilers and Circulators

1. You have been called to a job where the customer is complaining of a gas-like smell in the kitchen in which a wall mounted room sealed fan assisted boiler is sited. Which three things could be the cause of the problem?
   a)
   b)
   c)

2. An open flued circulator, which you have been asked to look at, has been described by the customer as making a loud 'bang-like explosive noise' when it lights up. What are the two possible causes to the problem?
   a)
   b)

3. You have been asked to look at a boiler which the customer says is making a boiling noise described as being like a steam train. This noise is being heard throughout the heating system pipework in the entire property. What is the most likely cause of the problem?

4. Yellow flames are being discharged from an open flued gas boiler burner which has not been serviced for three years. What is the most likely cause of the problem?

5. You have been called to a fanned draught boiler which heats up to approximately 50°C. The appliance then 'cuts out' and will not re-light without manual re-setting. The control thermostat is set at 70°C and appears to be operating adequately. What is the likely cause of the problem?

6. A fan assisted boiler incorporating an intermittent pilot fails to light and does not commence its pilot or main burner ignition sequence. It appears however that the combustion fan is operating correctly. What are the two likely causes of the problem?
   a)
   b)

7. A pilot light on an open flued natural draught boiler containing a standard multifunctional control valve operating on the thermo-electric flame failure principle will not remain alight, even though the manufacturer lighting procedure has been followed. What are the three possible causes?
   a)
   b)
   c)

BPEC   Module 17

Section 4 – Types of Appliances and their Operating Principles

1. What is the purpose of a slow ignition device fitted to an instantaneous hot water heater?

2. What is the purpose of an atmosphere sensing device (ASD) fitted to an open flued/flueless appliance?

3. Name the component fitted to a fanned draught boiler which prevents the boiler from operating if the fan fails.

4. The pilot assembly in a room sealed, natural draught instantaneous hot water heater incorporating a flame supervision device working on the thermo-electric principle usually contains three components. Name them.
    a)
    b)
    c)

5. What is the purpose of a water throttle on an instantaneous multipoint water heater?

6. Why would a scale reducer be fitted to a system incorporating an instantaneous water heater?

Section 5 – Installation and Commissioning of Instantaneous Hot Water Heaters

1. Can an open flued water heater be installed in a bathroom?

2. Which added safety device should be fitted to a flueless single point water heater of 7kW gross heat input to be installed in a bed-sitting room?

3. Can a flueless single point water heater be used to supply a shower?

4. Which four key requirements must be met when installing a water heater in a compartment?
    a)
    b)
    c)
    d)

5. When siting a water heater in an understairs cupboard in a four storey property, the cupboard must incorporate two additional features to those you have described in question 3. Name them.
    a)
    b)

April 2017   © BPEC

| BPEC | Domestic Central Heating and Water Heaters (CENWAT) |

6. Which seven requirements must be met for a water heater to be installed in a roof space?
   a)
   b)
   c)
   d)
   e)
   f)
   g)

7. Can a room sealed water heater be installed in a private garage?

Section 6 – Service, Maintenance and Repair of Instantaneous Hot Water Heaters

1. You have been called to a job where the customer is complaining of a gas-like smell in the kitchen, in which a wall mounted room sealed fan assisted water heater is sited. Which three things could be the cause of the problem?
   a)
   b)
   c)

2. An instantaneous water heater which you have been asked to look at has been described by the customer as making a loud 'bang-like explosive noise' when it lights up. What are two possible causes of the problem.
   a)
   b)

3. You have been asked to look at a water heater which the customer says is making a 'whining noise' when it operates. The heater is installed in a hard water area. What is the most likely cause of the problem?

4. Yellow flames are being discharged from an open flued water heater which has not been serviced for three years. What is the most likely cause of the problem?

5. A pilot light on a room sealed, C11 type water heater containing a standard multifunctional control valve operating on the thermo-electric flame failure principle will not remain alight, even though the manufacturer's lighting procedure has been followed. What are three possible causes of the problem?
   a)
   b)
   c)

6. You have been called to an open flued water heater which has black marks around the draught diverter.
   a) What is the likely cause of the problem?
   b) What action would you take?

© BPEC   April 2017

BPEC Module 17

Model Answers

Section 1 – Types of Appliances and their Operating Principles

1. To prevent the appliance from operating in the event of spillage occurring and a depletion of oxygen levels.
2. a) Constant pressure governor.
   b) Flame supervision device.
   c) Solenoid valve.
3. a) To control the temperature of water within the boiler.
   b) To provide added temperature protection in the event of control thermostat failure.
4. Air pressure switch.
5. To prevent lint from entering the main burner via the air supply.
6. The boiler operates at low flue gas temperature with the majority of the water vapour in the products of combustion in liquid form. This liquid must be drained away from the appliance for it to operate correctly.
7. Yes.
8. a) Pilot burner.
   b) Ignition/detection electrode.

Section 2 – Installation and Commissioning of Central Heating Boilers and Circulators

1. No.
2. Atmosphere sensing device (ASD).
3. You should have chosen four of the following:
   a) Be fixed, rigid structures with internal surfaces that comply with any special requirements of the appliance manufacturer. If these are not known, combustible materials should be at least 75mm from the boiler, or where this is not possible, a non combustible shield of at least 25mm thickness should be provided.
   b) Allow access for inspection.
   c) Allow access for maintenance.
   d) Utilise a warning notice advising against:
      – It being used for the purposes of storage.
      – Blocking or restricting of any air vents or grilles into the compartment.
   e) Be ventilated in accordance with the requirements of BS 5440 Flues and ventilation.
4. a) All the internal surfaces of the compartment must be non combustible, or be lined with a material providing 30 minutes fire resistance.
   b) All air vents must communicate directly with the outside air.
5. 50mm.
6. 225mm.
7. You could have chosen seven of the following:
   a) Flooring area is provided – sufficient for access and servicing of the appliance.
   b) For wall mounted appliances, mounting arrangements are capable of supporting the weight of the filled boiler and associated equipment.
   c) For floor standing appliances, the base must be of non-combustible materials of at least 12mm thickness.
   d) Permanent access is required to the roof space, for instance with a fixed retractable loft ladder.
   e) The roof space exit must be protected with a guard rail, to protect against falls.

April 2017 © BPEC

    f) Fixed lighting should be provided.
    g) Stored articles should be separated from the appliance (where required) by means of a guard.
    h) Gas, water and electrical isolation points should be provided outside the roof space, so the boiler can be isolated without having to gain access to the space.
    i) Ventilation requirements also need to be considered.
8. Yes.

Section 3 – Service, Maintenance and Repair of Central Heating Boilers and Circulators

1. a) Carry out a tightness test on the system and associated components.
   b) Terminal incorrectly sited in relation to an openable door or window.
   c) Leakage from the appliance case seals.
2. a) Poor size of pilot flame – either requiring adjustment or with a partially blocked injector.
   b) The pilot burner is not correctly positioned in relation to the main burner.
3. Defective control thermostat.
4. Burner choked/blocked with lint.
5. Defective overheat thermostat.
6. a) Defective air pressure switch/split kinked tubes.
   b) Defective printed circuit board.
7. a) Inadequate pilot flame.
   b) Defective thermocouple.
   c) Defective flame supervision section of the multifunctional control valve.

Section 4 – Types of Appliances and their Operating Principles

1. To minimise noisy ignition of the gas at the main burner by encouraging smooth lighting by opening the gas valve slowly.
2. To prevent the appliance from operating in the event of incorrect combustion taking place.
3. Air pressure switch.
4. a) Pilot burner.
   b) Ignition electrode.
   c) Thermocouple.
5. To control the water temperature leaving the appliance.
6. To minimise the build up of scale (hard water deposits) in hard water areas.

Section 5 – Installation and Commissioning of Instantaneous Hot Water Heaters

1. No.
2. Atmosphere sensing device (ADS).
3. No.
4. You could have chosen four of the following:
   a) Be fixed, rigid structures with internal surfaces that comply with any special requirements of the appliance manufacturer. If these are not known, combustible materials should be at least 75mm from the boiler, or where this is not possible, a non combustible shield of at least 25mm thickness should be provided.
   b) Allow access for inspection.

c) Allow access for maintenance.
   d) Utilise a warning notice advising against:
      – It being used for the purposes of storage:
      – Blocking or restricting of any air vents or grilles into the compartment.
   e) Be ventilated in accordance with the requirements of BS 5440: 2000 Flues and ventilation.

5. a) All the internal surfaces of the compartment must be non combustible, or be lined with a material providing 30 minutes fire resistance.
   b) All air vents must communicate directly with the outside air.

6. You could have chosen seven of the following:
   a) Flooring area is provided – sufficient for access and servicing of the appliance.
   b) For wall mounted appliances, mounting arrangements are capable of supporting the weight of the filled boiler and associated equipment.
   c) For floor standing appliances, the base must be of non-combustible materials, of at least 12mm thickness.
   d) Permanent access is required to the roof space, for instance with a fixed retractable loft ladder.
   e) The roof space exit must be protected with a guard rail, to protect against falls.
   f) Adequate fixed lighting should be provided.
   g) Stored articles should be separated from the appliance (where required) by means of a guard.
   h) Gas, water and electrical isolation points should be provided outside the roof space so the boiler can be isolated without having to gain access to the space.
   i) Ventilation requirements also need to be considered.

7. Yes.

Section 6 – Service, Maintenance and Repair of Instantaneous Hot Water Heaters

1. a) Gas leak on the installation or appliances.
   b) Appliance terminal incorrectly sited in relation to openable doors or windows and the products of combustion are able to re-enter the room.
   c) Defective appliance casing seals allowing products of combustion to enter the room.

2. You could have chosen two of the following:
   a) Poor size of pilot flame – either requiring adjustment or with a partially blocked injector.
   b) The pilot burner is not correctly positioned in relation to the main burner.
   c) Incorrectly adjusted, or faulty slow ignition device.

3. Scaled heat exchanger.

4. Burner air ports.

5. a) Inadequate pilot flame.
   b) Defective thermocouple.
   c) Defective flame supervision section of the multifunctional control valve.
   d) Overheat device needs re-setting.
   e) ASD faulty.

6. a) Appliance spilling products of combustion into the room.
   b) Endeavour to rectify the problem or alternatively apply industry unsafe situations procedure.

Contents

	Page
Introduction	2
Section 1 – Types of Appliances and their Operating Principles	3
Section 2 – Installation and Commissioning of Gas Cookers	12
Part 1 – Permitted installation locations for appliances	12
Part 2 – Ventilation requirements for cookers	14
Part 3 – Installation of cookers	15
Part 4 – Commissioning of cookers	18
Section 3 – Service, Maintenance and Repair of Gas Cookers	21
Part 1 – Service and maintenance of cookers	21
Part 2 – Typical gas component faults on cookers	22
Practical Tasks	25
Knowledge Questions	32
Model Answers	34

Introduction

The objective of this module is to enable you to successfully complete assessment across the following range of cookers:

- **Freestanding:**
  - Eye level grill.
  - Slide in cookers – this includes fold down lid and low level grill types.
- **Oven:**
  - Built under worktop.
  - Built-in oven housing.
- **Grill:**
  - Combined with oven.
  - Individual wall mounted.
- **Hob:**
  - Lidded.
  - Non lidded.

You will be required to prove that you can install, disconnect, service, repair, breakdown and commission domestic gas cookers.

Practically, you should be able to ensure the following:
- The gas supply pipe is of adequate size and terminates at an acceptable position for the appliance connection.
- The gas hose and bayonet connection conform to requirements.
- The appliance stability device is correctly located and secure.
- The appliance assembly is complete and is fit for use and purpose.
- The gas supply is isolated prior to work being commenced.
- A plug-in socket is fitted to the existing point.
- A flexible hose is fitted to the appliance and connected to the plug-in socket.
- The gas supply is re-established.
- The work carried out is gas tight.
- The appliance is correctly located, level and stable.
- The appliance's operational gas safety components are dismantled and cleaned, using appropriate cleaning methods and agents (e.g. burners, injectors, primary air ports, ignition devices, thermostats, taps, flame supervision devices and lid safety cut-off device).
- The appliance is commissioned as follows:
  - The appliance is purged of air.
  - The working pressure at the appliance is correct.
  - All burner flame pictures, stability and ignition are correct.
  - The user controls are operating correctly.
  - The safety control devices are operating correctly.
  - The temperature controls are operating correctly.
- Defects on gas safety components are identified.
- The safe operation and use of the appliance is explained.

Additionally, you should know the following:
- Identification of unsafe conditions.
- Diagnosis of gas safety faults.
- Recognition of suitable and unsuitable appliance room/space locations.
- Clearance requirements – proximity of combustible materials.

Section 1 – Types of Appliances and their Operating Principles

Introduction
In this module we shall be taking a look at the various types of appliances and the key operating principles of gas cookers.

What is a gas cooker?
Since the mid 1800's gas cookers have evolved to become one of the most important and widely used domestic appliances in our homes. With their easy-to-use and sophisticated controls they have taken the drudgery out of the art of cooking and made it a pleasure.

However, today's cooker looks quite different to the one your grandmother may have used. This can be seen by the number of categories of cooking appliances which are available:

- **Freestanding** – Eye level grill.
  – Slide in cookers (this includes fold down lid and low level grill types).
- **Oven** – Built under worktop.
  – Built-in oven housing.
- **Grill** – Combined with oven.
  – Individual wall mounted.
- **Hob (hotplate)** – Lidded.
  – Non-lidded.

The categories have their own sub-categories depending on the customer's preference. Remember, cookers can also be multi-fuelled by a combination of gas and electricity supplies. Therefore, when it comes to choosing a gas cooker, the choice is quite immense.

Note: All new cookers must carry a CE Mark. The CE Mark is followed by the last two figures of the year in which it was marked on the appliance.

Freestanding gas cookers
British Standard – BS 6172: 2010 defines a freestanding cooker as:

A cooking appliance resting directly on the floor comprising:

- A hotplate including one or more burners.
- One or more ovens with or without thermostats.
- Possibly a grill and/or griddle.

Figure 1 shows a typical selection of freestanding gas cookers.

Figure 1: Freestanding cookers

Let us look at the various parts of a gas cooker and their controls in more detail.

Grill

BS 6172: 2010 defines a grill as an appliance for cooking food by means of radiant heat. Figure 2(a) below shows a surface combustion grill. A grill can be an integral part of a freestanding cooker or an individual appliance.

The surface combustion version tends to be the most common type used on modern cookers. The grill has a metal gauze and gas burns on the surface of the gauze producing an even radiant heat across its surface.

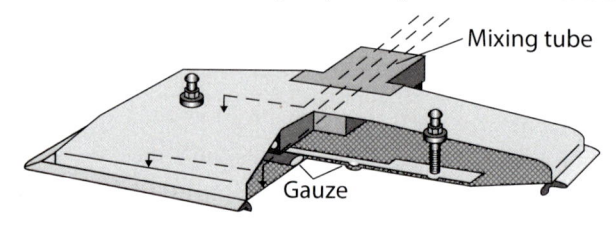

Figure 2(a): Surface combustion grill

More conventional grills, such as that shown in Figure 2(b), have a single burner at the rear, firing forward beneath an expanded metal fret. Sometimes the burner runs from front to back with grill frets at either side.

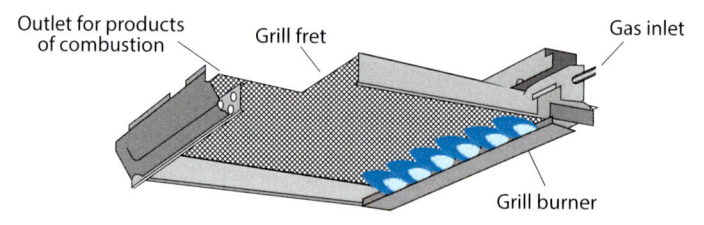

Figure 2(b): Conventional grill

When looking at a conventional grill burner, do not expect each flame to be the same size. Manufacturer's produce the burners with some large burner ports and some small burner ports. This is to give a more evenly distributed heat across the grill fret.

Grill fret

This is a thin metal mesh which absorbs the heat from the flame, then transfers this heat via radiation to the food located below on the grill pan.

Injector

An injector is positioned in the gas supply pipework to the appliance to control the rate of gas flow. The grill tap controls the flow of gas to the grill burner assembly. An ignition system will also be included to light the grill burner.

When the grill is situated in the oven, a safety valve controlling the gas supply to the main grill burner may be fitted. The purpose of the safety valve is to prevent gas flow through to the grill burner when the oven door is shut. As an alternative to the safety valve, a mechanical door spacing device may also be used.

| BPEC | Module 18 |

Gas hob (hotplate)

British Standard – BS 6172: 2010 defines a hob (hotplate) as an appliance comprising one or more covered or uncovered burners and designed to support cooking vessels. Figure 3 below shows a typical hob (hotplate).

Figure 3: Hob hotplate

Spillage tray

This is a semi-decorative panel which eliminates the possibility of spillage from cooking being able to come into contact with the internal components of the appliance.

Hotplate tap

The hotplate tap is the method by which the flow of gas is controlled to the burner. The internal components of the tap may require periodic greasing to maintain ease of operation.

Injector

An injector is a unique part of the appliance which determines the gas rate to the burner, i.e. a boiling or simmering burner.

Burner head assembly

This assembly contains the flame burner ports and retention ports (stabilisation for main burner flames).

A burner cap is positioned on top of the burner head and is usually finished with a vitreous enamel coating for decorative purposes.

As with many hobs, removal of the burner head will reveal the burner ignition electrode fixed to the burner mixing tube.

Pan support

Pan supports take many forms – round or square for single burners or pairs – but they all do the same job. They support the cooking ware, i.e. pot or pan, at a sufficient height above the burner to allow complete combustion.

April 2017 © BPEC

Burner mixing tube

More and more hobs are integrating the mixing tubes with the spillage tray. Figure 4 shows this more clearly. The figure is simplified as so many components go together to produce a complete cooker burner assembly.

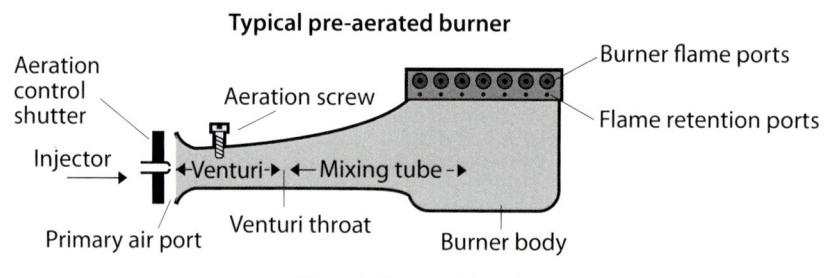

Typical pre-aerated burner

- Aeration control shutter
- Aeration screw
- Burner flame ports
- Flame retention ports
- Injector
- Venturi
- Mixing tube
- Primary air port
- Venturi throat
- Burner body

Figure 4: Burner mixing tube

Note: The aeration control shutter and aeration screw components are not a common feature with modern natural gas appliances due to developments in modern burner design. They are however still used with LPG.

Hobs (hotplates) may include closable lids which fold down to cover the appliance burner. These types of appliances should include a device designed to prevent the flow of gas through the burners when the lid is closed (see Figure 5).

On some models, when the lid is raised a re-set button may need to be depressed to allow gas to flow through the burners; on other models the gas is re-established when the lid is raised.

Note: The lid should be in the open position when carrying out tightness testing.

Figure 5: Safety device

One manufacturer has patented a system of gears and drives which actually turns off the hotplate control taps when the lid is lowered. Its trade name is the Switchback System.

Gas oven

British standard – BS 6172: 2010 defines an oven as an appliance which is a closed compartment for cooking roasts, pastries, etc. Figure 6 shows a typical gas oven.

Figure 6: Gas oven

| BPEC | Module 18 |

How does the gas oven work?

The oven is basically a metal box wrapped with insulation in order to maintain heat for efficiency and also to restrict the excessive heating of exterior panels.

The box has an air intake and a flue outlet to assist with combustion. There are a number of further control devices to control its temperature and allow the oven to operate safely.

The oven can be of the natural convection type by which convection currents are set up around the oven.

These create different temperature zones within the oven, i.e. heat rises, as seen in Figure 7 below. In this type of oven the difference between the top and bottom shelf positions would be approximately two gas marks (approx. 25°C).

However, with forced convection (fan assisted) ovens the burner is positioned beneath the base of the oven and an electric fan rapidly circulates the heat throughout the oven, as seen in Figure 8. This means that the entire oven is heated to a uniform temperature and is ideal for the cooking of large numbers of the same item in batches.

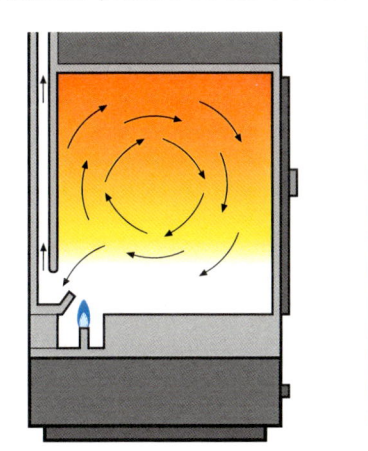

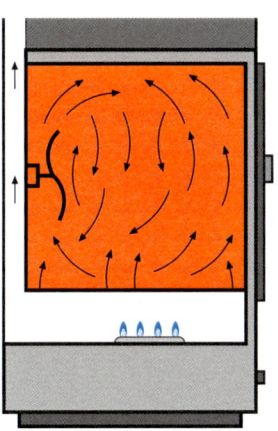

Figure 7: Convection oven

Figure 8: Fan assisted oven

Oven burner

A bar burner has the purpose of heating the oven (see Figure 9).

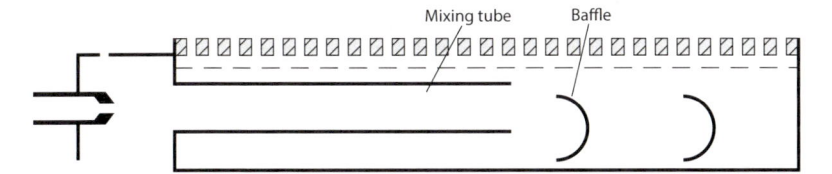

Figure 9: Bar burner

April 2017 © BPEC

Flame supervision device – Vapour pressure principle

This allows a two stage light-up of the oven burner:

Stage 1 This stage allows a small gas rate through to the oven burner whose flame is ignited by the ignition system. The low rate flame heats the flame supervision device phial, which causes the liquid within the capillary to vapourise and expand, and in turn moves the lever in the flame safety device to the fully open position, so allowing full gas flow to the main burner.

Stage 2 The low rate flame is increased to high flame by the increased gas rate to the appliance. This safety device will not allow the main gas to flow until there is a flame.

Figure 10 below shows a typical flame safety device which may be used in a gas oven.

Vapour Pressure Flame Protection Device

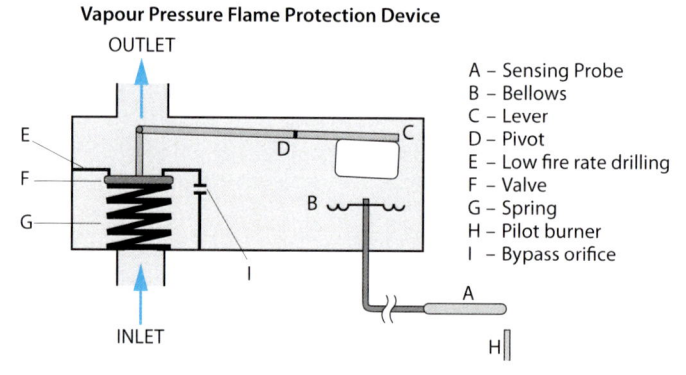

A – Sensing Probe
B – Bellows
C – Lever
D – Pivot
E – Low fire rate drilling
F – Valve
G – Spring
H – Pilot burner
I – Bypass orifice

Figure 10: Flame safety device

Oven dome and side panels

Internal surface panels are sometimes coated with a self cleaning material. The side panels are grooved for the oven shelf positions depending on sizing of cookware and oven position required.

Oven thermostat (thermotap) – Liquid expansion type

A control tap combined with a thermostatic assembly housing to control the oven temperature is usually used (see Figure 11). The thermostat phial is usually connected to the thermostat assembly via a capillary tube and is commonly sited in the upper level of the oven, most likely below the oven dome panel.

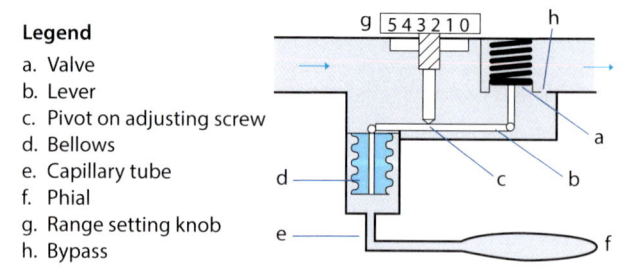

Legend
a. Valve
b. Lever
c. Pivot on adjusting screw
d. Bellows
e. Capillary tube
f. Phial
g. Range setting knob
h. Bypass

Figure 11: Oven thermostat

Thermostats on modern gas cookers utilise a combined gas tap and liquid expansion thermostat to turn on and off the oven and to control the temperature within the oven. In Figure 11, the gas tap has been omitted in order to concentrate on the operation of the thermostat.

When the thermostat control is turned on and set using the range setting knob, the gas valve is fully open and gas flows to the next control in line, which is the flame safety device shown in Figure 10. This is the reason that the main burner of the oven does not light at full rate immediately. Once the flame supervision device is satisfied that a flame exists, control of the gas to the main oven burner passes back to the thermostat.

Valve A is spring loaded and operated by lever B, which moves due to the fulcrum point C pivoting because of the movement of the bellows D.

Turning the range setting knob G will move the fulcrum, and thereby alter the distance the valve is from its seating, thus setting the temperature as required. The bellows movement is produced by the expansion of liquid due to the heat in the oven.

The thermostat contains a by-pass. The by-pass rate should be equal to the oven heat loss; the purpose of the by-pass is to prevent the flame being extinguished at high oven temperature. The by-pass H is usually in the form of a drilling in a screw sited in the thermostat.

The ignition of the grill, hob and oven

Ignition can be satisfied either by the use of a battery or an electrical mains supply (older ignition systems may have used a permanent gas pilot light, or be lit by a match).

Figure 12 shows an illustrated wiring diagram of a cooker ignition system operating with a battery, while Figure 13 translates this to a functional flow wiring diagram.

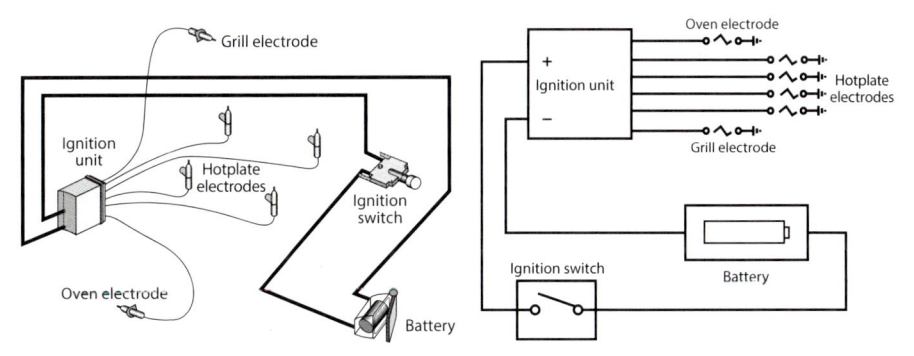

Figure 12: Cooker ignition system

Figure 13: Cooker ignition system – Wiring diagram

Ignition unit

The ignition unit, commonly known as a spark generator, is a component which transforms low voltage electricity to a charge of between 10,000 and 17,000 volts. The voltage travels down the high tension electrode lead to the electrode, where it arcs the electrode gap and produces a spark capable of igniting the gas from the burner.

What about automatic cooking?

Not all ovens have auto cooking facilities. This is mainly due to the cost of the associated components.

The cooker requires a timer and a mains electric supply.

Figure 14 shows a typical auto cooking facility translated into a functional flow wiring diagram. The wiring system may operate on mains voltage or in some cases low voltage.

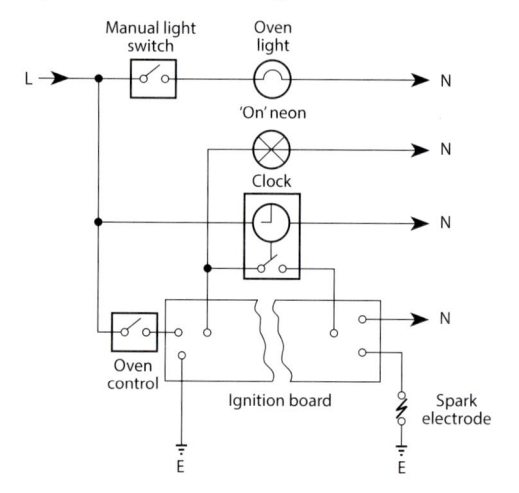

Figure 14: Auto-cooking facility – Wiring diagram

Let us look at a typical auto-cooking facility translated into a functional flow gas supply diagram in Figure 15.

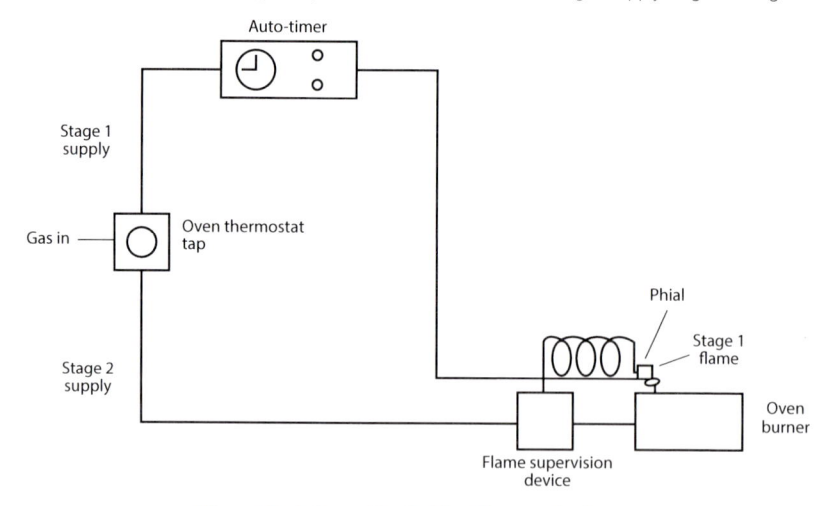

Figure 15: Auto-cooking facility – Gas supply diagram

The operation of automatic cooking – Mechanical and electrical controls

Though there is more than one method, here is a typical example:

(1) On turning on the oven control:

    Gas (stage 1)   – Flows from control to valve assembly in clock.

    Gas (stage 2)   – Flows from control to oven flame safety device.

    Electric   – Flows via micro-switch connected to oven control to clock timer micro-switch.

(2) When cooking time starts:

    Gas (stage 1)   – Flows through clock valve assembly to stage 1 oven burner assembly.

    Electric   – Flows via clock timer micro-switch to ignition unit, which in turn produces spark which ignites stage 1 oven burner gas.

Flame supervision device will operate approximately 30-45 seconds later due to the stage 1 flame heating the flame supervision device phial. Thus stage 2 main flame ignites.

The thermostat will now regulate the oven temperature throughout the cooking period.

(3) When cooking time ends:

    Gas (stage 1)   – Flow stops to stage 1 burner, thus stage 1 flame extinguishes, the flame supervision device phial cools and the stage 2 main flame goes out.

    Electric   – Clock timer micro-switch opens, thus stopping power flowing to the ignition unit, therefore no spark will occur when the flame goes out.

Why does the ignition unit stop sparking when the oven flame ignites?

There is more than one method that ensures the ignition unit stops sparking when the oven flame ignites. Some manufacturers employ the use of micro-switches integrated within the flame supervision device. When the flame supervision device opens, the micro-switch is also opened and breaks the ignition circuit.

However, a more common method is by the use of 'flame suppression'. The system uses rectification; a solenoid valve is powered shut until 'cook start', then ignition is applied. When the flame lights, half wave rectification takes place. The flame supervision control board recognises if the flame is lost and sparking restarts.

There are various sophisticated ignition, auto cooking and oven control arrangements, some employing solenoids, flame convection and rectification devices and printed circuit boards as the gas control (controllers) and flame safety (supervision) arrangements. The manufacturer's instructions should be consulted for further guidance.

Section 2 – Installation and Commissioning of Gas Cookers

Introduction
In this section we shall focus on the key installation and commissioning aspects of gas cookers.

Part 1 – Permitted Installation Locations for Appliances

Can cookers be installed in any room?
Cookers cannot be installed in any room, as there are specific sitting requirements which must be complied with.

Appliances over 14kW gross heat input must be room sealed. As from 1st January 1996, appliances rated at under 14kW gross heat input may be installed. However, the appliance(s) must also have a safety device (atmosphere sensing device) for automatic shut down of the appliance in the event of a build up of products of combustion.

You would naturally anticipate that cookers would be fitted in kitchens or the kitchen areas of bed-sitting rooms. British Standards – BS 6172: 2010 Installation of domestic gas cooking appliances identifies the following:

Multi dwelling premises
(Reference Gas Safe Register Technical Bulletin 015 – The requirement to install gas appliances (including cooking appliances) with flame supervision in flats and other multi-dwelling premises).

Since January 2008 it became a requirement based on the Institution of Gas Engineers publication IGE/G/5 – *Gas in flats and other multi dwelling buildings,* (now in it's second edition) that all **new** flueless appliances installed in multi dwelling premises incorporate Flame Supervision Devices (FSD) on all burners (including cooker hobs) rated at 600W or more. The instruction does not apply to previously used (second hand) appliances, however, where an operative discovers any cooker without FSD on all burners installed in multi-dwelling premises it should be classified as NCS in accordance with the Gas Industry Unsafe Situations Procedure.

The definition of multi-dwelling premises is not confined to blocks of flats but also includes single storey maisonette type situations or any other domestic dwellings where the premises have been sub-divided into a number of individual dwellings such as bed-sits etc.

Bathrooms/shower rooms
Cookers should not be fitted in bathrooms or shower rooms.

Sleeping accommodation
A cooker should not be installed in a bed-sitting room with a volume of less than 20m^3. This requirement does not apply to a single burner hotplate.

Other siting issues
There are further limitations placed on the sitting of cookers, namely:
- The appliance should be positioned to take account of the requirements of the customer, i.e. proximity to the sink or work surfaces.
- Sitting adjacent to doors or openable windows should be avoided wherever possible so as to avoid the effects of draughts.
- The position of the cooker should not restrict the use of doors or kitchen furniture such as drawer units.
- The cooker should not be sited near combustible furnishings such as curtains.
- Sitting on long pile carpets and on carpets that are not securely fixed should be avoided.
- Free-standing cookers should be sited on a stable base and if connected by a flexible connector, an adequate space should be provided in front of the appliance to allow it to be moved forward for disconnection purposes.

Proximity of kitchen furniture

The appliance manufacturer will usually specify minimum dimensions for cooker positions in relation to kitchen furniture. In the absence of clear manufacturer guidance, Figure 16 should be used.

(a) Free-standing cooker with high level grill

610mm
150mm
150mm
760mm
50mm
20mm
20mm

(b) Hob unit

760mm
50mm
50mm

(c) Hob unit in relation to kitchen units

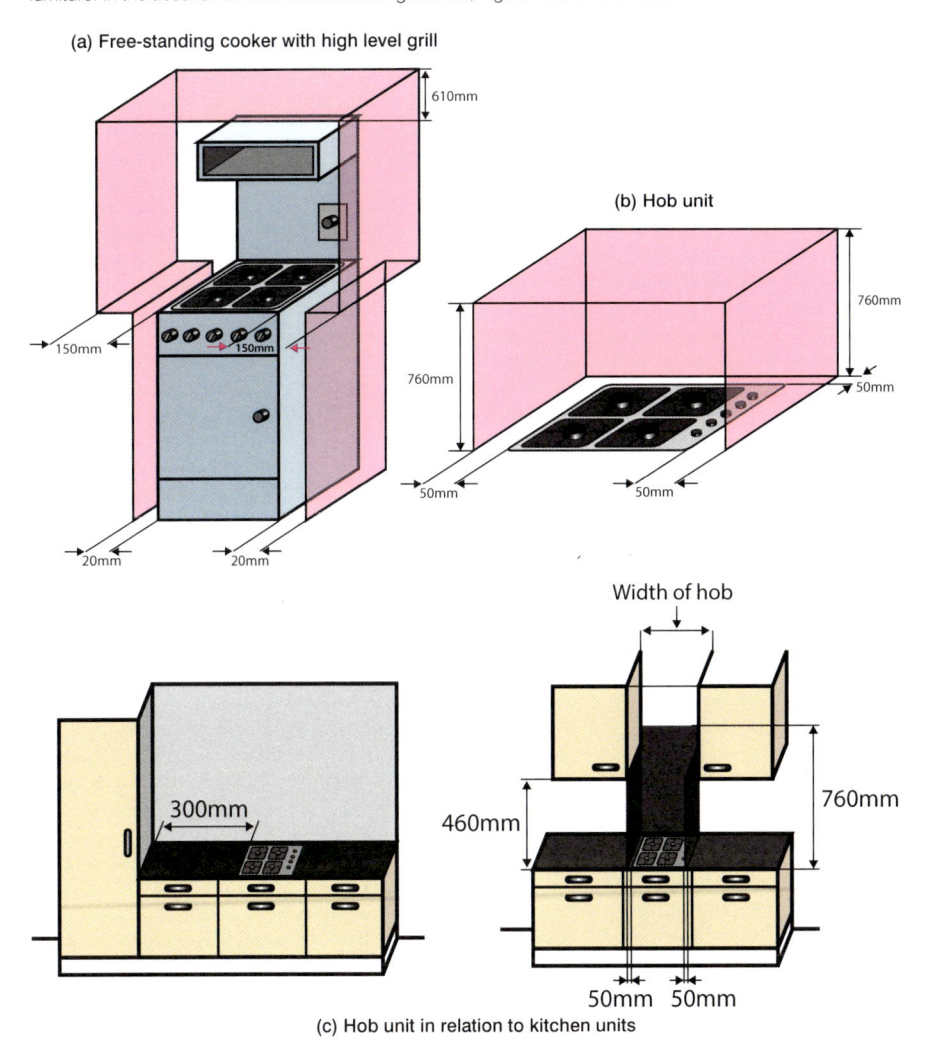

300mm
460mm
Width of hob
760mm
50mm 50mm

Figure 16: Minimum dimensions for cooker positions

Note: Free-standing cooker hotplates should usually be level with surrounding work surfaces.

These dimensions are recommended clearances where the manufacturer's instructions **do not** give clear guidance.

BPEC
Domestic Cookers (CKR1)

Electrical connections

Electrical connections in terms of connection method, fuse rating, earth connection and voltage range should comply with manufacturer's instructions.

The electrical connection should be readily accessible and sited adjacent to the cooker (within 1.5m).
The connection should provide a facility for electrical isolation conforming to the IET 17th Edition Regulations.

Electrical components should be kept away from hot flue products and hot surfaces.

Part 2 – Ventilation Requirements for Cookers

Ventilation requirements for domestic gas cookers should comply with British Standard – BS 5440-1: 2008 Flueing and ventilation:

- Any room containing a gas cooking appliance must have ventilation direct to outside via an openable window or other opening such as a hinged panel or louvre.

- If the volume of the room is between $5m^3 - 10m^3$, an air vent of $50cm^2$ free area is required unless there is a door which opens to outside air. If the room is less than $5m^3$ in volume, then an air vent of $100cm^2$ free area must be provided.

Table 1: Minimum air vent free area for domestic cooking appliances

Appliance type	Max heat input limit (net)	Room volume m^3				Openable window hinged panel, adjustable louvre etc. direct to outside required
		Less than $5m^3$	$5m^3$ to $10m^3$	Over $10m^3$ to $20m^3$	More than $20m^3$	
Oven, hotplate, grill or any combination in room with a door outside.	None	$100cm^2$	Nil	Nil	Nil	Yes*
Oven, hotplate, grill or any combination in room without a door outside.	None	$100cm^2$	$50cm^2$	Nil	Nil	Yes*
Boiling ring (single ring only).	None	Nil				No

* If there is not an openable window, the Building Regulations can provide alternatives such as mechanical ventilation, passive stack or additional permanent ventilation.

Part 3 – Installation of Cookers

Obviously, we cannot detail the exact procedure for installing every type of cooker which is manufactured. The best source of information is the manufacturer's installation instructions.

By studying the following we should have an overview of the general procedures associated with installing domestic cookers:

- Free-standing cookers.
- Additional requirements of built-in ovens.
- Additional requirements of hobs.

Before you can commence with the installation of the cooker, you will need to carry out the following preliminary checks.

Preliminary checks for free-standing cookers

Confirm that:

- The appliance is suitable for the gas supplied, i.e. either natural gas or LPG.
- The appliance is complete and in acceptable working order.
- The room is suitable for the appliance.
- The proposed cooker position meets the following requirements:
    - Acceptable to the customer.
    - Proximity to doors and windows.
    - Proximity to kitchen furniture.
    - Permits cooker oven/grill doors to be opened.
    - With free-standing cookers using flexible connections, permits disconnection of the appliance.
    - Proximity to other combustible materials including suitability of the floor covering material.
- Room ventilation should comply with the requirements highlighted above.
- Any existing gas supply pipework should be proved adequate for supply and the inlet working pressure is sufficient for the appliance meeting the requirements of BS 6891: 2015 Installation of low pressure pipework of up to 35mm (R1¼) in domestic premises.
- Proposed electrical connections should meet the requirements given above.

Gas connections

There are two methods of making gas connections to cookers:

- Flexible connections.
- Rigid connections.

The appliance manufacturer will usually identify which types of gas connections may be used.

Flexible connections must conform to BS 669-1: 1989 for 1st and 2nd gas families (manufactured and natural gas) and BS 3212: 1991 for 3rd gas families (LPG).

Flexible connections

Flexible connections are usually used on free-standing/slide-in cookers (see Figure 17). They may also be used on hobs, where the hob is sited directly above a built-in oven. A rigid connection will normally be required, however, as the space above the oven may rise to a temperature greater than 70°C.

- A gas supply of 15mm diameter is usually supplied to a backplate elbow or micro-point. The flexible connection must incorporate a spring loaded valve for isolation purposes.
- The valve must permit the disconnection of the appliance and isolation of the gas supply.
- The gas connection should not be subjected to excessive force.
- The gas connection should not be subjected to excess heat. Where flexible hoses come into contact with heat sources of over 70°C, a rigid connection must be used.
- The bayonet connector should be accessible for disconnection of the appliance.
- The backplate elbow (or similar) should be firmly fixed and positioned so that the appliance flexible connector hose hangs freely downwards to avoid undue stress on the hose itself.

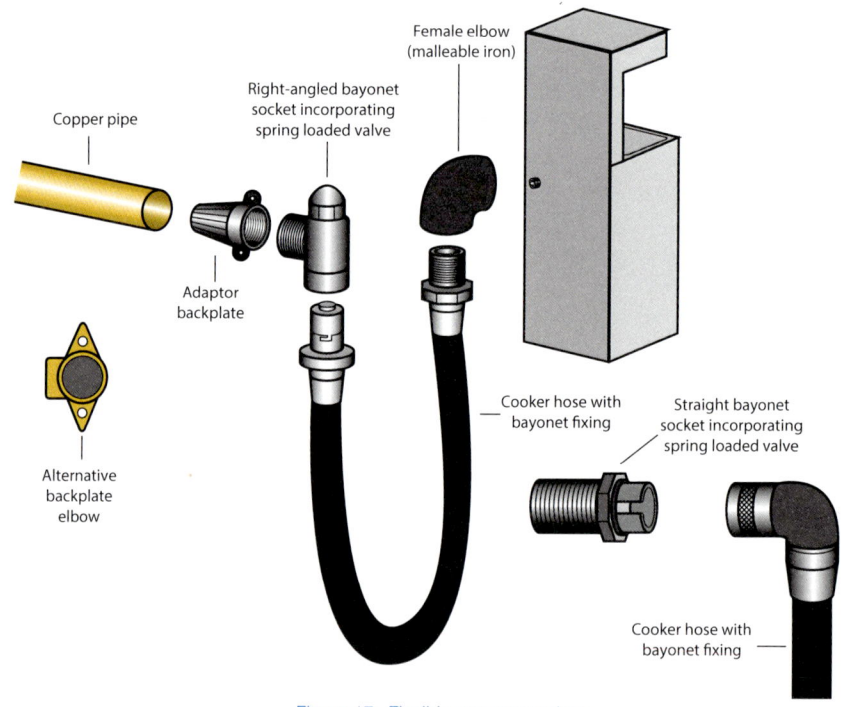

Figure 17: Flexible gas connections

Rigid connections

Rigid connections will usually be provided to built-in cookers and hobs. Pipework materials will usually be copper. An appliance isolation tap should be provided with suitable means of disconnection in a readily accessible position.

| BPEC | Module 18 |

Cooker stability

With free-standing cookers using flexible connectors, appliance stability needs to be considered and a stability device must be used (see Figure 18).

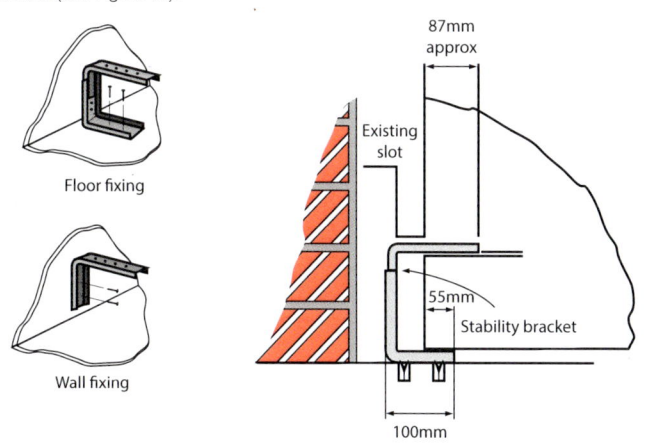

Floor fixing

Wall fixing

87mm approx
Existing slot
55mm
Stability bracket
100mm

Figure 18(a): Cooker stability bracket (for cookers specifically designed with bracket engagement slot)

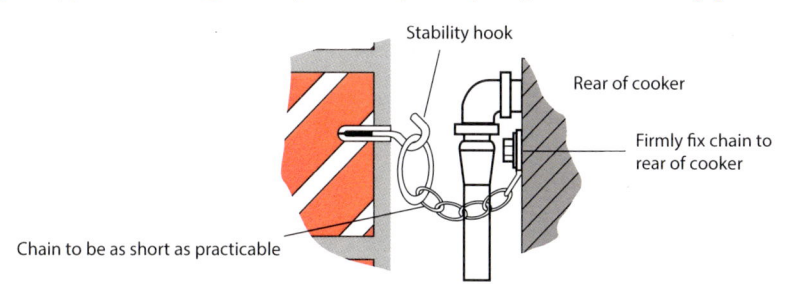

Stability hook
Rear of cooker
Firmly fix chain to rear of cooker
Chain to be as short as practicable

Figure 18(b): Cooker stability chain for other cooker types

- The bracket should be adjusted to give the smallest practical clearance between the bracket and the bottom of the engagement slot in the rear of the cooker. The bracket should extend approximately 90mm through the slot.

Other requirements for free-standing cookers:

- The electrical supply (if required) should be made to the appliance and earth continuity/polarity tests and fuse rating carried out – usually 3 amp fuse should be checked.
- The gas installation must be purged and tested for tightness in accordance with IGE/UP/1B.
  - Particular attention needs to be given to the test procedure adopted when the appliance contains a fold-down lid safety shut off valve or grill-door shut off valve, as the test should be carried out with the lid or door open to permit gas flow to all parts of the appliance.
- Make sure that the cooker is level.

The installation is now ready for commissioning.

| BPEC | Domestic Cookers (CKR1) |

Additional requirements of built-in ovens

The additional requirements of built-in ovens are as follows:

- The cabinet must be firmly fixed in position together with any supporting shelves. Care must be taken to ensure that the appliance is level.
- The cabinet must be suitably sized in accordance with the gas appliance manufacturer's requirements.
- The oven should be fixed in position following manufacturer's requirements.
- Rigid connections will usually be required with this type of appliance, depending on the requirements of manufacturer's instructions. The isolation tap will usually be situated outside the cabinet for access purposes.

Additional requirements of hobs

A typical hob installation is shown in Figure 19. In particular, the hob should:

- Be sited in a worktop of adequate thickness.
- The cut-out in the worktop should meet manufacturer's requirements.
- Access from underneath in terms of cut-outs in back panels; plinths should be in accordance with manufacturer's requirements.
- The hob should be effectively secured and sealed to the worktop.
- Rigid connections incorporating a gas tap will usually be required, particularly where the hob is sited above a built-in oven.

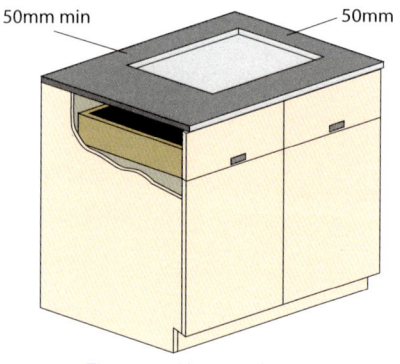

Figure 19: Hob installation

Part 4 – Commissioning of Cookers

We shall now complete the installation module by taking a look at the commissioning of cookers.

If you have not installed the cooker you are about to commission, you should first carry out the installation checks as described in Part 3 of this section.

Once the installation checks have been completed you can go on to commission the appliance. The following procedure may be used.

- Assemble all the appliance components (burners, etc.).
- Check the electrical supply to the appliance (if fitted). Ensure that a battery is fitted (battery ignition systems). Turn the supply on.
- Check the operation of the ignition system, i.e. that a spark occurs at the ignition electrodes.
- Check that the appliance gas control taps operate smoothly.

© BPEC   April 2017

- Check that the appliance burner pressure is correct at the test point using a manometer. The burner pressure cannot usually be adjusted. If the burner pressure is incorrect, you should check the pressure at the meter governor and/or review the gas pipework size to the cooker.
- Light all the burners and check the flame height and aeration against manufacturer's requirements.
- Light the oven (which should commence with a low rate flame). Once the flame safety (supervision) device senses the presence of a flame, the main burner should light on full flame.
- Check the operation of the flame supervision device (FSD) by extinguishing the flame (if possible). The gas flow should cease within the maximum fail safe time, i.e. ovens – 60 seconds; hotplates, griddles, etc. – 90 seconds.

The following procedure is a guide for use when testing the operation of domestic ovens fitted with a liquid expansion device, however, the principle can also be used elsewhere. The FSD has two tasks to perform: The first and simplest is to check that the burner is coming to a full flame. The requirement is that when the oven burner is turned on and is operating at 'low fire', the FSD should come into operation and allow the burner to rise to full gas rate. This operation should take approximately 30 seconds, and is an operational test which will usually be highlighted in the manufacturer's commissioning procedures. The second task is that it shuts off the gas supply if the flame is extinguished.

The safe operation of the FSD must be checked. To do this the oven burner should reduce to 'low fire' within the specified time following the flame being extinguished. A procedure that may be adopted to check this is as follows:
  - Ensure all safety checks and procedures have been carried out and it is safe to ignite the appliance.
  - Turn on and ignite the burner which should come on at 'low fire' rate when the FSD is cold.

After a short time the flame should increase to a 'high flame' to allow the appliance to reach its normal working temperature.
  - Ensure all thermostats are set to full.
  - Turn off the oven control tap and wait 30 seconds.
  - Turn the oven on again. If the oven burner rate has reduced to 'low fire' the FSD has passed the test and may be left on.
  - If the oven remains at full rate, turn off, wait a further 30 seconds and re-check. If the burner is still at full rate you may allow a further 30 seconds; if the FSD has not come into operation after this time the test has failed. The appliance must then be turned off and the FSD replaced.

- Check the operation of the oven fan (if applicable).
- Ensure the correct operation of the thermostat by referring to the manufacturer's instructions. In the absence of specific instructions the following checks can be applied:

Note: This is a commissioning check only and if problems with cooking have been highlighted then a more thorough check must be made and the temperature control assessed. The calibration of the thermostat is generally outside the gas operative's remit of responsibility.
  - Turn the cooker oven on and set the thermostat to gas mark 5.
  - Check that the FSD energises and the burner rises to main flame.
  - With oven door closed, allow approximately 15 minutes for the oven to warm up.

- After approximately 15 minutes the thermostat should operate and reduce the burner to 'low fire'.
- It is essential to check that the burner does not extinguish at this stage.
- If the burner gas rate does not reduce, the cause should be investigated.
- If the thermostat has reduced the gas rate, it must be checked that the main gas rate will return. Leave the oven door open until this occurs.

This procedure is for an oven thermostat, although the principle of allowing a system to search for an operating temperature, watching the thermostat come into operation and then allowing the system to cool down in order to observe the system re-ignite or boost output, can be used for any thermostat.

- Check the operation of hotplate drop down lid safety cut off devices where applicable. The device is fitted on the hotplate burner supply pipe at the rear of the appliance. This stops the flow of gas to the hotplate if the lid is closed when the burners are lit. The valve is operated by a push down spindle connected to the hotplate lid, which closes the valve as the lid drops.

- Check the oven door seal(s) in line with manufacturer's procedures. If no manufacturer guidance is available, by inserting a piece of paper between the door and its seal, contact should just be made with the piece of paper.

- Check the operation of the automatic cooking controls and the oven timer.

Finally, you should demonstrate the use the of appliance to the occupant of the building and leave the manufacturer's appliance instructions on site for future reference purposes. You should advise the occupant of the parts which they should regularly clean, i.e. hotplate burners.

We have now covered the installation and commissioning requirements of cookers. If you are unsure about any of the topics covered, you should go back and study them again.

BPEC   Module 18

Section 3 – Service, Maintenance and Repair of Gas Cookers

Part 1 – Service and Maintenance of Cookers

The following identifies a general procedure for carrying out service/maintenance of cookers:

Step 1 – Preliminary checks – Ask the customer if there are any problems

- Check to establish that the appliance location is acceptable including provision of stability bracket, method of gas connection isolation, floor coverings, etc.
- Test the operation of electrical components on the appliance, e.g. auto timer, ignition system; check appliance is fitted with correct fuse (3 amp) where applicable.
- Check the operation of the cooker gas control devices.
- Light the appliance and put into full operation; check flames are stable.
- Check the condition of the appliance and identify whether correct combustion is taking place by looking at the flame picture. Check that the installation conforms to manufacturer's instructions and current standard requirements.
- Check to ensure that sufficient free area of ventilation has been provided. Check the operation of the oven on low thermostat setting to ensure that a flame is still maintained.

Note any defects and advise the customer prior to the service taking place.

Step 2 – Appliance servicing

- Isolate the gas and any electrical supply to the appliance.
- Check the condition of any exposed wiring and connections; carry out polarity and continuity checks.
- Ease and grease/replace any stiff gas control taps.
- Check condition of oven door seals (replace as necessary). Check to ensure that effective oven door seal is made.
- Renew batteries (if fitted).
- Check the condition of the flexible connector (if fitted), ensuring correct type is fitted.
- Remove and clean air ports, e.g. burners and igniters. Where the parts may normally be cleaned by the customer, but are not being cleaned, advise the customer of the need to clean such parts, e.g. hotplate burners (see Figure 20).
- Check and clear the oven flueway.
- Check operation of fan, lighting sequence, igniter operation, etc.
- Replace parts as necessary.
- Tightness test all disconnected joints, using leak detection fluid where necessary. Repair any gas escape.
- Assemble all components.

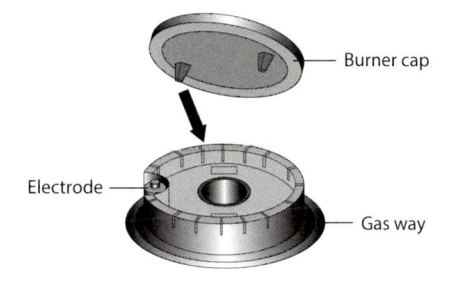

Figure 20: Common hotplate burner

April 2017   © BPEC

Step 3 – Final checks

- Check the appliance working pressure. If it is not within manufacturer's tolerances, check meter control and/or supply pipework.
- Check the operation of all controls, including gas shut off devices such as those used with hot plate lids.
- Check to ensure that the ignition system works.
- Check the appliance flame picture(s) – they should be suitably stable and of the correct shape and colour
- Check the operation of the flame supervision device, ensuring that the FSD responds within the recommended time period.
- Check the operation of the oven thermostat and ensure that when reaching thermostat temperature the flame reduces. Check that the oven works at by-pass rate.
- Check that the stability device is operative and is fixed to meet requirements.
- Check that the appliance is level (in all directions).
- Clean and tidy the work area.

Remember to consult the appliance manufacturer's instructions, as these are an important source of specific appliance details. Ensure that the customer understands the appliance operation.

Part 2 – Typical Gas Component Faults on Cookers

This section focuses on the diagnosis of typical faults associated with cookers. This section will focus on:

- Unsatisfactory ignition of burners/defective flame supervision devices.
- Constant 'ticking' of repetitive, regenerative ignition systems.
- Unstable flame picture at full and simmer rate.
- Oven burner which goes out at thermostat by-pass rate.
- Stiff burner control tap.
- Oven burner does not achieve full flame.
- Inoperative lid closure safety cut-off device.

You may need to use electrical test equipment to identify faults on components (particularly on electronically operated ovens).

Unsatisfactory ignition of burners

Typical faults associated with unsatisfactory ignition of burners include:

- Failure of the ignition system.

Failure of the ignition system is usualy caused by blockage or partial blockage of jets or burner ports, due to:
- Corrosion.
- Deposits.
- Burnt on oils and fats.
- Moisture.

BPEC   Module 18

The flow chart in Figure 21 shows what to do if there is a failure in the ignition system.

START Ignitor does not spark.

Check gas supply.
Check mains voltage, at appliance terminal block.
If there is no voltage, check fuse in plug and that there is a mains supply.

Gas to burner? (Light manually). — YES → Check operation of switch. — YES → Attempt to light using ignition system. Does system spark? — YES → Repeat ignition. Does ignitor spark? — YES → Does burner light? — YES

NO ↓ Replace/repair switch

NO ↓

NO ↓ Exchange ignitor unit.

NO ↓ Check spark gap.

Ignition system is now in working order.

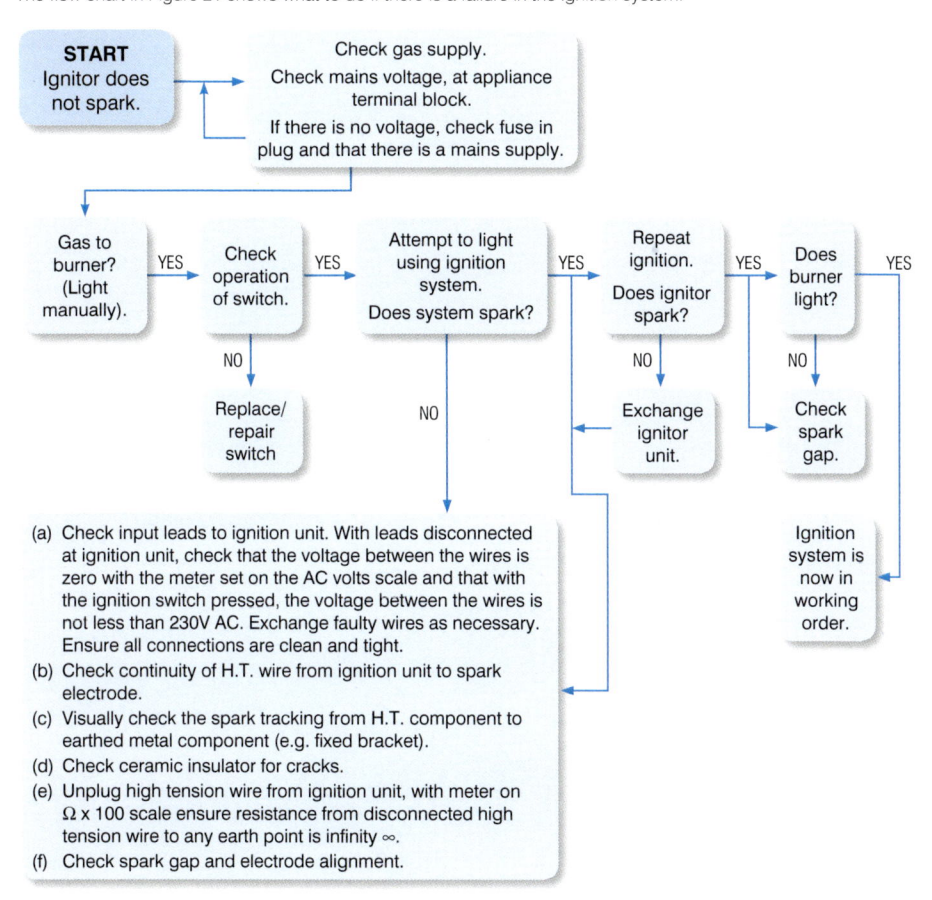

(a) Check input leads to ignition unit. With leads disconnected at ignition unit, check that the voltage between the wires is zero with the meter set on the AC volts scale and that with the ignition switch pressed, the voltage between the wires is not less than 230V AC. Exchange faulty wires as necessary. Ensure all connections are clean and tight.
(b) Check continuity of H.T. wire from ignition unit to spark electrode.
(c) Visually check the spark tracking from H.T. component to earthed metal component (e.g. fixed bracket).
(d) Check ceramic insulator for cracks.
(e) Unplug high tension wire from ignition unit, with meter on Ω x 100 scale ensure resistance from disconnected high tension wire to any earth point is infinity ∞.
(f) Check spark gap and electrode alignment.

Figure 21: Ignition system flow chart

Common problems resulting from blockages

Essentially the burner jets may be blocked adjacent to the ignition electrode or pilot flame. Burnt on oils and fats tend to block spark gaps or bridge flame rectification circuits causing lighting failure. This can cause constant ticking of the ignition system device. The cleaning of components will usually cure the problem.

With ovens, blocked stage 1 jets will cause the oven flame supervision device to fail to safe, so preventing the oven lighting sequence commencing. A defective flame supervision device may also result in the same problem. Oven lighting procedures may also be affected by incorrectly adjusted or defective oven timers, which prevent the main burner from coming into full operation. The solution here is to adjust or repair/replace the timer.

April 2017   © BPEC

Unstable flame picture

Unstable flame pictures are generally caused by:

- An inadequate supply of combustion air by the burner combustion air ports/grill frets become partially blocked/blocked with cooking deposits and the combustion process becomes affected, i.e. incorrect flame picture (slack flames with yellow tips). Remember, grills often burn with relatively slack blue flames. The cooker flue-way can also become blocked, causing combustion problems.
- Blocked cooker burners/injectors. These result again in poor appliance flame pictures. Cleaning the appliance components will usually rectify the problem. A faulty gas tap may result in an incorrect supply of gas to the burner, creating similar problems.
- Incorrectly set gas rate. The main problem here tends to be with a partial blockage or incorrectly sized injectors.

In the case of a partial blockage in the injectors, insufficient gas flow will be available. Wrongly sized injectors may result in over gassing of the appliance.

Oven thermostat which goes out at by-pass rate

The oven thermostat by-pass may sometimes become blocked, causing the flame to be extinguished when the oven reaches temperature and the flame size reduces, i.e. gas flow is interrupted through the by-pass.

The solution here is to clean the by-pass orifice/screw. Re-assemble and check the cooker operation. When cleaning be careful not to enlarge the orifice to the bypass.

Stiff burner control tap

Identifying the signs of a stiff gas control tap are obviously quite easy to determine. There are two possible solutions to the problem:

- Strip down the control tap and grease the spindle and tap components in line with manufacturer's procedures, replacing any seals as necessary, or
- In the event that greasing the tap does not work, then it should be replaced.

Remember that the tap should be checked for tightness after undertaking any work. This can be done by using leak detection fluid.

Oven burner does not achieve full flame

If the oven burner does not achieve full flame rate whilst in operation, this is generally caused by:

- A faulty flame supervision device.
- Incorrectly aligned phial, wrongly located or broken sensing tube.

Inoperative lid closure safety shut-off valve

This device will usually fail to safe, which means that when the hotplate lid is closed, gas will not be available at the hotplate burners. The safety cut-off valve will usually require replacement.

It is also possible for the valve to fail in the open position, in which case the gas supply to the hot plate burners continues, even when the lid is in the closed position.

Remember that an oven incorporating a grill may have a similar device, which prevents the oven from operating when the door is opened for grilling purposes. The device will operate on a similar basis to the hotplate lid shut-off device.

Practical Tasks

The practical tasks link directly with the performance criteria of the Nationally Accredited Certification Scheme (ACS) assessments for CKR1 – Domestic Gas Cookers.

Your tutor will assess your practical training requirements before undertaking the practical tasks and may require you to:

- Complete all the tasks identified, or
- Complete some of the tasks identified (based on previous experience).

You should have access to the appliance manufacturer's instructions. You may also use the knowledge manuals associated with the course.

You will be given the following tasks to be carried out:

- Installation (or exchange) of a gas cooker.
- Commissioning a gas cooker.
- Servicing a gas cooker.
- Diagnosing typical faults on a range of gas cookers.

To assist you in the process of carrying out the work, you should complete the information required in the following pro-forma.

Note – To complete all the tasks you will be required to work on more than one appliance.

BPEC	Domestic Cookers (CKR1)

Pre-installation checks

Task 1
Visually check the existing pipework system and note any defects below, and any remedial actions necessary, e.g. pipework fixings, pipe size, materials etc.

Task 2
Visually check and establish that the appliance to be installed is within minimum requirements for the proximity of kitchen furniture and combustible materials.

Task 3
Check to ensure that the gas supply has been effectively isolated prior to the work commencing.
Has the gas supply been effectively isolated?   Yes   No

If no, what remedial action is necessary?

© BPEC   April 2017

Task 4

Carry out a gas tightness test of the existing pipework installation prior to the work commencing.

Does the tightness test indicate that the pipework system is leak free?　　Yes　　No

If no, what remedial actions are necessary?

Task 5

Visually check the appliance to be installed and identify whether there are any obvious defects.

Is the appliance in suitable condition?　　Yes　　No

If no, what remedial action is necessary?

Task 6

Visually check and establish that the gas hose and bayonet provided are fit for the purpose intended.

Installation (or exchange) of the appliance

Task 7
A backplate elbow and plug-in socket is connected to the gas pipework.

Task 8
A flexible hose is fitted to the appliance and connected to the plug-in socket.

Task 9
A gas tightness test is carried out.
Is the reading acceptable?   Yes   No

Task 10
The appliance is correctly located, level and stable, and ventilation requirements are adequate.

Task 11
The appliance stability device is correctly fitted.

Commissioning the appliance

Task 12
Is the appliance/installation purged of air?   Yes   No

Task 13
Is the working pressure at the appliance correct?   Yes   No

Task 14
Are burner flame picture, stability and ignition correct?   Yes   No

Task 15
Are the user controls operating satisfactorily (timer, etc.)?   Yes   No

Task 16
Are the safety control devices operating correctly?   Yes   No

| BPEC | Module 18 |

Task 17
Are the temperature controls operating satisfactorily?   Yes   No

Tasks 12-17 – Note any deficiencies in the commissioning procedure in this box:

Task 18
Subject to the installation being satisfactorily commissioned, explain the safe operation of the appliance.

Servicing an appliance

Task 19
Carry out a full service on a gas cooker. The following table is included for your use. Note details of any components which may need replacement.

Component	Serviced/Cleaned Yes/No	Requiring replacement Yes/No	Not fitted to appliance
Burner(s)/injectors			
Primary air ports			
Flueways			
Ignition devices			
Control taps			
Flame supervision devices			
Oven thermostat including by-pass rate			
Oven lining(s), shelves, grill frets etc.			
Timing devices/other controls			

Note further details here:

Fault diagnosis

Task 19

You will be given a number of appliances with specific gas safety faults. Your tutor will advise on the number of faults per given appliance. You should list the faults associated with each appliance below.

Appliance 1 – Faults identified:

Appliance 2 – Faults identified:

Appliance 3 – Faults identified:

Appliance 4 – Faults identified:

Appliance 5 – Faults identified:

Knowledge Questions

Domestic Cookers – CKR1

Section 1 – Types of Appliances and their Operating Principles

1. What is the purpose of a flame safety (supervision) device fitted to a gas oven?

2. Why does an oven thermostat include a by-pass port?

3. What is the purpose of an injector feeding a gas cooker grill?

4. What is the purpose of a hotplate lid safety cut-off valve?

5. What are two possible ignition arrangements for hotplates?
   a)
   b)

6. Why does a gas oven use a two stage lighting procedure?

7. What are four of the main components used on domestic cooker ignition systems?
   a)
   b)
   c)
   d)

Section 2 – Installation and Commissioning of Gas Cookers

1. Can a gas cooker can be installed in a bathroom?

2. Is it acceptable to site a cooker directly below some curtains?

3. Is it acceptable to site the wall units above a built-in hob within a vertical height of 800mm of the hob?

4. Is it acceptable to place a gas cooker's electrical isolation point 3m away from a cooker position?

5. What permanent area of ventilation should be provided for a cooker which is to be installed in a room of $8m^3$?

6. Is it permissible to site a gas cooker in a bed-sitting room measuring 2.5m x 2.5m x 2.5m?

7. Which gas component should be fitted to the supply to a built-in oven, where a rigid connection is used to connect the oven to the gas supply?

8. Which safety device should be secured to a slide-in cooker, which is to be fitted into a space between two kitchen units?

Section 3 – Service, Maintenance and Repair of Gas Cookers

1. You have been asked to investigate the likely fault of an oven which heats up successfully, but the flame goes out during the cooking process. What is the likely cause of the problem?

2. Yellow flames are being discharged from a grill burner which has not been serviced for three years. What are three possible causes of the problem?
    a)
    b)
    c)

3. One burner on a hotplate fails to light. The burner is covered in oil spilled during the cooking process. What are two possible causes of the problem?
    a)
    b)

4. You have been called to a property where the customer advises that it has been necessary to operate one of the cooker control knobs with a pair of pliers. What is the likely cause of the problem?

5. Gas fails to flow through the hotplate burners on a cooker with a fold down lid. What is the cause of the problem?

Model Answers

Section 1 – Types of Appliances and their Operating Principles

1. To prevent the main burner from lighting in the absence of a flame in the oven.

2. To permit a low gas rate equal to the rate of heat being lost from the appliance to by-pass the thermostat, so that a flame is maintained in the oven while it is being used.

3. To control the flow of gas through the grill burner.

4. To prevent gas being supplied to the hotplate burners when the lid is closed.

5. You could have chosen:
   a) Mains ignition.
   b) Battery ignition.
   c) Permanent pilot ignition.

6. A two stage lighting procedure is employed for safety purposes:
   Stage 1 – A small gas flow and pilot flame heats the flame supervision device.
   Stage 2 – Once sufficient heat from the small pilot flame is established, the flame safety device opens fully and permits full gas flow to the main burner.

7. You could have included four of the following:
   a) Spark generator.
   b) Electrode.
   c) HT lead.
   d) Ignition switch.
   e) Battery.

Section 2 – Installation and Commissioning of Gas Cookers

1. No.
2. No.
3. Yes.
4. No.
5. 50cm^2.
6. No.
7. Isolation tap permitting disconnection of the supply.
8. Stability device.

Section 3 – Service, Maintenance and Repair of Gas Cookers

1. Blocked by-pass on oven thermostat.

2. a) Blocked grill fret – impeding combustion air supply.
   b) Partially blocked injector impeding gas flow to the grill burner.
   c) Linted burner air ports.

3. a) Igniter and spark gap choked with spillage from cooking products.
   b) Hotplate burner partially blocked with spillage from cooking products.

4. Gas control tap needs greasing/replacing.

5. Faulty lid safety cut-off valve.

Contents

	Page
Introduction	2
Section 1 – Types of Appliances and their Operating Principles	**4**
Part 1 – Gas fires	4
Part 2 – Wall heaters	18
Section 2 – Installation and Commissioning of Space Heaters	**20**
Part 1 – Permitted installation locations for appliances	20
Part 2 – Flue and ventilation requirements for space heaters	21
Part 3 – Hearth requirements for space heaters	43
Part 4 – Installation of space heaters	44
Part 5 – Commissioning of space heaters	53
Section 3 – Service, Maintenance and Repair of Space Heaters	**56**
Part 1 – Service and maintenance of space heaters	56
Part 2 – Appliance fault finding	59
Part 3 – Typical gas component faults on space heaters	61
Practical Tasks	67
Knowledge Questions	74
Model Answers	78

Introduction

The objective of this module is to enable you to successfully complete assessment across the following range of space heaters:

- Open flued gas fires.
  - Radiant convector.
  - Inset live fuel effect (ILFE).
  - Decorative fuel effect (DFE).
- Room sealed natural draught gas fires.
- Open flued fanned draught gas fires.
- Room sealed natural draught and fanned draught wall heaters.

You will be required to prove that you can install, disconnect, service, repair, breakdown and commission domestic open, room sealed and fan assisted flued gas fires and wall heaters.

Practically, you should be able to check the following:

- The fire place opening and hearth construction and dimensions conform to requirements.
- The chimney/flue is complete throughout its length and is correctly terminated.
- The flue flow test confirms that the flue discharges correctly only to atmosphere.
- The catchment area conforms to requirements.
- The appliance assembly is complete and is fit for use and purpose.
- The gas supply is isolated prior to work being commenced.
- The flue spigot restrictor is correctly installed if required.
- The fire is correctly sealed to surround/wall (inset).
- The closure plate is correctly fitted and sealed to the fire place opening (radiant convector).
- The appliance is correctly connected and sealed to the pre-installed flue set.
- The gas supply is re-established.
- The work carried out is gas tight.
- The appliance is correctly located, level and stable.
- The coal/log effect fuel is correctly positioned.
- The radiant element is correctly positioned.
- The appliance operational gas safety components are dismantled and/or cleaned, using appropriate cleaning methods and agents (e.g. burners, injectors, primary air ports, combustion chambers, ignition devices, taps, flame supervision devices and fuel effects where appropriate).

- The appliance is commissioned as follows:
  - The appliance is purged of air.
  - The working pressure at the appliance is correct.
  - The burner's flame picture, stability and ignition are correct.
  - The user controls are operating correctly.
  - The safety control devices are operating correctly.
  - The spillage test is carried out.
- Defects on gas safety components are identified.
- The safe operation and use of the appliance is explained.

Additionally, you should know the following:

- Identification of unsafe conditions.
- Diagnosis of gas safety faults.
- Recognition of suitable and unsuitable appliance room/space locations.
- Ventilation location requirements for decorative fuel effect gas fires.
- Minimum flue sizes for inset live fuel effect fires.
- Requirements for the installation of metal flue systems and flue boxes for gas fires.
- Requirements for direct flue connection appliances.
- Types and installation requirements of heating stoves.
- Electrical gas safety control devices required for fanned draught gas fires.
- Canopy requirements for decorative gas fires.
- Requirements for fire protection including user and floor.
- Advice to user including operation and maintenance.
- Requirements for fitting appliances in raised builder's openings.
- Flue testing procedures.
- The operation of mechanical and electrical gas safety control devices.
- Clearance requirements (proximity of combustible materials).
- Requirements of components.

Section 1 – Types of Appliance and their Operating Principles

Introduction
In this module we shall be taking a look at the various types of appliances and the key operating principles of:

- Gas fires.
- Room sealed wall heaters.

Part 1 – Gas Fires

Types of gas appliances
There are five types of gas fire available:

a) Radiant or radiant/convector gas fire to BS 5871-1: 2005

Flue size: There shall normally be a minimum of 125mm across the axis of the flue.

Location: This type of gas fire will normally be sited in front of a closure plate, which is fixed to the fireplace opening or flue box.

Ventilation: Purpose provided ventilation is not normally required for these appliances, if they have a rated heat input up to 7kW (gross or net).

Figure 1: Radiant gas fire

Comment: The room is heated by either radiated heat or convected heat from a heat exchanger within the appliance, or as in this case both. For this type of appliance the radiating surface can be in the form of either ceramic radiants or an imitation fuel bed.

b) Inset live fuel effect gas fire (ILFE) to BS 5871-2: 2005

Flue size: There shall normally be a minimum of 125mm across the axis of the flue.

Location: The appliance is either fully or partially inset into the builder's opening or fireplace recess (for a recess, the chairbrick may need removal, dependent upon the design of the appliance).

Ventilation: Purpose provided ventilation is not normally required for these appliances, if they have a rated heat input up to 7kW (gross or net) not exceeding 15kW.

Figure 2: ILFE gas fire

Comment: The room is heated by either radiated heat or convected heat from a heat exchanger within the appliance, or as in this case both. For this type of appliance the radiating surface will be in the form of an imitation fuel bed.

c) Decorative fuel effect gas fire (DFE) to BS 5871-3: 2005

Flue size: There shall normally be a minimum of 175mm across the axis of the flue.

Location: The appliance is either fully inset into the builder's opening or fireplace recess, flue box or installed beneath an associated independent canopy (for a recess, the chairbrick may need removal, dependent upon the design of the appliance).

Ventilation: Purpose provided ventilation of at least 100cm^2 is normally required for these appliances, if they have a rated heat input up to 20kW (net).

Comment: The room is heated by radiated heat only and for this type of appliance the radiating surface will be in the form of the imitation fuel bed (it should be noted that the efficiency of these appliances is in the region of 35%).

Figure 3: DFE gas fire

d) Independent gas-fired flueless space heaters of nominal heat input of not exceeding 6kW to BS 5871-4: 2007

Flue size: No flue of chimney required.

Location: The appliance has a wide range of siting options, but are not suitable for bath and shower rooms, rooms with sleeping accommodation and rooms with a volume of less than 40cm^3.

Ventilation: Permanent ventilation will be required. This will be dependent upon manufacturer's requirements.

Comment: Appliances of this type are available as stoves or inset fires. All types have glass panel fronts and have an energy efficiency rating of 100%.

Figure 4: Freestanding flueless appliance

All but the flueless gas fires are available in a variety of flue types. Some types of open flue gas fires may also incorporate a fan as part of a fanned draught arrangement, which decreases the size of flue required and makes their positioning more flexible. With ILFE and DFE appliances incorporating fanned flueing arrangements, the appliance flue system will more than likely be open-flued, with combustion air being drawn from the room in which the appliance is sited.

Radiant/convector fires are available as room sealed models in both natural draught and fanned draught options.

BPEC   Domestic Space Heaters, Gas Fires and Wall Heaters (HTR1)

e) Cassette gas fires

The term 'cassette' fire is a generic term given to a modern generation of appliance which is designed to slot into a fabricated firebox installed within a builders opening if flued or be wall mounted if flueless.

Their appearance is designed to be modernistic to blend with latter-day domestic household appliances such as flat screen TVs, computer screens etc.

Open flued radiant and radiant/convector gas fires

In the early days of gas fire construction, the vast majority of gas fires were of the radiant only type. This meant that all the heat given off from the fire to the room was radiated from the ceramic radiants fitted within the appliance and some from the hot fire case.

Radiant only fires had the advantage of almost immediate heating of the occupants, however, as radiated heat only warms an object directly in its path, not all occupants benefited from the warmth.

Figure 5: Radiant/convector gas fire

In an attempt to improve overall room heating, heat exchangers were incorporated into the design of radiant gas fires to make them radiant/convectors (see Figure 5). The radiant convector not only heats the occupants in front of the fire, but also sets up convection currents to heat the whole room and therefore all the occupants, giving an overall appliance efficiency of approximately 70%.

Due to the fact that the hot products of combustion are passing over a heat exchanger, the radiant/convector fire is more efficient than an equivalent radiant only fire and is therefore more popular today.

Components of a radiant/convector fire

Heat exchanger

Figure 6 shows a section through a radiant/convector gas fire and clearly identifies the air paths as they pass through and around the heat exchanger.

Combustion products travel through the heat exchanger before passing out of the flue spigot to be safely disposed into the flue. Cooler room air enters beneath the fire, is drawn up via the heat exchanger, becomes heated and is convected back into the room via the front grills in the fire case.

Under no circumstances should the products of combustion and the convection air mix with each other. If this were to happen, the possible cause would be a damaged or split heat exchanger, which is an extremely serious defect, and must be dealt with in accordance with the gas industry unsafe situations procedures.

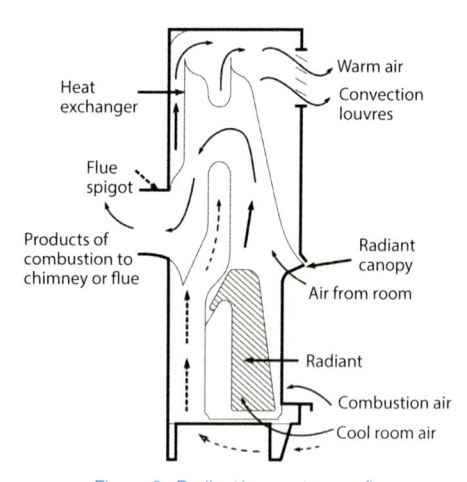

Figure 6: Radiant/convector gas fire

© BPEC   April 2017

Firebox

Is an aluminised steel box, which contains the radiants and sometimes a firebrick or insulation pad. The top of the firebox is formed into a canopy, which draws products of combustion into the heat exchanger or flue spigot and acts as a draught diverter.

Firebrick

The firebrick is a refractory brick which minimises overheating of the firebox by refracting heat from the radiants away from the internal parts of the fire, and also helps maintain the radiants at the highest possible temperature.

Radiants

Radiants are specific to the model of fire for which they are produced, therefore they cannot be interchanged with radiants from other fires. They are fragile and can reach temperatures of approximately 1,000°C. From Figure 7 we can see that a radiant has thorns and slots.

The purpose of the thorns is to create a greater surface area and to distribute the heat from the gases and achieve an even, luminous appearance.

The purpose of the slots is to allow secondary air to enter into the radiant in order to produce complete combustion.

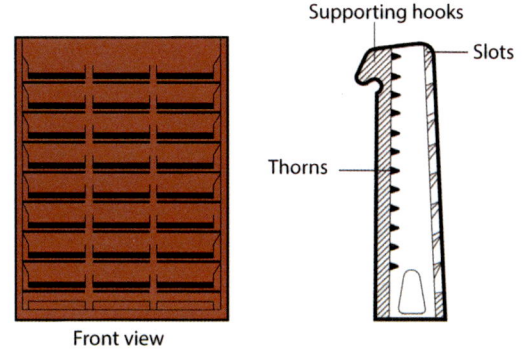

Figure 7: Radiant

Today, modern radiant convector fires may also have a living flame fire effect, as a possible alternative to the use of radiants, e.g. imitation coals or logs.

Burner

Burners may be either simplex or duplex.

Simplex

The flames on a simplex burner (see Figure 8) are supplied through a single injector controlled by a Simplex tap. It feeds one injector and this type of burner is less common on radiant fires, as the highest radiant efficiency is when the burner is full on and much reduced if the gas flow is decreased. More flexibility is afforded by using a duplex burner.

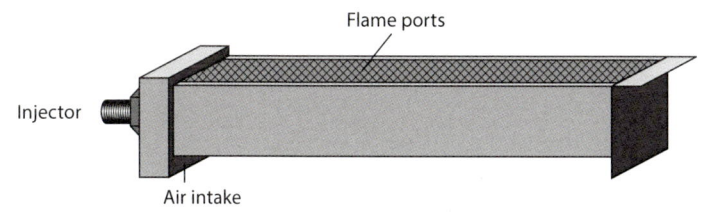

Figure 8: Simplex burner

Duplex

A duplex burner allows various permutations of burners to be used at a given time (see Figure 9). This is done by having more than one injector and the burner being divided into sections, controlled by a duplex tap. This is a more complex burner set-up, but gives the added advantage of greater selection of heat output settings.

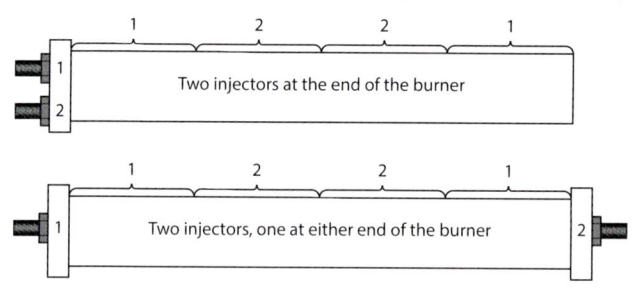

Figure 9: Duplex burner

The burner will normally include a lint arrestor. Its purpose is to filter out and prevent lint from entering into the main burner air supply.

Gas controls

Figure 10 shows the gas fire controls, which incorporate:

- User controls to adjust the gas flow to the burner.
- The control tap itself, which usually permits gas to flow to a varying number of sections of the burner.
- Piezo ignition unit to light the burner; older models may use a permanent pilot lit by match or a glow coil. Rotation of the control tap to a fixed point will cause gas to flow to the burner and the piezo unit to create a spark at the burner, resulting in ignition of the gases.

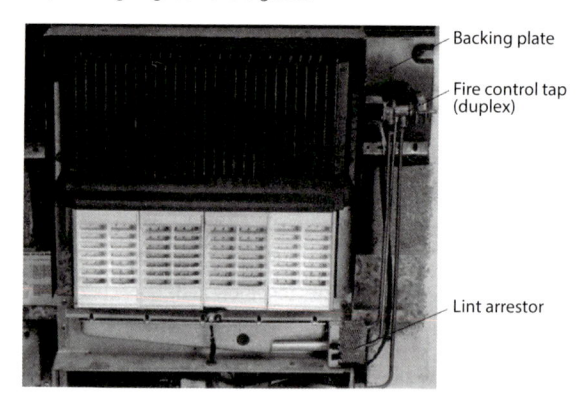

Figure 10: Gas fire controls

Older fires may include a constant pressure regulator; this is usually factory pre-set. Modern fires, however, do not have regulators, but rely upon the correct gas pipework sizing to supply a pressure of 20mbar to the appliance inlet.

Additional controls

All modern gas fires incorporate a flame supervision device (FSD) in the form of an electro-magnet unit connected via a thermo-couple to a pilot burner assembly, i.e. a thermo-electric valve.

With this type of control arrangement a pilot light fed through an injector is lit by the piezo igniter. When the pilot flame is ignited, it heats the thermocouple tip and small voltage EMF energises the magnet, thus holding the armature to it in the spring-operated gas valve and allowing gas to flow to the main burner (see Figure 11).

Should the pilot be extinguished, the thermocouple cools down and stops producing an EMF, thus allowing the spring to close the valve. As with all other heat related flame supervision devices, there is a delayed reaction between failure of the flame and closure of the valve, usually in the region of 60 seconds.

The time allowed before the FSDs reaction falls short of the requirement depends upon the appliance to which it is fitted; for gas fires other than DFEs the maximum time is 180 seconds.

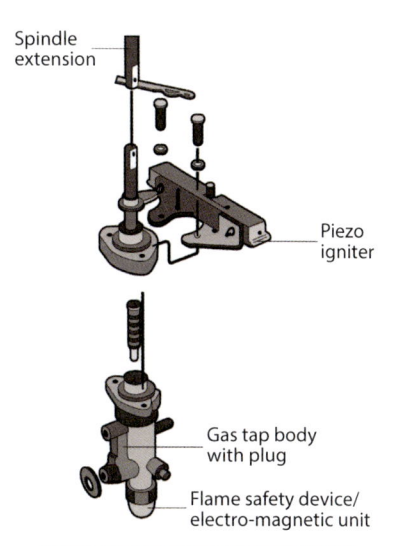

Figure 11: Gas control tap with (EMF) energised magnetic field

In order to comply with the Gas Safety (Installation and Use) Regulations 1998 regarding open flued appliances fitted in rooms intended to be used as sleeping accommodation, newer appliances tend to be fitted with an atmosphere (vitiation) sensing device shown in Figure 12.

ASD operating correctly with adequate oxygen supply.

As the oxygen level fails, the sensing flame lifts away from the thermocouple tip.

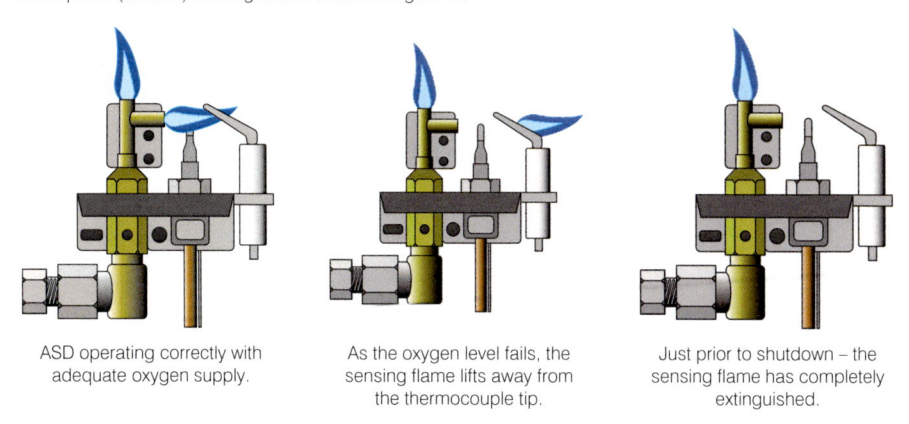

Just prior to shutdown – the sensing flame has completely extinguished.

Figure 12: Pilot assembly incorporating atmosphere sensing device

This type of atmosphere sensing device (ASD) uses a controlled flame to heat a thermocouple, being part of a thermo-electric flame supervision device. As the oxygen level decreases in the atmosphere, this controlled flame 'lifts' in search of oxygen, thus reducing the heat applied to the tip of the thermocouple until, at a predetermined point, the electric current is reduced sufficiently to shut off the gas supply to the appliance burner.

Domestic gas fire design allows for excess air under normal operating conditions to be entrained into the combustion area and hence to the atmosphere via the flue. When there is a spillage of combustion products into the room where the appliance is installed, complete combustion will occur for a period, even though the oxygen level is decreasing and the carbon dioxide (CO_2) level is rising. However, as the oxygen level falls further, incomplete combustion occurs and carbon monoxide (CO) starts to be produced.

Typically when CO_2 levels within the room and in the combustion air to the pilot burner reaches 1.5 to 2.0%, and the corresponding carbon monoxide (CO_2) concentrations reaches a level less than 200ppm (parts per million), which is within the safety limits, the ASD will cause the appliance to shut down.

Other features of radiant convector fires

Figure 13: Radiant/convector gas fire

Radiant convector gas fires will usually have a fire dress guard fitted over the front of the radiants to minimise contact with combustible materials (see Figure 13).

As mentioned previously, radiant convector fires can also use a living flame fire-bed as an alternative to radiants. In this case, the fire dress guard is usually replaced by a glass panel.

The glass panel reduces the amount of air drawn through the appliance and therefore increases the energy efficiency. The inclusion of the glass panel does, however, mean that an integral draught diverter must be provided to prevent any down draught from passing combustion products over the appliance burner. It is at the skirt of the draught diverter that spillage testing must be carried out.

Radiant convector – Room sealed, natural draught

A balanced flue fire is sealed from the room in which it is installed and obtains air for combustion from outside the building, through a duct in the wall. The products of combustion are vented by a smaller duct which usually passes through the air duct. The two ducts are usually concentric, passing from the rear of the fire to outside air.

At the terminal, it is usual for the air inlet duct to terminate close or even flush with the external surface of the structure. The flue duct usually terminates a short distance beyond the face of the combustion air inlet. This prevents products of combustion being drawn back into the appliance. Figure 14 illustrates the principles of operation of a natural draught balanced flue live fuel effect radiant/convector gas fire.

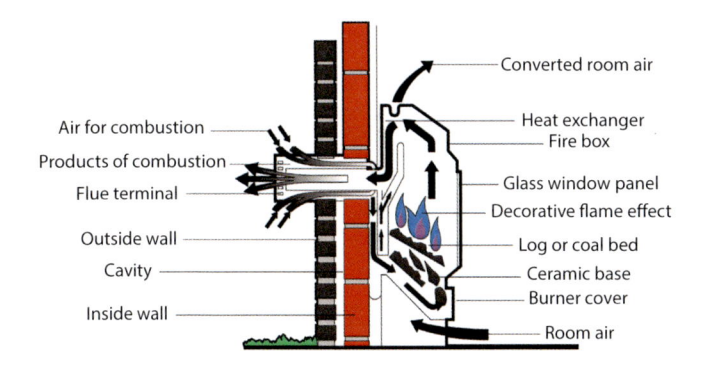

Figure 14: Room sealed radiant convector fire

Room sealed appliances differ from open flued appliances, in that they take their air for combustion from outside the room in which they are installed. In most cases, the air for combustion will be sourced from the area into which the products of combustion are discharged. So, any leak between the appliance and room or internal space will prevent the fire and flue from operating effectively. It is for this reason that the fire and flue system will contain a number of seals. With a seal damaged or missing, it is possible for incomplete combustion to take place, resulting in the products of combustion entering the property in which the fire is installed.

It should be remembered that on all room sealed fires the glass front forms a combustion seal. Under no circumstances should a room sealed fire be left operating if a seal is missing or damaged, or if the glass front is broken or will not fit correctly.

Radiant convector – Open flued, fan assisted

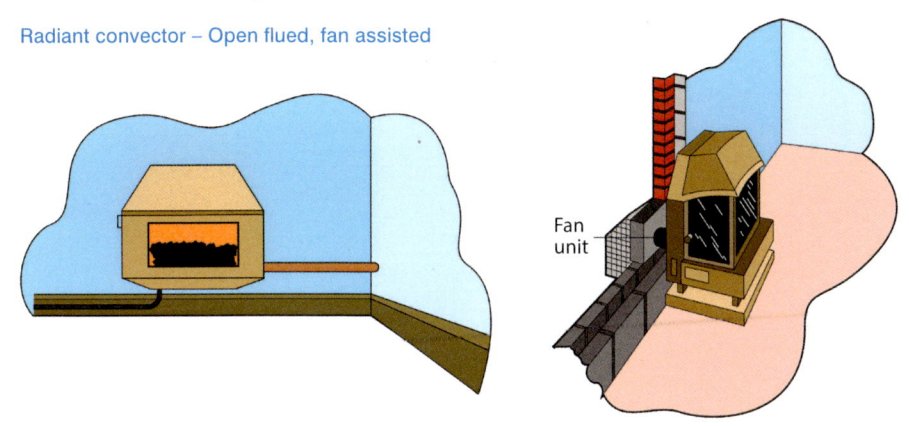

Figure 15: Open flued fan assisted gas fire

Figure 16: Through flue system

Gas fires may use fan-assisted flues, which are usually of the open flued type. This design allows a gas fire to be installed in a situation where there is no flue or a flue which is not working correctly. The flue may be either with a side flue exit as shown in Figure 15 or a through flue system as in Figure 16. The through flue system permits the appliance to discharge its products of combustion through the rear of the appliance to outside air.

If the fan to be used in the flue system is incorporated within the fire, the additional safety controls will be incorporated in the appliance. If the fan is to be fitted remotely from the appliance, the gas operative must ensure all necessary safety controls are incorporated into the fire and flue installation.

The safe operation of the fire and flue system will usually be under the control of some form of a printed circuit board (PCB) and associated controls. These may give the appliance an automatic safety control system.

Any open flue system which incorporates a fan should have some form of safety control, which will cut off the gas supply to the main burner if, for more than 6 seconds, the flow in the secondary flue becomes insufficient, to ensure that all the products of combustion will be cleared. If the flue draught were to fall below the pre-set minimum, it would usually be detected by a flow detection switch, e.g. a diaphragm operated air pressure switch, and this would be related back to the PCB, which would cut off the gas supply to the main burner.

After the safety control has operated, manual intervention will be required to re-establish the gas supply to the main burner.

The operating sequence for a fanned draught open flue is listed below:

- Appliance is manually turned on.
- Controls call for heat.
- Air pressure switch proved in the no flow position prior to start.
- Pre purge – fan begins:
  - Air flow proves.
  - Air flow monitored continually throughout burner run period.
- Ignition device begins.
- Pilot gas valve opens and pilot flame ignites:
  - FSD proves flame.
- Ignition ceases.
- Main gas valves open and main flame ignites.
- Main flame run period:
  - FSD monitors flame throughout main flame run period.
- Control(s) satisfied (for example the fire thermostat reaches its required temperature).
- Pilot and main gas valves close.
- Post purge.
- Fan stops.

Fanned draught open flue systems fitted to appliances that do not have an automatic control sequence must have additional features, which do not allow the appliance to be used if the fan is not operating or the flue flow is insufficient.

The controls in the appliance vary from manufacturer to manufacturer. Shown in Figure 17 is a functional flow diagram for a typical appliance.

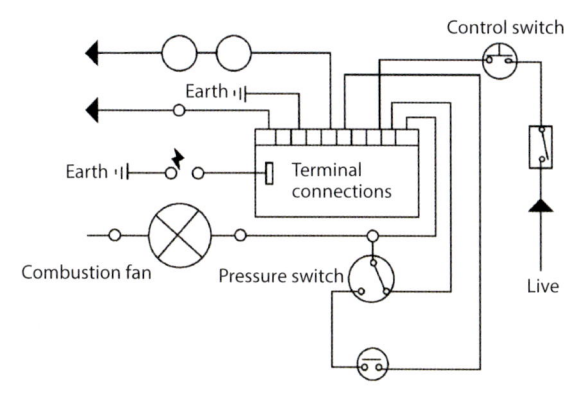

Figure 17: Functional flow diagram

The fire is controlled by a printed circuit board (PCB). Key additional safety features include:

- Air pressure switch, designed to prevent the gas fire lighting procedure from commencing in the event of combustion fan failure.
- Thermostats designed to control fire operation and shut down the appliance in the event of over-heating.
- Solenoid valves – designed to control gas flow through the appliance.

With other types of fan assisted flue systems, such as the side flue system, the fan may be sited separately from the appliance in a fan box.

Flueless catalytic gas fire

There are many old types of flueless gas fire in existence. These are usually, but not exclusively, to be found installed in the hallways of older domestic dwellings.

Technology advances have seen the introduction of a new generation of flueless gas appliances which incorporate a catalytic converter similar to those used on motor cars (see Figure 18). The converter takes the waste gas emissions produced by the fire and chemically changes the potentially dangerous carbon and hydrocarbon products of combustion into harmless gases.

Flueless gas appliances require no flue or chimney, which means they offer an incredibly wide range of siting options. There is no minimum room size requirement although they should not be installed in rooms with a volume less than 40m^3. Wherever flueless appliances are installed some form of permanent ventilation will be required. These appliances are available as stoves or inset fires and all have glass panel fronts. The energy efficiency of a flueless gas fire is 100%.

Figure 18: Flueless catalytic gas fire

On installation, flueless gas appliances must be tested in accordance with manufacturer's instructions. This process may require the use of a flue gas analyser.

Inset live fuel effect fire

The inset live fuel effect (ILFE) gas fire is inset into a builder's opening or fireplace recess (see Figure 19).

In recent times this type of gas fire has become very popular with buyers of new fires. The reason for this is purely aesthetic; these fires are attractive to look at but are less efficient, at 45-55% compared with the equivalent radiant/convector fire. In an attempt to improve efficiency, the fire uses a heat exchanger/convector box.

These appliances have either a log or coal effect, and may use a burner bed with granular infill or burner and fuel bed support. The manufacturers are continually developing new fuel effects in order to improve the appearance of these fires; the current trend is pebble or driftwood fuel bed effects.

Figure 19: ILFE gas fire

Back brick fitting (a)

Clay granules infill (b)

Side cheek fitting (c)

Coal support grid (d)

Imitation fuel (e)

Completed installation (f)

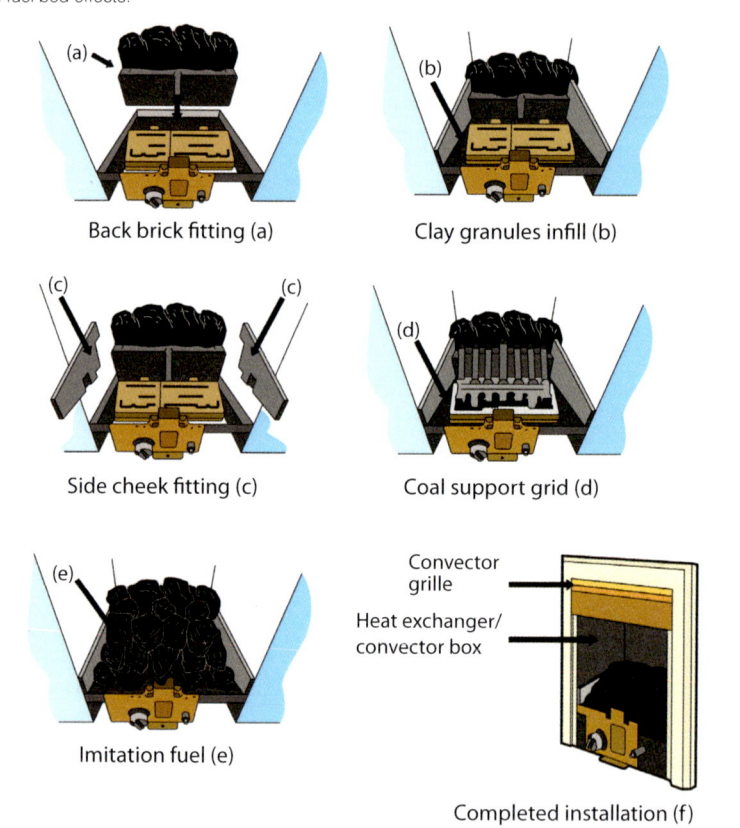

Figure 20: Typical ILFE fire component parts

Fanned draught ILFE

Open flued fanned draught ILFE fires are available with either built in fan units or remote fans with skirting type flue assembly. Fanned draught flue systems must be installed in accordance with BS 5440-1: 2008 and only when permitted by the appliance manufacturer's instructions. Prior to installation the following factors should be taken into consideration:

- Fires with a built-in integral fanned draught flue system must be installed in accordance with BS 5440-1: 2008.
- The flue system is suitable for its proposed location ensuring that the distance between the fire and the outer wall face on which the flue is to terminate is recommended by the fire manufacturer.
- The terminal from the flue must be positioned to allow the free passage of air across its external face, as well as conforming with the flue system manufacturer's specifications, concerning the minimum acceptable distance from ground level to the bottom of the terminal, ensuring that there are no obstructions around the terminal openings.
- Fanned draught flue systems are required by the Gas Safety (Installation and Use) Regulations 1998 to shut down the appliance in event of failure of draught, e.g. fan failure.

Additional components of an ILFE (see Figure 20)

Back brick and side cheeks (20(a) and (c))
As well as having a decorative effect, they carry out the same function as the firebrick on a radiant/convector gas fire. That is to refract any heat away from the internal parts of the fire.

Burner
This can be of a simplex or duplex arrangement. Some ILFE gas fires have a duplex arrangement where a primary set of burners gives an under-firing arrangement, producing efficient blue coloured flames.

This under-firing pre-heats the coal bed in order to minimise sooting and condensation from the live effect flames of the secondary burners.

We must remember that these yellow burning flames are a sign of incomplete combustion and therefore these flames will produce carbon deposits in the form of soot. This sooting is unavoidable and is a characteristic of this type of appliance.

The efficiency for this type of gas fire will only be in the region of 45-55%.

Coal support grid (20(d))
This grid is positioned directly above the burner. It assists in distributing the flames evenly and supports the coals.

Coals (20(e))
Sometimes known as imitation fuel, these carry out the function of the radiants, but not as efficiently, and simulate pieces of solid fuel. It is very important that these coals are correctly fitted, as spillage can occur if excessive or poorly fitted coals are used.

Heat exchanger/convector box
The burner bed and tray are located within this designed chamber. It allows heat to be stored so that air passes across the heat exchanger section, thus setting up a convection current as seen with the radiant/convector fire in Figure 20.

Gas controls

A new design for gas taps has evolved in recent years, whereby slide controls have replaced the traditional rotary gas tap. The slide control incorporates gas tap, ignition microswitch and flame supervision device.

The operating principles of ILFE fires are in most other cases similar to those already described for the radiant convector fire, based upon whether the fire is to be natural draught or fan assisted.

Decorative fuel effect (DFE) fire

This type of fire tends to be much less efficient than both the ILFE and radiant convector options, at approximately 25%. As its name suggests, it is usually used primarily for decorative purposes.

What is the purpose of some of these components?

Refractory coals

With this type of fire, decorative coals are produced from refractory materials in order to transfer heat into the room.

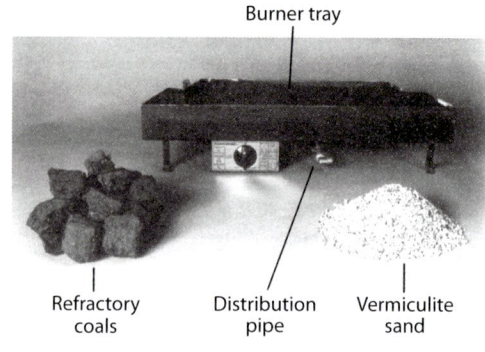

Figure 21: Decorative fuel effect fire

Vermiculite/sand

This is a material used to fill the burner tray of the appliance. When packed loosely, it will allow the gas to permeate to the surface whereupon it can be burnt.

Distribution pipe

The distribution pipe has been factory pre-drilled for an even distribution of gas into the vermiculite/sand bed.

Burner tray

The burner tray of the DFE fire is normally manufactured from steel and holds the above mentioned components.

Gas controls

On this type of appliance, the burner used is of the simplex type, being a pre-drilled tube laid around the base of the burner tray. The controls which are fitted to this type of appliance may include a simple thermo-electric valve and thermocouple. The therm-electric valve cuts the gas flow to the burner when the presence of heat is not detected by the thermocouple. Ignition controls include a pilot assembly and piezo igniter for safe lighting. Added controls include a pilot assembly and piezo igniter to prevent the appliance from being manually ignited each time it is required.

There are no essential differences in the way in which the appliance operates to those previously described for the radiant convector fire.

Note: Purpose provided ventilation of at least 100cm^2 is normally required up to 20kW input (net).

Cassette fires

Open flued cassette fires will normally be installed into a raised builders opening where the flue connection is on top of the fire box. They are normally installed into a lined chimney but may be installed into an unlined chimney if the appliance manufacturers approve it with a specially designed optional flue kit for unlined chimneys.

The flue kit is designed such that debris is prevented from entering the flue box by a debris deflector and must be installed strictly in accordance with manufacturers' instructions.

When using a flue kit with a direct flue connection the chimney needs to be 50mm bigger than the maximum cross sectional area of the debris deflector.

Where the appliance is fitted into an unlined chimney a label will need to be prominently displayed indicating that fact and therefore the manufacturer's instructions have to be adhered to for removal of any debris build up.

The catchment space should be measured from below the lowest point of the debris collector and should be at least 12 litres.

Flueless cassette fires should be installed strictly in accordance with manufacturer's instructions with particular respect to siting and ventilation. They should not be installed into a chimney breast unless the manufacturers approve it or the chimney is sealed off from the appliance as the flue pull may adversely affect the combustion by causing flame disturbance.

Figure 22: Open flued cassette fires

Part 2 – Wall Heaters

Wall heaters operate by supplying their heat to a room or space by the principle of convection. They are sometimes referred to as convector heaters (see Figure 23).

Wall heaters can be:

- Flueless.
- Room sealed.
- Fanned draught.

The two most common options used are room sealed natural draught and room sealed fanned draught.

Flueless wall heaters tend to be of low heat output and their installation is restricted in terms of where they may be sited. Their operating principles are similar to those for the room sealed natural draught model.

Figure 23: Typical wall heater

Room sealed, natural draught wall heater

The principle of operation is similar to the room sealed radiant convector gas fire and is illustrated in Figure 24.

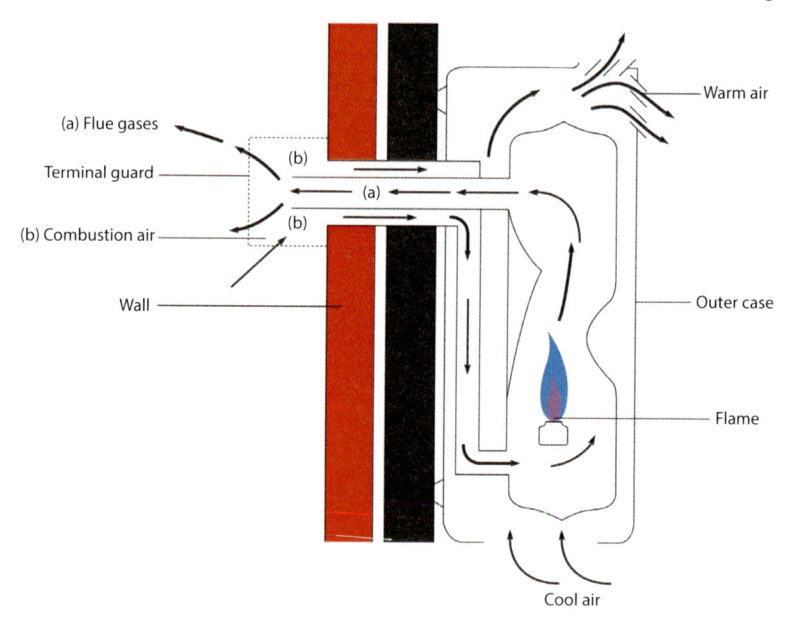

Figure 24: Room sealed natural draught wall heater

Gas is supplied to the main burner, where it is mixed with air supplied from outside via the air duct. The products of combustion flow through the appliance heat exchanger (raising its temperature) and discharge to the atmosphere through the flue duct.

Air from within the room circulates naturally across the heat exchanger due to the convection currents set up during the heating process, warm air being discharged back into the room.

The gas controls incorporate a permanent pilot light, which is lit by a piezo igniter.

The key safety device used is a thermocouple and electro-magnet unit working on the thermo-electric principle. The flame supervision device (FSD) turns off the supply of gas when a flame is not present at the thermocouple. The gas flow rate to the main burner can usually be adjusted by the means of a control knob to meet the heat requirements.

More sophisticated models may include an air thermostat to sense the room air temperature.

Room sealed fanned draught wall heater

The flue and air duct system size on appliances of this type are smaller than for other wall heaters, usually between 65 – 75mm diameter. This reduction is achieved by incorporating a combustion fan in the flue assembly (see Figure 25).

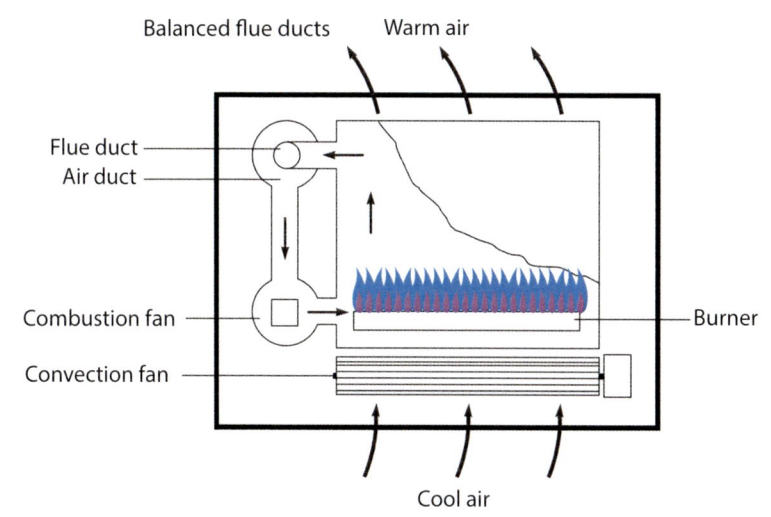

Figure 25: Room sealed fanned draught wall heater

The controls used vary according to the appliance manufacturer. There should always be a device fitted within the appliance which sensors whether the combustion fan is operating correctly or not. This is usually an air pressure switch.

More sophisticated fanned draught wall heaters incorporate a time clock and electronic ignition, which are used to operate the appliance automatically. The key controls are similar to those described for the fanned draught convector fire.

We have now covered the various types of space heaters and their operating principles. This provides important preliminary learning before progressing onto the installation and commissioning and service and maintenance modules.

Section 2 – Installation and Commissioning of Space Heaters

Introduction

In this section we shall focus on the key installation and commissioning aspects of domestic space heaters by looking at:

- Permitted installation locations for appliances.
- Flue and ventilation requirements for space heaters.
- Hearth requirements for space heaters.
- Installation of space heaters.
- Commissioning of space heaters.

Part 1 – Permitted Installation Locations for Appliances

There are a number of locations into which certain gas fires may not be installed. The restrictions are generally based upon the appliance flue type and the rated input of the fire.

Wherever possible, it is preferable to install a room-sealed appliance. This is always the safest option, and may be installed in most locations with access to an outside wall. However, with gas fires the user will generally choose the appliance based upon aesthetics, not safety.

The following text looks at restricted locations.

Bathrooms/shower rooms

Open flued or flueless appliances may not be installed in bathrooms or shower rooms or rooms in which it is intended to install a bath or shower.

Room sealed appliances may be installed providing the installation conforms to the requirements of BS 5440: Parts 1 and 2. There are also restrictions placed on the actual appliance location when the appliance incorporates electrics. If there are any doubts regarding these restrictions, the advice of a competent electrical installation operative should be sought.

Private garages

The Gas Safety (Installation and Use) Regulations 1998 and British Standards endorse the installation of open flued fires in private garages. However, great care is required when siting a fire in a position where a build up of flammable gases can occur (including workshops).

Again, where possible a room sealed appliance should be considered.

Sleeping accommodation

Appliances over 12.7kW heat input net (14kW gross) must be room sealed when fitted in a room used or intended to be used for sleeping.

As from 1st January 1996, open flued appliances rated under 12.7kW heat input net (14kW gross) may be installed. However, the appliance(s) must also have safety devices (atmosphere sensing device), which will cause automatic shut down of the appliance before there is a dangerous build up of products of combustion within the room.

Where a combined appliance is used, such as a back boiler and gas fire, the 12.7kW heat input net (14kW gross) limit applies to the total heat input of both appliances, i.e. input for gas fire should be added to input for back boiler to determine whether the appliance may be installed.

Clearance from combustible materials

There are further limitations placed on the siting of space heaters, namely the distance that an appliance must be installed from combustible materials such as carpets or wooden surrounds. Some examples are given below.

Gas fires and stoves

- Where a gas fire is wall mounted, it must be installed so that the top of the burner is at least 225mm from the carpet or other combustible floor covering.
- Certain gas fires may be floor mounted in accordance with manufacturer's instructions. Should the floor be likely to be covered, the top of the burner must be at least 300mm above floor level in order to take into account any subsequent floor covering.
- Any hearth must be made of non combustible material with a minimum thickness of 12mm. The hearth must extend at least 300mm from the back plane of the fire, and at least 150mm from the side of the burner.
- Manufacturer's instructions should be consulted regarding the proximity of curtains and other combustible furnishings.
- No part of a combustible side wall should be within 500mm of the burner of a gas fire, unless differing figures are specified in the manufacturer's instructions.
- Combustible material adjacent to the appliance should be protected against the effects of heat transmission. The manufacturer may provide specific guidance.
- Any part of a canopy or un-insulated flue pipe within 1 metre of the naked flame or incandescent material source should be separated from any combustible material by at least a gap of 300mm. Otherwise, the canopy or flue pipe should be such that the flue gases are separated from any combustible materials by a distance of not less than 50mm.

Wall heaters

- No part of a combustible side wall should be within 150mm of the warm air outlet, unless differing figures are specified in the manufacturer's instructions.

Part 2 – Flue and Ventilation Requirements for Space Heaters

The flue system can have considerable impact on where the appliance can be located.

Let us take a look at how the flue system and ventilation requirements apply to the following:

- Flueless heaters.
- Room sealed flue systems – natural draught and fanned draught.
- Open flued systems for radiant convector and inset live fuel effect gas (ILFE) fires and wall heaters:
  – Masonry chimneys.
  – Pre-cast flue blocks.
  – Prefabricated sheet metal flue system.
  – Lining an existing flue.
  – Proprietary fanned draught flue systems.
  – Catchment spaces and voids.

- Flue termination.
- Flues for multi-appliance installations.
- Flues for condensing appliances.

• Open flued systems for decorative fuel effect (DFE) fires:
- Masonry chimneys.
- Flue boxes.
- Flue and fireplace sizes.
- Terminals.

• Open flued systems for gas fired heating stoves:
- Masonry chimneys.
- Pre-fabricated flue systems.

• Ventilation requirements for multiple appliance installations.

Flueless heaters

Flueless heaters are generally rated for domestic purposes up to a maximum heat input of 4.3kW (4.75kW gross). BS 5871-1: 2008 does, however, place restrictions on the size of heater which may be installed in a room based on the room volume.

Table 1 is reproduced from BS 5440-2: 2009 and concerns the ventilation of flueless space heaters.

Table 1: Minimum permanent opening free area for flueless appliances

Type of appliance	Maximum appliance rated input limit (net)	Room volume (m^3)	Permanent vent size (cm^2)	Openable window or equivalent also required [A) B)]
Space heater in a room	45W/m^3 of heated space		100 plus 55 for every kW (net) by which the appliance rated input exceeds 2.7kW (net)	Yes
Space heater in an internal space	90W/m^3 of heated space		100 plus 27.5 for every kW (net) by which the appliance rated input exceeds 5.4kW (net)	Yes
Space heaters conforming to BS EN 449: 2002 and A1: 2007 in a room	50W/m^3 of heated space	>15	25cm^2/kW with a minimum of 50cm^2 at high and low level	Yes
Space heaters conforming to BS EN 449: 2002 and A1: 2007 in an internal space	100W/m^3 of heated space	>15	25cm^2/kW with a minimum of 50cm^2 at high and low level	Yes

[A)] Alternative acceptable forms of opening include any adjustable louvre, hinged panel or other means of ventilation that opens directly to outside air. This is additional to the permanent vent requirement.

[B)] Where no openable window direct to outside is available, other products shall be sought.

NOTE: Ventilation requirements for flueless appliances specified in BS EN 14829: 2007 should be in accordance with the appliance manufacturer's instructions. BS 5440-2 may be used for general guidance on ventilation and room volume calculations.

It is clear to see the rated heat input should be limited to 45W/m^3 in a smaller room, or 90 W/m^3 in a small internal space other than a room, e.g. hallway. The example below shows the method for calculation of ventilation.

Example:

If a hallway measures 2.4m x 4.0m x 1.5m, calculate the maximum rated heat input of flueless heater which may be installed.

Room volume = 2.4 x 4.0 x 1.5 = 14.4m^3
Maximum rated heat input = 14.4 x 90 = 1,296W or 1.29kW

When siting a flueless heater, the room or space into which it is to be installed will usually require an openable window and an air vent, which communicates directly with the outside air.

For rooms, the air vent free area requirements are the air vent free area requirements are 100cm^2 plus 55cm^2/kW, by which the rated input exceeds 2.7kW(net). For internal spaces, the air vent free area requirements are 100cm^2 plus 27.5cm^2/kW, by which the rated input exceeds 5.4kW (net).

As technology advances, other types of flueless heaters are entering the market. One example is the catalytic flueless heater. These are decorative, high efficiency heaters that can be fitted anywhere within a property. You should refer to manufacturer's instructions for installation, service and maintenance requirements.

Independent greenhouses

Where the rated heat input to a greenhouse heater exceeds 2.7kW (net), two air vents, one at low level and one at high level, shall be fitted. The minimum effective area of each air vent shall be 39cm^2 for every 1kW of the total rated heat input in excess of 2.7kW (net).

The term "independent greenhouse" covers those types of greenhouse which are completely independent of a dwelling. Air vents are not required where the heat input to the greenhouse heater does not exceed 2.7kW (net).

Design considerations for flueless appliances

For installations other than in a greenhouse, particular matters that should be considered are:

a) potential for problems of condensation;

b) whether the appliance input is such that the appliance may be installed in its intended location in conformity with the input and ventilation requirements

c) presence of any flues which might have an adverse effect on the appliance performance unless closed off

d) presence of other heating appliances in the room space;

e) position of heating appliances in relation to probable position of fixtures, furniture and curtains;

f) availability of gas supplies;

g) availability of electrical supply (where applicable);

h) positioning of air vent(s);

i) installation of an independent electrical carbon monoxide alarm conforming to BS EN 50291 in accordance with BS EN 50292 and the appliance and/or alarm manufacturer's instructions.

Collaboration is essential between those concerned with the design and installation, both at the planning stage and during the execution of the work.

Flueless heaters might give rise to problems of condensation in the room. These appliances are intended as a secondary heat source and it is recommended that a primary heat source, such as a radiator or night store heater, is present in the room and that the room volume and ventilation are adequate for the output of the appliance selected.

Appliances fitted in conservatories might give rise to extra condensation due to low insulation values and rapid cooling below the Dew Point. The installer will have to make an independent assessment of the suitability of a flueless appliance for such an application and advise the customer if they envisage problems with condensation; the following is a list of circumstances to be considered when making this assessment:

- overall insulation value of conservatory;
- likely cold surfaces, such as single glazed panels and roofing materials, on which condensation might readily form;
- construction of floor and amount of insulation built in;
- location and type of primary heating source;
- aspect of building: a north facing conservatory will be much more likely to suffer condensation than one on a south facing aspect;
- proposed usage pattern: the customer may only wish to use the heating on occasional days and condensation could be acceptable in these instances; other customers may wish to use the conservatory as a living room and expect the same level of comfort as the rest of the house;
- method of sealing from main house: a conservatory that has an external type door between it and the main house will experience much quicker cooling than one with a lightweight door, leading to increased condensation risk;
- location of conservatory with respect to altitude, latitude, aspect, and prevailing weather conditions.

Where an independent electrical carbon monoxide alarm is not fitted in the room or internal space where the appliance is to be installed, the user should be made aware of the potential contribution to safety, for all fuel burning appliances, that such an alarm can make. However, it should be stressed that such alarms are to be regarded only as a "back-up precaution" and not a substitute for proper installation and maintenance of appliances and ventilation.

Only an independent electrical carbon monoxide alarm conforming to BS EN 50291 should be installed. The installer is strongly advised to consider the desirability of using an alarm for which the manufacturer can demonstrate that they have obtained third party certification/inspection/testing of product conformity with BS EN 50291.

Appliance fixing

The following guidelines should be observed when fixing flueless appliances.

- Appliances must be installed in accordance with the manufacturer's instructions.
- Flueless appliances should not be connected to a flue.
- Where fitting into an existing fireplace opening or canopy under the base of the existing flue, the flue should be sealed off from the appliance, unless otherwise specified in the manufacturer's instructions.
- Attention should be drawn to the Gas Safety (Installation and Use) Regulations, which control all aspects of the ways in which gas-fired appliances are installed, maintained and used in premises where they apply and the classes of persons who may undertake gas work.

- A flueless heater fitted:
  - into an opening under an existing flue,
  - in front of a fireplace opening,
  - close to an existing flue, or
  - in close proximity to an air vent and any other ventilator, e.g. one serving a redundant chimney, can experience one or more of the following due to excessive air movement: flame disturbance/reversal, overheating, incomplete combustion and sooting.
- Unless the appliance manufacturer's instructions advise otherwise, it is recommended that the base of the flue is sealed with a fire-resistant material to prevent these adverse effects.
- Consideration should also be given to the closure of the flue outlet using a proprietary ventilator flue cap in order to prevent entry of rain, moisture, etc., and the fitting of a ventilator to ensure that the redundant chimney is sufficiently ventilated.

Commissioning

The following guidelines should be observed when commissioning flueless appliances.

- All gas fittings forming part of the installation shall be tested for gas tightness, and purged.
- The gas rate or appliance operating pressure shall be checked and corrected, where necessary, to the setting specified in the appliance manufacturer's instructions, or as indicated on the appliance data plate.
- It is recommended that a combustion test is carried out at the time of installation. This should be in accordance with the appliance manufacturer's instructions or, in the absence of a specific instruction, in accordance with the appropriate method specified in BS 7967.
- The ventilation provision shall be checked for conformity with manufacturer's instructions and appropriate standards.
- The appliance should be commissioned in accordance with then appliance manufacturer's instructions.
- Where any room of the premises is fitted with a fan (e.g. re-circulating ceiling fan, an extract fan, or a fan incorporated within an appliance), operation of the fan(s) shall not adversely affect the appliance's flame stability.
- Correct and safe appliance operation must be checked in accordance with the appliance manufacturer's commissioning instructions.

Note: It should be noted that the Gas Safety (Installation and Use) Regulations require the appliance to be disconnected from the gas supply with an appropriate fitting and labelled if it cannot be fully commissioned.

Maintenance considerations for flueless appliances

If the premises in which the appliance is installed are owned by the occupier, the occupier should be advised in writing that, for continued efficient and safe operation of the appliance, it is important that adequate and regular maintenance is carried out by a competent person (i.e. a Gas Safe registered gas installer) in accordance with the appliance manufacturer's recommendations.

If the premises are tenanted and the landlord owns the gas appliance, the landlord should be advised in writing of the duty imposed by the Gas Safety (Installation and Use) Regulations to ensure that the appliance installation is maintained in a safe condition and checked for safety every 12 months.

The Gas Safety (Installation and Use) Regulations 1998 impose a general obligation on landlords providing gas appliances in tenanted premises to have these maintained in a safe condition and checked for safety every 12 months.

Where any defects that cannot be rectified are identified as part of any maintenance or safety check activity, reference should be made to the requirements of the Gas Industry Unsafe Situations Procedure.

A combustion test should be carried out during maintenance or checks for safety. This test must be in accordance with the appliance manufacturer's instructions or, in the absence of a specific instruction, in accordance with the appropriate method specified in BS 7967.

Room sealed flue systems

Natural draught

Only appliances specifically designed to be used in balanced flue natural draught applications shall be used.

The air supply and flue system form an integral part of a balanced flue appliance design. All components for this type of flue installation will be provided by the appliance manufacturer. The appliance and flue assembly must be installed in accordance with the manufacturer's instructions.

The cross sectional area of the air inlet duct and flueway for a balanced flue appliance is determined by the appliance manufacturer. It should therefore be assumed to be of the correct size. The gas operative must not alter the cross sectional area of the flue duct components nor use components that were not supplied by the appliance manufacturer for use with the appliance.

The flue route and length will usually be governed by the appliance manufacturer. Natural draught balanced flue appliances are typically designed to be fitted directly to an outside wall. The flue assembly will be directed from the appliance directly through the wall.

Room sealed flue systems must be installed so that they:

- Terminate in an acceptable position.
- Are suitable for the wall thickness through which they are to discharge.

Fanned draught

In principle, the majority of the installation requirements for a fanned draught balanced flue fire are the same as for a natural draught balanced flue.

Only appliances specifically designed and incorporating a fan shall be used in balanced flue fanned draught applications.

The appliance manufacturer will usually govern the flue route and length. Fanned draught balanced flue appliances have greater flexibility in routing the flue system, which gives increased options for siting the appliance.

In addition to the requirements for natural draught flues, fanned draught flues need:

- The flue to be adequately supported.
- The flue system must comply with manufacturer's instructions in terms of jointing methods, length of run and number of bends used.

A room sealed space heater will not normally need any purpose provided ventilation for combustion.

Ventilation may be required for cooling purposes when installed in compartments; guidance and recommendations will be made in the manufacturer's instructions.

Note: To comply with the requirements of the Gas Safety (Installation and Use) Regulations any fan assisted means of combustion and/or ventilation must be interconnected to the gas supply such that the gas is isolated in the event of fan failure

Open flued system for radiant convector and ILFE gas fires and wall heaters

General requirements
These are the general requirements, unless otherwise stated in the manufacturer's installation instructions.

Radiant and radiant/convector gas fires
Open flues for these types of appliance should usually be of a minimum of 125mm across the flue axis. The cross sectional area shall be 12,000mm^2 if the flue is round, or 16,500mm^2 if the flue is rectangular, and have a minimum dimension of 90mm.

ILFE gas fires
Many fires of this type are suitable for use on a 125mm minimum across the axis flue system. However, when fitted to a masonry chimney and unless specified in manufacturer's instructions, open flues for this type of appliance should usually be of such a size as to contain a circle of not less than 175mm diameter across the axis. Any throat in the flue system should have a minimum cross-sectional area of at least 240cm^2. Where the flue is rectangular, it should have no dimension less than 100mm. Care should be taken that any purpose designed throat is not restricted when the fire is fitted in place.

Example:
The throat in a flue measures 100mm x 150mm. Determine whether an ILFE gas fire may be installed with this flue system.

Cross-sectional area of flue = 100 x 150mm = 15,000mm^2

There are 100mm^2 in 1cm^2, therefore 15,000/100 = 150cm^2

The cross-sectional area of the throat is less than 240cm^2. The flue is therefore unsuitable.

Masonry chimneys
Many houses are constructed with brick chimneys, primarily designed for solid fuel fires. These chimneys can be used, in most cases, for new or replacement gas fired appliances, but should be swept prior to installation. Older chimneys, generally built prior to 1965, may not meet the requirements of the current Building Regulations and must be carefully inspected to determine their suitability. If a brick chimney is badly built or in a poor state of decay, it is unlikely to clear the products of combustion safely and efficiently. Flue construction and condition of the chimney are, typically, beyond the gas operative's control, but they should be able to recognise an unsuitable flue, either directly or via poor flue performance test symptoms.

The minimum flue sizes for solid fuel appliances are, as a rule, in excess of the requirements for gas appliances, and should usually be suitable. In some cases the chimney may be oversized for certain gas appliances and so a means of controlling the total rate of flow through it may be required. If a method of control is advisable, it will be detailed in the appliance manufacturer's instructions, for example, with the use of a flue spigot restrictor.

| BPEC | Domestic Space Heaters, Gas Fires and Wall Heaters (HTR1) |

Additional guidance can be found in BS 5440: Part 1: 2008 and Part 2: 2009.

The route of the flue should rise continuously towards the termination. It should be so constructed that no bend is at an angle of more than 45° to the vertical and all horizontal flue runs should be avoided.

There should only be two openings into the chimney. The first should be the fireplace opening, the second opening should be at the termination.

Only one appliance or combined appliance shall be fitted to any one brick chimney. Installations have been found where a flexible flue liner has been fitted into a brick chimney connected to a freestanding boiler, and also connected directly into the chimney was a gas fire, with the space around the liner being used as the flue for the fire. This method is unacceptable and dangerous.

Installed within the throat of some brick chimneys the gas operative may find register plates, restrictors or dampers. These were used to reduce the pull of the flue, and allow the fire to stay alight for longer periods. This is quite acceptable when a solid fuel appliance is fitted, however, when a gas appliance, such as a gas fire, is installed an unrestricted flue must be ensured. Therefore, any register plates, restrictors or dampers shall be removed, except where it is not reasonably practicable to remove a sliding damper, where it shall then be permanently fixed in the fully open position.

A Baxi Grate or Baxi Overnight Hearth may be encountered when installing or maintaining gas appliances, such as gas fires. This is a vent found in the base of a fireplace opening. It has a duct which communicates with a ventilated floor void. These must be sealed.

This includes any similar type of ventilation openings/voids into the catchment space and any openings around pipes etc. These must be sealed prior to the installation and use of a gas fire. If these openings are not sealed, they could cause one of the following problems to occur:

- Reduction in flue pull/secondary flueing and air entrainment.
- Products of combustion entering a room or internal space.
- Flame distortion caused by excessive air movement under the appliance.

Figure 26 illustrates the second of these problems.

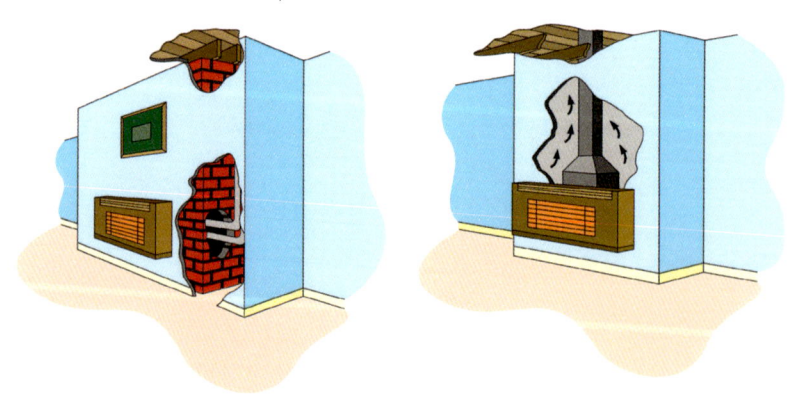

Figure 26: Products of combustion entering a room or internal space due to a lack of sealing

© BPEC   April 2017

Pre-cast flue block chimneys

Radiant and radiant convector fires can generally be fitted to pre-cast flue block systems where permitted by the appliance manufacturer. The flue system must comply with the requirements of BS 5440-1: 2008.

The flue opening/catchment space must comply with manufacturer's requirements.

It should be noted that pre-cast flue blocks are generally more restrictive to flow than chimneys or flue pipes of the same cross sectional area. Therefore, not all appliances, particularly some ILFE gas fires, are suitable for connection to a pre-cast flue block system. The appliance manufacturer's installation instructions must always be checked to ensure that an appliance is suitable to be connected to a pre-cast flue block system.

If a pre-cast flue has been incorrectly designed or badly built, it is unlikely to clear the products of combustion safely and efficiently. Flue design and bad construction are, typically, beyond the gas operative's control but they should be able to recognise bad construction, either directly or via poor flue performance test symptoms.

BS 5440-1: 2008 gives additional guidance as to the construction of pre-cast flues.

Pre-fabricated sheet metal flue systems

Sheetmetal flue systems should comply with BS EN 1856 Parts 1 and 2. The flue system usually incorporates a flue box sited in a chimney recess, where the flue box is discharging into a traditional flue. This will usually be lined with a continuous stainless steel flexible flue liner. Where the liner discharges into an independent flue system (not built into the building), this should usually be of twin wall design.

In general, flue boxes provide a means to accommodate an appliance where:

- No fireplace recess or builder's opening exists; or
- An existing fireplace recess or builder's opening is oversized; or
- The existing fireplace opening plane represents an unsuitable surface upon which to mount a closure plate or seal the appliance housing against (e.g. as necessary in the case of an inset live fuel effect gas fire). It should be noted that flue boxes are not suitable for solid fuel fired appliances and this should be stated (via a permanent badge/label) on the flue box.

Example

Warning – Fire risk!

The flue box is primarily for use with decorative gas fires (DGF) conforming to BS EN 509: 2000, but a fire conforming to BS 7977-1 may also be fitted. A solid fuel fire must not be fitted in this box or chimney.

Joints to be well made where the closure plate or the flue box is sealed to the face of the opening or fire surround.

Flue liner conforming to BS EN 1856-2

Methods of installation using a flue box, flue pipe and flexible flue liner are shown in Figure 27.

When using a flue box, particularly with ILFE fires, the appliance and flue box manufacturer's instructions must be checked to ensure that they are compatible, conforming to the relevant British Standards.

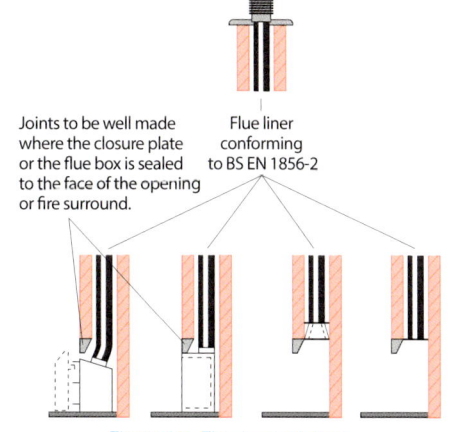

Figure 27: Flue box with liner

Lining an existing flue

Where a chimney has been found to be unsound, it is possible to renovate the flue by lining it with a flexible liner as shown in Figure 27 above.

Alternatively, from 1987 any existing poured lightweight insulated concrete cast in situ lining systems or new linings may be used to form a continuous flueway to line and refurbish the existing brick built constructional chimney. Such methods shall only be used where the British Board of Agreement (BBA) has independently certified such lining system methods (not applicable to new masonry constructed chimneys).

This form of lining is specialist in nature and it is essential the requirements of BS 5440-1: 2008 are fully met in respect of such systems. The names of certified cast in situ chimney lining systems may be obtained by reference to the BBA. The process may be used to insulate, refurbish and/or reduce chimney free areas to match appliance chimney design requirements.

Proprietary fanned draught flue systems

Before an appliance is installed for use with a proprietary fanned draught flue system, the gas appliance manufacturer's instructions shall be checked to confirm that it is an acceptable combination.

The installation shall be in accordance with the instructions supplied by the manufacturer(s) of both the appliance and of the flue system. Where a replacement fire is to be fitted to an existing fanned draught flue system, the gas fire manufacturer's fixing kit shall be used and all requirements of BS 5440-1: 2008 must be satisfied.

Catchment spaces and voids

The gas fire shall be fitted so that there is a void below the base of the spigot for the collection of debris. The minimum volume of the void and its depth below the fire spigot shall be as given in Table 2 below.

The finished opening into the void shall be large enough to permit the clearance of any debris when the closure plate and/or the gas fire are removed. The void, including that which may be created by any ledge, shall not be so large as to adversely affect the flue's performance by creating abnormal flow. All openings other than the flue outlet and front opening should be sealed.

Where an oversized void is encountered, it may be reduced in size by lining with bricks or suitable blocks or alternatively by installing a metallic flue box.

The nominal dimensions of the void should not exceed 650mm wide by 475mm deep by 800mm high.

Table 2: Minimum void dimensions required below appliance connections

Circumstances	Depth mm	Volume m^3
Any appliance fitted to an unlined brick chimney	250	0.012 (12 litres)
Any appliance fitted to a lined brick chimney (new or unused, or used with gas)	75	0.002 (2 litres)
Any appliance fitted to a lined brick chimney (previously used with solid fuel or oil)	250	0.012 (12 litres)
Any appliance fitted to flue block chimney/metal chimney (new or unused, or previously used with gas)	75	0.002 (2 litres)
Any appliance fitted to flue block chimney/metal chimney (previously used with solid fuel or oil)	250	0.012 (12 litres)

Table 2 uses some unusual dimensions for measuring volume, so let us look at an example.

Example
The void volume below the fire flue spigot in a previously used flue system measures 0.4m x 0.35m x 0.3m. Calculate and establish whether the void volume meets the requirements of the above table.

$0.4 \times 0.35 \times 0.3 = 0.042 m^3$

There are 10 dm per metre. There are therefore 10 dm x 10 dm x 10 dm = 1,000 dm^3 in a cubic metre.

Void volume = $0.042 m^3$ x 1,000 = 42 dm^3. The void volume is therefore satisfactory.

Where an oversized void is encountered, it may be reduced in size by lining with bricks and suitable blocks. The nominal dimensions of the void should not exceed 650mm wide x 475mm deep x 800mm high.

To assist the correct operation of the fire, a fireplace recess or builder's opening shall have only an entrance through the fireplace opening and an exit via the flue. All other openings, in particular gaps/cracks inside the builder's opening (including in or around any chair brick), those between any surround and the builder's opening, those which may exist in respect of an existing underfloor air supply and those made for the passage of gas and flue pipes and electric cables, shall be sealed.

The reason for sealing these openings is that they reduce the flue's pull on the fire and can allow combustion products into the room. An acceptable way of sealing these openings would be by use of, for example, cement or fire clay. In the case of a dry lined wall construction, attention is drawn to the need to seal any gaps or voids between the plasterboard and the wall.

When the catchment space contains an existing solid fuel boiler, where practical the boiler should be emptied of water and drilled with a hole of minimum diameter 6mm. This action should prevent a dangerous build up of pressure occurring within the boiler.

Flue termination

Pre-cast flue blocks and sheet metal flue systems will usually be terminated with an approved terminal.

British Standards state that a chimney with a flue of 170mm diameter or less needs to be fitted with a terminal. It is, however, sometimes considered to be best practice to fit a terminal, as this will guard against the possibility of birds nesting in the flue system, or it becoming blocked by snow or leaves, particularly in circumstances where the fire is not used very often.

Where there is evidence that a chimney is used by birds for nesting or there is a known problem of birds nesting in chimneys in the neighbourhood, a guard or terminal should always be fitted to the chimney.

Birds nesting in chimneys are particularly prevalent in areas where jackdaws are known to roost. Before fitting a terminal or guard, the chimney should be inspected and, if necessary, reinforced to ensure it will support such a terminal or guard.

Bird guards should be fabricated from corrosion and weather resistant material, and should be securely fixed. Any opening in the bird guard accessible to birds should have a minor dimension of not more than 20mm.

Flues for multi-appliance installations

Where, for whatever reason, two or more chimneys serve a common space, for example where a wall between two rooms has been removed, the draught of the stronger chimney can influence the pull of the weaker and cause spillage at the appliance to occur.

This will happen with gas fired appliances of different types and even more so, if one of the chimneys is serving a solid fuel appliance. With this in mind, it is important that both appliances are of a similar type and heat input.

Flues for condensing appliances

An appliance designed to operate in a condensing mode shall be installed in accordance with the manufacturer's installation instructions, which will detail provisions for condensate, disposal and any requirements on the size and length of flue.

Appliances of this type normally incorporate a fanned draught flue system, thus enabling small-bore flue piping, which may be non-metallic, to be used both for evacuating the products of combustion and for the drainage of any condensate build up.

With such flue systems, special jointing techniques may apply and any instructions should be followed. The maximum length of flue pipe, including bends etc. Together with permitted flue materials, will be specified in the manufacturer's instructions.

Unless otherwise specified in the manufacturer's instructions, there should be a continuous horizontal fall of the flue pipe from the appliance to the point of termination of 1:50. The flue pipe should project a minimum of 75mm from the point of exit on an external wall to avoid condensate dripping back onto the wall.

Further details on the installation of condensing appliances are given in BS 5440-1: 2008.

Ventilation requirements for radiant radiant convector and ILFE gas fires

An open flued appliance with a rated input not exceeding 7kW (net) and which generates a clearance flue flow not greater than 70m^3/h under specified conditions (generally all except DFEs), does not normally require an air vent in the room or internal space in which it is installed.

This is due to natural or adventitious ventilation through, for example, floorboards, cracks in window frames and doors. However, the availability of such ventilation should never be taken for granted, as the air tightness of a dwelling can be affected by double glazing, cavity insulation, draught proofing, its method of construction, the installation of extraction fans and so on.

For open flued fires with a rated heat input exceeding 7kW, purpose provided ventilation of at least 5cm^2 per kilowatt (net) of heat input should be provided, unless otherwise specified in the manufacturer's instructions.

Areas identified as requiring action for radon gas will be known due to local publicity, but in case of doubt, further advice can be obtained from a Building Control Officer at the Local Authority Headquarters. In these areas ventilation shall not be taken from below floor level or interfere with measures taken to prevent the entry of radon into the dwelling. For the purposes of this standard and safety reasons, a conservatory should be treated as a habitable room.

Where an appliance is to be installed in a room or space. Which already contains one or more fuel burning appliances, the ventilation requirements shall be as specified in BS 5440-2: 2009 for multi-appliance installations. If permanent ventilation is required for a multi-appliance installation, this should, wherever practicable, be sited between the appliances.

Where an interconnecting wall has been removed between two rooms and the resultant room contains two similar chimneys and each is fitted with a gas fire or inset live fuel effect gas fire, an air vent is not normally required if the total rated heat input of the appliances does not exceed 14kW.

Open flues for decorative fuel fires (DFE)

Any DFE gas fire shall be flued in accordance with the same standards as previously mentioned for fires and additionally the following as appropriate.

A visual check of the flue system shall be carried out to confirm that:
- There is a smooth tapered transition (gather) to the flue.
- There is no apparent structural damage to the flue system.
- The flue system is continuous from its inlet to the point of termination.
- Termination conforms with requirements of BS 5440-1: 2008.

Where the appliance is installed under an associated independent canopy, the canopy flue outlet shall be positioned at the top of the canopy. The flue outlet shall have the same dimensions as the required flue system and be securely fixed and sealed into the flue. The canopy shall have no openings other than at its base and top.

Any flue that cannot be seen must be clean and unobstructed throughout its length and shall be thoroughly swept before installing an appliance.

Suitable flue systems may include the following:
- An existing masonry chimney.
- Single or double wall metal flue pipe which is approved by the appliance manufacturer.
- An existing masonry chimney lined with a stainless steel double wall flue liner or single skin stainless steel liner satisfying the requirements of BS 715: 2005 (not flexible flue liner).
- Existing masonry chimney lined with a system which has been approved by an accredited test house as being suitable for use with a solid fuel fired appliance.
- A lined masonry chimney (e.g. to BS 6461-1).
- A pre-cast flue block chimney for use with a solid fuel fired appliance.
- Any other pre-cast flue block chimneys which have been approved by an accredited test house as being suitable for use with solid fuel fired appliances.

Where un-insulated single wall flue pipe is used, there should be a minimum clearance of 25mm between the flue pipe and combustible material. In the case of double wall flue pipe, a clearance of 25mm, measured from the inner wall, should be provided.

Un-insulated single wall flue pipe should not be used externally, in loft or roof spaces, and in other exposed locations, e.g. unheated rooms or spaces. This is to prevent chilling of the flue, resulting in poor flue performance.

Flue and fireplace size

The flue serving the appliance shall have no cross-sectional dimension less than 175mm, other than in the case of an appliance which has been certificated for use on a flue of a smaller size.

The fireplace size shall be such that there is no spillage from the appliance. Where an appliance has been certificated for use on a flue of less than 175mm across its axis, this will be stated in the manufacturer's installation instructions.

Typical fireplaces into which appliances may be installed are shown in Figure 28.

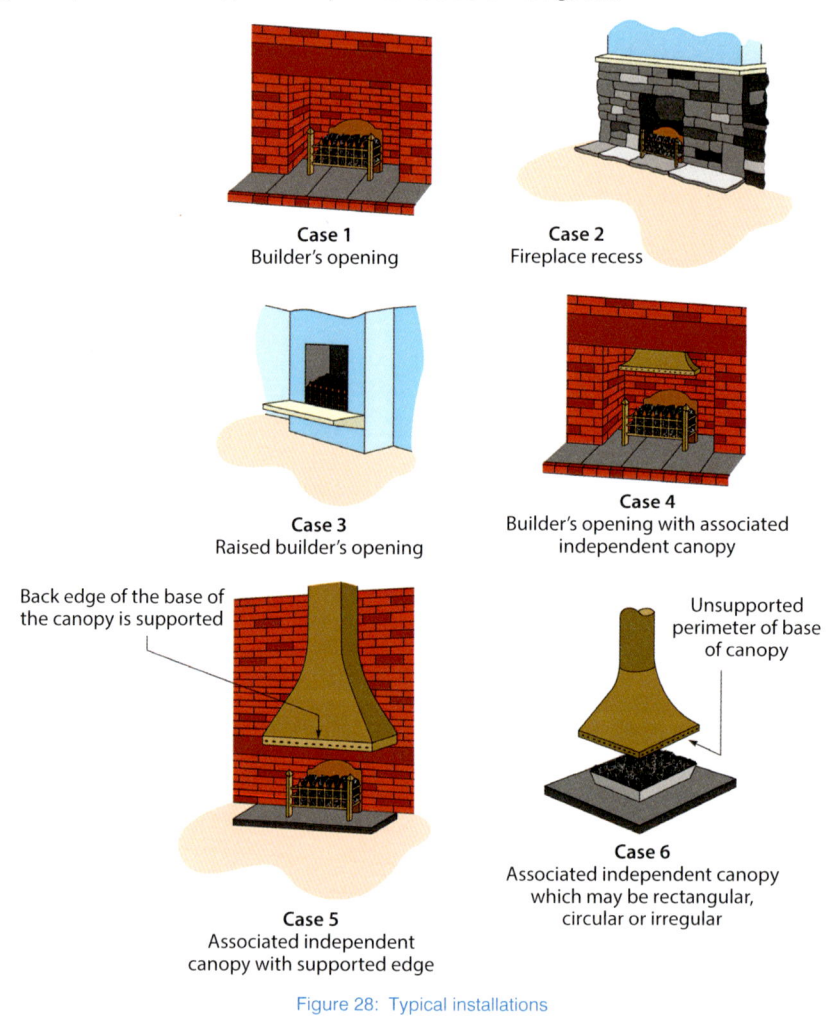

Case 1
Builder's opening

Case 2
Fireplace recess

Case 3
Raised builder's opening

Case 4
Builder's opening with associated independent canopy

Back edge of the base of the canopy is supported

Unsupported perimeter of base of canopy

Case 5
Associated independent canopy with supported edge

Case 6
Associated independent canopy which may be rectangular, circular or irregular

Figure 28: Typical installations

BPEC	Module 19

Case 1 shows a builder's opening. The fireplace opening area is taken as the multiple of the width and the height of the vertical face of the opening into the fireplace from the room.

Case 2 shows a fireplace recess. The fireplace opening area is taken as in Case 1 above.

Case 3 shows a raised builder's opening (sometimes referred to as a "hole-in-the-wall" fireplace), which may or may not have fireplace components installed to form a fireplace recess. In both cases, the fireplace opening area is taken as in Case 1 above.

Cases 4, 5 and **6** show fireplaces incorporating a canopy. Such fireplaces, and flues, may be sized from Figure 30 by either of two methods:

Method 1. The fireplace opening area may be taken as the area of the horizontal entry into the base of the canopy **provided that** all the relevant constraints shown in Figure 30 are followed, or;

Method 2. The fireplace opening area may be taken as the multiple of the unsupported perimeter of the base of the canopy and the height of the base of the canopy above the fire bed.

Appliances in raised builder's opening

Where the appliance to be installed in a hole in the wall fireplace, a hearth conforming with BS 476-4 or materials classified as "Class 0" in accordance with Approved Document B of the Building Regulations shall be fitted on the floor beneath the hole as to protect combustible material from the radiant heat, unless:

a) the appliance is installed in accordance with the manufacturer's instructions and the instructions state that no hearth is required to protect the floor covering from radiant heat: or

b) the appliance is installed so that every part of any flame or incandescent part of the fire bed is at least 225mm vertically above any carpet or floor covering: or

c) the hearth beneath the appliance , or into which the appliance is set, extends in front of any flame or incandescent part of the fire bed such that the sum of the x + y dimensions in Figure 29 is at least 225mm to any carpet or floor covering.

Note: Although it is stated in BS 5871 that any flame or incandescent material should be at least 225mm above the finished floor level, it is usually advisable to use a figure of 300mm to allow for the subsequent fitting of any carpet or floor covering.

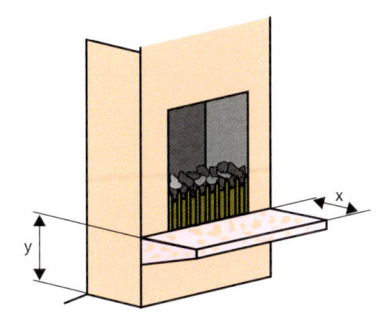

Figure 29: Sizing a hearth for appliances in raised builder's openings

April 2017 © BPEC

When installing an appliance into an existing fireplace arrangement, it is not normally necessary to alter the flue size if the flue system has been proven to work safely with a solid fuel open fire.

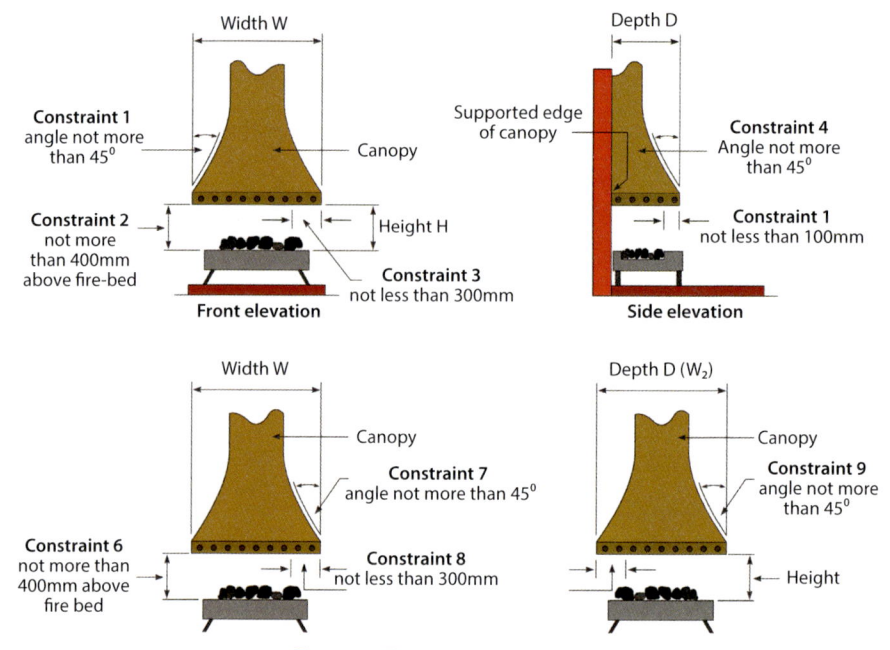

Front elevation
- Width W
- **Constraint 1** angle not more than 45°
- **Constraint 2** not more than 400mm above fire-bed
- Canopy
- Height H
- **Constraint 3** not less than 300mm

Side elevation
- Depth D
- Supported edge of canopy
- **Constraint 4** Angle not more than 45°
- **Constraint 1** not less than 100mm

Front elevation (lower)
- Width W
- Canopy
- **Constraint 7** angle not more than 45°
- **Constraint 6** not more than 400mm above fire bed
- **Constraint 8** not less than 300mm

Side elevation (lower)
- Depth D (W_2)
- Canopy
- **Constraint 9** angle not more than 45°
- Height

Figure 30: Typical canopy installation

For a flue and fireplace to operate without spillage, there is a necessary relationship between the flue size, the flue height and the fireplace opening area. The chart shown in Table 3 gives practical guidance on this relationship.

Table 3: DFE flue sizes

Fireplace openings			Flue heights				
Width	Height	Area	3.0m	4.5m	6.0m	9.0m	5.0m
35cm	55cm	1925cm^2	175mm	175mm	175mm	175mm	175mm
40cm	55cm	2200cm^2	175mm	175mm	175mm	175mm	175mm
46cm	46cm	2116cm^2	175mm	175mm	175mm	175mm	175mm
46cm	55cm	2530cm^2	200mm	175mm	175mm	175mm	175mm
46cm	61cm	2806cm^2	200mm	200mm	175mm	175mm	175mm
61cm	46cm	2806cm^2	200mm	200mm	175mm	175mm	175mm
61cm	61cm	3721cm^2	250mm	225mm	200mm	200mm	175mm
61cm	76cm	4636cm^2	300mm	250mm	250mm	225mm	200mm
76cm	46cm	3496cm^2	225mm	225mm	200mm	200mm	175mm
76cm	61cm	4636cm^2	250mm	250mm	250mm	225mm	200mm
76cm	76cm	5776cm^2	300mm	300mm	250mm	250mm	225mm
76cm	91cm	6916cm^2	350mm	300mm	300mm	250mm	250mm
91cm	46cm	4186cm^2	250mm	225mm	225mm	200mm	200mm
91cm	61cm	5551cm^2	300mm	300mm	250mm	250mm	225mm
91cm	76cm	6916cm^2	350mm	300mm	300mm	250mm	250mm
91cm	91cm	8281cm^2	350mm	350mm	300mm	300mm	250mm
91cm	107cm	9737cm^2		350mm	350mm	300mm	300mm
107cm	46cm	4922cm^2	300mm	250mm	250mm	225mm	200mm
107cm	61cm	6527cm^2	300mm	300mm	300mm	250mm	250mm
107cm	76cm	8132cm^2	350mm	350mm	300mm	300mm	250mm
107cm	91cm	9737cm^2		350mm	350mm	300mm	300mm
107cm	107cm	11,449cm^2			350mm	350mm	300mm
107cm	122cm	13,054cm^2				350mm	350mm
122cm	46cm	5612cm^2	300mm	300mm	250mm	250mm	225mm
122cm	61cm	7442cm^2	350mm	300mm	300mm	300mm	250mm
122cm	76cm	9272cm^2		350mm	350mm	300mm	300mm
122cm	91cm	11,102cm^2			350mm	350mm	300mm
122cm	107cm	13,054cm^2				350mm	350mm
122cm	122cm	14,884cm^2				350mm	350mm
152cm	46cm	6992cm^2	300mm	300mm	300mm	250mm	250mm
152cm	61cm	9272cm^2		350mm	350mm	300mm	300mm
152cm	76cm	11,552cm^2			350mm	350mm	300mm
152cm	91cm	13,832cm^2				350mm	350mm
152cm	107cm	16,264cm^2					350mm
152cm	122cm	18,544cm^2					

Example

A fireplace opening measures 107cm wide x 76cm high. The flue length is 6.0 metres. Determine from the table the flue diameter required.

Fireplace openings			Flue heights				
Width	Height	Area	3.0m	4.5m	6.0m	9.0m	5.0m
107cm	76cm	8132cm^2	350mm	350mm	300mm	300mm	250mm

From the table the flue diameter should be 300mm.

Terminals

When fitted, a terminal must comply with the following:

- Not restrict the safe exit of the combustion products from the flue.
- Outlet openings shall be provided either all round or on all sides of the terminal.
- Outlets shall admit a 6mm diameter ball, but not a 16mm diameter ball.

When a chimney pot is fitted, no dimension across the axis of its outlet, or outlets, should be less than 175mm and no chimney pot inserts should be used.

Sometimes it is difficult to gain access to check the outlet opening sizes of terminals.

Figure 31 should assist you to make a preliminary assessment as to the suitability of the pot or whether it is a chimney pot insert.

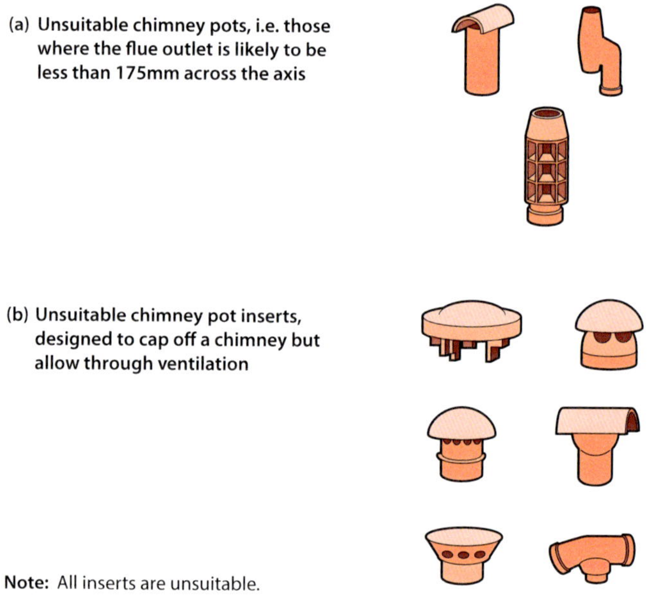

(a) Unsuitable chimney pots, i.e. those where the flue outlet is likely to be less than 175mm across the axis

(b) Unsuitable chimney pot inserts, designed to cap off a chimney but allow through ventilation

Note: All inserts are unsuitable.

Figure 31: Unsuitable chimney pots and inserts

Ventilation requirements for DFE fires

Purpose provided ventilation is usually required for these appliances. British standards – BS 5871-3: 2005 recommends that 100cm^2 free area is provided. Greater requirements may be specified by the appliance manufacturer.

In some cases where the appliance is of below 7kW heat input, the manufacturer may advise that additional permanent ventilation is not required.

Table 4: Ventilation requirements for DFE/multiple gas appliance installations

No	Installation – rate input	Appliance(s) location	Ventilation requirement to outside air
1	DFE up to 7kW		Normally 100cm^2 minimum but check manufacturer's instructions as some models may not require any ventilation.
2	DFE 7kW-20kW		Normally 100cm^2 minimum or as in manufacturer's instructions.
3	Two DFE's up to 20kW	Room or space with more than one flue	Normally 200cm^2 (or as in manufacturer's instructions) plus 35cm^2 (adventitious air).
4	One or two DFEs plus other appliance(s)		DFE requirement based on options 1-3, plus whichever is the greatest of: a) 5cm^2 per kW input (net) of all open flue space heating appliances, such as central heating boilers, ILFE's, etc., or b) The total flueless space heating requirement, such as hall/cabinet convector heater, or c) 5cm^2 per kW input (net) of a single, open flue non-space heating appliance, such as a water heater
5	DFE plus other appliance(s)	Through room with two similar, open flues	DFE requirement based on options 1-3, plus whichever is the greatest of: a) 5cm^2 per kW input above 7kW of all open flue space heating appliances, such as central heating boilers, ILFE's etc., or b) The total flueless space heating requirement, such as hall cabinet convector heater, or c) The requirement for other single, flueless or closed flue appliance d) 5cm^2 per kW input above 7kW of a single, open flue non-space heating appliance, such as water heater.
6	Two DFEs plus other appliance(s)		DFE requirement based on options 1-3, plus whichever is the greatest of: a) 5cm^2 per kW input (net) of all open flue space heating appliances, such as central heating boilers, ILFE's etc., or b) The total flueless space heating requirement, such as hall/cabinet convector heater, or c) The requirement for other single, flueless or closed flue appliance d) 5cm^2 per kW input (net) of a single, open flue non-space heating appliance, such as water heater.

- Where the appliance is installed in a builder's opening or fireplace recess that has a supply of air entering from below, 20% of the air vent requirement may be supplied from this source.
- If the appliance fails the spillage test, it may be necessary to provide extra ventilation; a DFE fitted in a property with a solid floor, double glazing and cavity wall insulation may not have sufficient adventitious air to allow correct operation of the flue.
- Treat oil and solid fuel appliances as if they were gas and calculate input as being 166% of output. For a solid fuel fire or small closed fire of unknown input, provide (100 cm^2) of permanent opening.
- Air vents shall not be communicate directly with a builder's opening or fireplace recess.
- Where a builder's opening, fireplace recess, or inglenook installation is served by an existing underfloor air supply, the air vent/grill should be sealed to avoid draughts interfering with the correct operation of the flue and the appliance burner. Outside of the hearth area, the use of underfloor ventilation is permitted.

BPEC Domestic Space Heaters, Gas Fires and Wall Heaters (HTR1)

Open-flued system for heating stoves

Open flued heating stoves are available in two basic types; freestanding and those which have a rear flue spigot which passes through a closure plate in a similar manner to a gas fire. Three different installations are shown in Figure 32 below.

The manufacturer's instructions for each form of appliance will specify the permissible types of flue and any special fixing instructions which should be followed.

Where a flexible flue liner is used in conjunction with a register plate as in Figure 32 and 34, the liner should protrude through the plate by a minimum of 150mm. Where a closure plate is used, it is essential that any air relief opening is not obstructed.

Flue pipe connections from the stove either to a flexible liner or sealed to the closure plate above the appliance

Flue system to terminate with a flue terminal conforming to British Standards - BS5440: Part 1: 2008

A flexible liner shall always be used to line the entire chimney where an existing masonry structure has not been built with a clay liner. Otherwise it is an optional requirement depending on the appliance manufacturer's installation instructions

Flue pipe to project not less than 150mm above register plate

Dilution air through integral draught diverter

Flue pipe sealed to debris or register plate

Dilution air through integral draught diverter

The flue system used should be in accordance with the appliance manufacturer's installation requirements

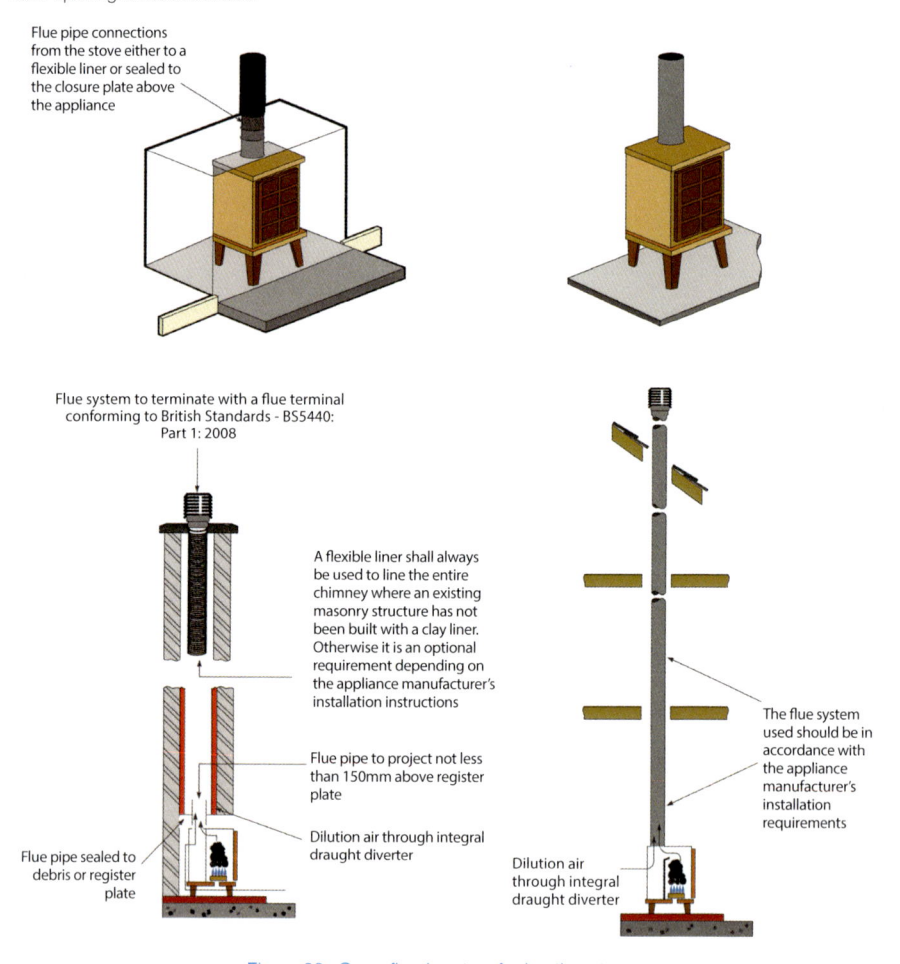

Figure 32: Open-flued system for heating stoves

Requirements for direct flue connection appliances

A direct flue connection to a gas fire or convector shall only be made where the appliance has been designed for such use and this method is permitted in the manufacturer's installation instructions

Flue system to terminate with a flue terminal conforming to BS5440-1

A flexible liner shall always be used to line the entire chimney where an existing masonry structure has not been built with an integral liner

Otherwise it is an optional requirement depending on the appliance manufacturers installation instructions

In either case, the flue system is to terminate with a flue terminal conforming to BS5440-1

Twin wall flue pipe to BS EN 1856-1

Integral chimney liner

Flexible flue pipe sealed to plate

Flexible metal flue liner section to BS EN 1856-2

Draught diverter opening

Flue pipe sealed to appliance outlet spigot

Sealed register plate

Mechanical fixing of the flue liner sealed to the appliance outlet spigot

Draught diverter opening

a) Top outlet direct flue connection

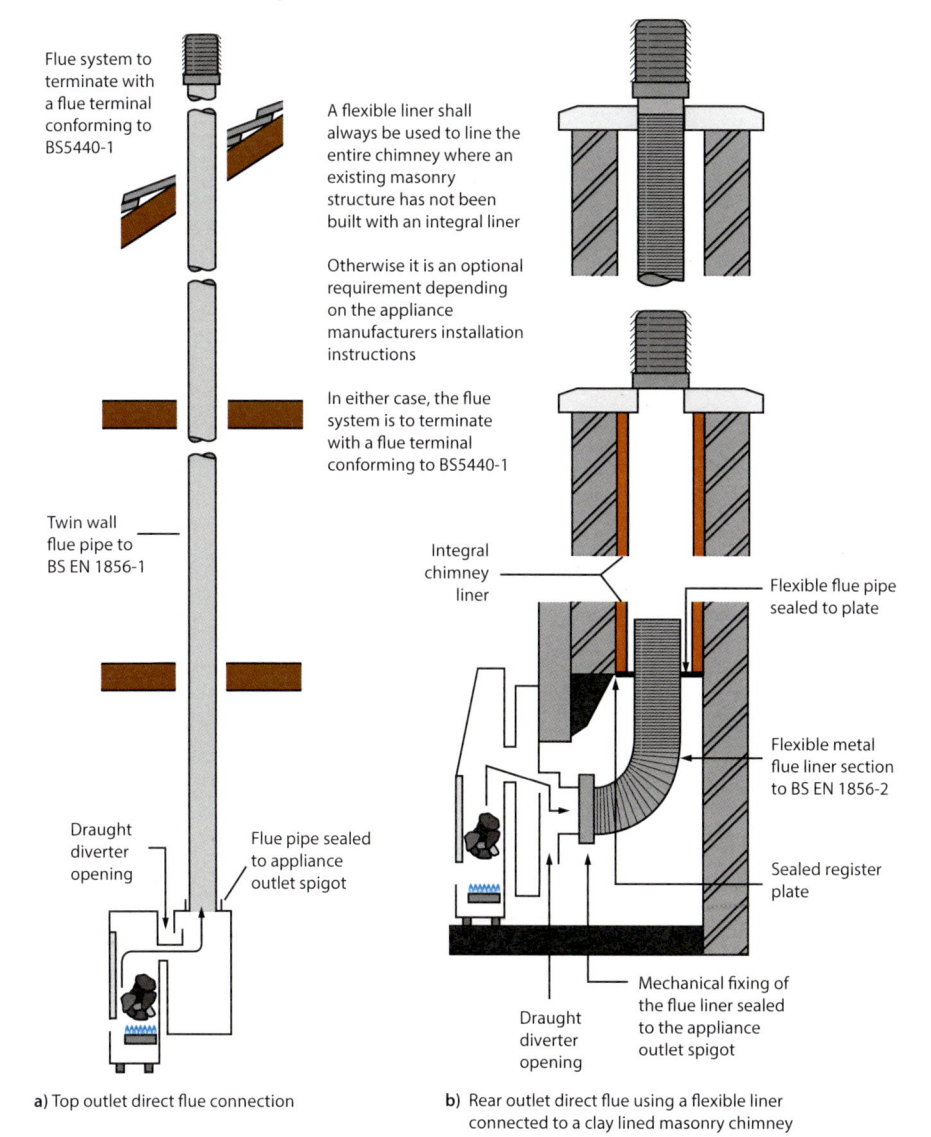

b) Rear outlet direct flue using a flexible liner connected to a clay lined masonry chimney

Figure 33: Direct flue connections

| BPEC | Domestic Space Heaters, Gas Fires and Wall Heaters (HTR1) |

Flue system to terminate with a flue terminal conforming to British Standards – BS5440: Part 1: 2008

Existing masonry chimneys may be lined using a flexible liner to British Standards – BS5440: Part 1:2008

Debris or register plate

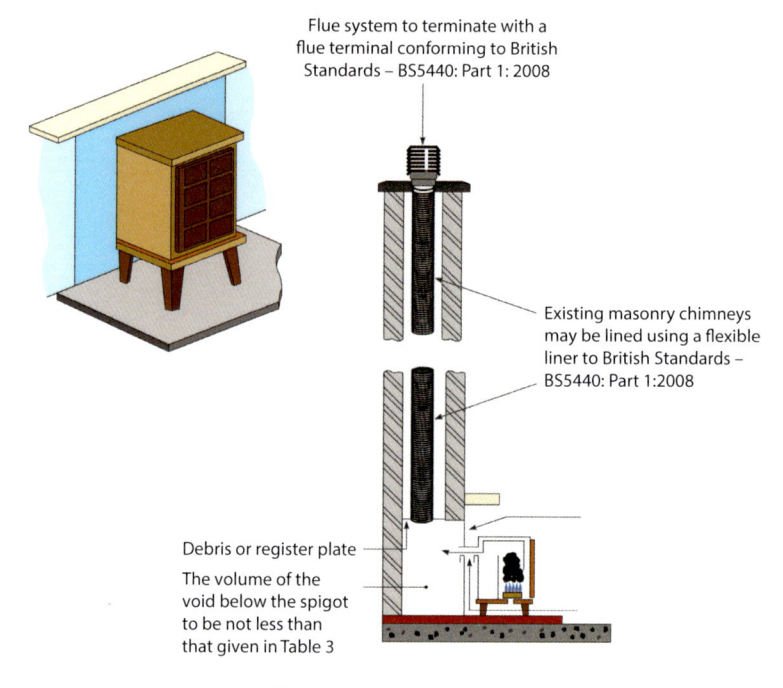

The volume of the void below the spigot to be not less than that given in Table 3

Figure 34: Heating stoves

Ventilation requirements for multiple appliance installations

Care needs to be taken when identifying the ventilation requirements of a room containing two or more open flued/flueless gas appliances. With radiant convector and ILFE gas fires and wall heaters, the ventilation requirements should be based on the greatest of the following:

- The total rated input of **flueless space heating** appliances, or

- The total rated input of **open flued space heating** appliances, except where the interconnecting wall between two rooms has been removed and the resultant room contains two similar chimneys, each fitted with similar gas fires, no air vent is required if the total rated input of the gas fires does not exceed 14kW gross or net heat input; or

- The maximum individual rated input of any other type of appliance.

Note: Where a room contains an oil or solid fuel appliance of unknown heat outputs, the appliance ventilation requirements should be taken as 100cm^2.

BPEC   Module 19

Part 3 – Hearth Requirements for Space Heaters

Before we can get into the installation section, we need to address the issue of the suitability of hearths for use with space heaters.

Wall heaters are usually wall mounted and therefore they should be sited according to manufacturer's requirements.

Radiant convector gas fires may be suitable for wall mounting, in which case the fire's flame or incandescent material source should be installed at least 225mm above a carpet or any floor covering. Where the floor is of the type that is likely to be covered, any flame or incandescent materials should be at least 300mm above the floor in order to make allowance for floor coverings beneath the appliance.

The Building Regulations (England and Wales) approved Documents J (ADJ) require that when competent registered gas operatives install new open flues fire places or hearth, or modify existing chimney/flue systems, that the client/gas user is provided with a commissioning certificate (check list) detailing the work carried out. The Commissioning Certificate can also be used by the user of gas, as a means of confirming to the local Building Control Body that the work completed conforms to the requirements of the Building Regulations.

ADJ also require that when new open flue fireplaces or hearths are installed, or existing chimneys/flue systems are altered, a Notice Plate is provided detailing the performance capabilities and that it is suitable for the particular chimney/flue installation design. The Notice Plate should be securely attached to the fabric of the building in a unobtrusive, obvious location.

Requirements for siting an appliance on a hearth

Figure 35 illustrates which hearth dimensions to use, and these apply to all types of gas fires:

- The hearth depth should be a minimum of 300mm from the rear of the appliance. In the case of a DFE fire the hearth should project at least 300mm in front of the naked flame or incandescent material source (as shown at (a) in Figure 35).

- The hearth should project at least 150mm beyond each side of the naked flame or incandescent material source (as shown at (b) in Figure 35).

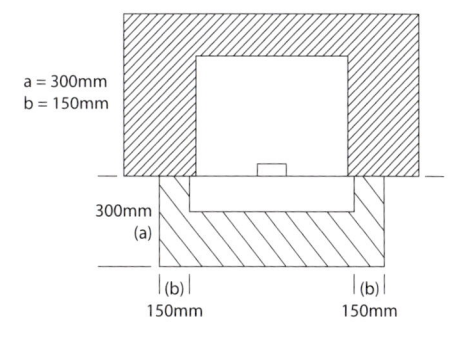

a = 300mm
b = 150mm

Figure 35: Hearth dimensions

In terms of the thickness of the hearth, there are specific requirements based on the type of gas fire used:

- With all appliances the hearth should be manufactured from non-combustible material which is at least 12mm in thickness.
- With ILFE and DFE fires the hearth should be at least 50mm above floor level.
- With DFE fires the hearth should not give rise to a temperature greater than 80°C on its underside.

April 2017   © BPEC

User Protection

The user, or other persons in the room in which the appliance is fitted, shall be protected as far as is reasonably possible, from the risk of burns or ignition of their clothing from the heat from the flames and incandescent parts of the appliance by either:

a) Installing an appliance that is fitted with an integral guard which conforms to DD CEN/TS 15209:2008, or

b) A tactile separator, in the form of either:

   i) a hearth provided in accordance with BS 476-4 or materials classified as "Class 0" in accordance with Approved Document B of the Building Regulations

   ii) a fender, kerb, horizontal bar or other barrier, being fixed not less than 50mm above floor level and not more than 1000mm above floor level, and positioned at least 300mm in front of and 150mm beyond the edge of any naked flame or incandescent part of the fire bed

Part 4 – Installation of Space Heaters

Now that we have covered all the necessary appliance siting requirements which must be met, we can go on and look at the installation of the appliances.

Obviously we cannot detail here the exact procedure for installing every type of gas fire or wall heater which is manufactured. The best source of information is the manufacturer's installation instructions.

But studying the following we should have an overview of the general procedures associated with installing gas fires and wall heaters:

- Open flued radiant convector gas fire installation.
- Additional requirements of ILFE gas fires.
- Additional requirements of DFE gas fires.
- Additional requirements of fanned draught open flued gas fires.
- Additional requirements or room sealed wall heaters.

Before you can commence with the installation of the gas fire you will need to carry out the following preliminary checks.

Preliminary flue checks

Confirm that:

- The room is suitable for the appliance.
- The flue system meets the requirements of BS 5440-1: 2008 and the requirements of Section 2 of this module.

As the flue is a vital part of the fire installation, then if the flue is inadequate or faulty the fire cannot be fitted.

With this in mind, before unpacking the fire, the following flue checks will need to be made (all checks may not be necessary dependent upon installation).

Visually inspect the entire flue including any section in the roof space, disconnecting and removing any gas appliance, closure plate, etc. as required to allow access to flue to ensure:

- A flue previously used with other fuels has been swept.
- Only one appliance is connected to the flue, unless the flue has been specifically designed for the connection of more than one appliance.
- The flue is constructed from suitable materials.
- The flue is complete and continuous throughout its length.
- The flue is not corroded or cracked and is in good condition; in the case of ridge terminals, check the integrity of the adaptor and their fixing bolts.
- The flue is the correct size and suitable for the appliance.
- The catchment space/starter block is accessible via a suitably sized builder's opening.
- The catchment space/starter block is of the correct size, free of debris and any air gaps into the space are sealed.
- The flue is clear of obstructions and dampers/restrictors have been removed or permanently fixed in the open position.
- Flexible flue liners are suitably sealed.
- The flue route is acceptable.
- All flue and appliance joints/seals are correctly made and suitable adaptors are used as required.
- The use of bends meets the appliance flue requirements.
- The flue is adequately supported.
- The flue is a sufficient distance from any combustible material.
- The termination is correct, suitably located and fitted with an appropriate terminal as required.
- Check for any visual signs of spillage or wall staining etc.
- The flue should operate in a satisfactory manner. Carrying out a flue flow test using a smoke pellet can check this. It is advisable to carry out the test by covering the flue opening with a closure plate. All doors and windows should be closed. The smoke should discharge at the correct terminal, there should be no leakage from elsewhere in the flue system, nor should there be any spillage into the room.

With these checks completed, it is a reasonable assumption that the flue is now suitable for the fire to be installed.

Preliminary installation and appliance checks

It is now important to check the suitability of the fire and its location before installation begins. These checks should be carried out prior to fire installation.

Check the general condition of the fire and that it is suitable for the gas being used and that it can be installed in accordance with current regulations and appropriate standards including:

- Check the correct distances from and location of the appliance in proximity to other fixtures, fittings and combustible materials.
- Check that the appliance location will allow for stability.

- Check the suitability of any hearth and/or surround as required.
- Check installation pipework is suitably sized, correctly installed, protected and the correct materials have been used up to the point of connection. Carry out tightness test where applicable.
- Inform the customer of any damage that exists on the appliance and/or surroundings before commencing work.
- Check ventilation is adequate, where applicable.
- Check visually for signs of spillage on any appliance to be replaced and/or adjacent decoration.

Gas connection

There are two methods of making gas connections to gas fires:

(a) Concealed connection.

(b) Unconcealed connection.

a) Concealed connection

A typical concealed gas fire connection is shown in Figure 36.

The concealed connection tends to be the most favoured option, as pipework is hidden within the fireplace opening:

- An appliance service cock must, where practical, be provided adjacent to the appliance.
- Where the pipework passes through a wall or floor, it must be enclosed in a gas-tight sleeve and take the shortest practicable route and be sealed.
- Any pipework leading into, and within, the fireplace opening must be protected from corrosion by wrapping (PVC tape) or sleeving the pipework.

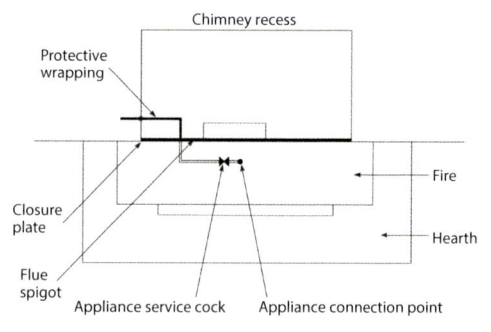

Figure 36: Concealed connection (aerial view)

b) Unconcealed connection

This tends to be the easiest option and is illustrated in Figure 37.

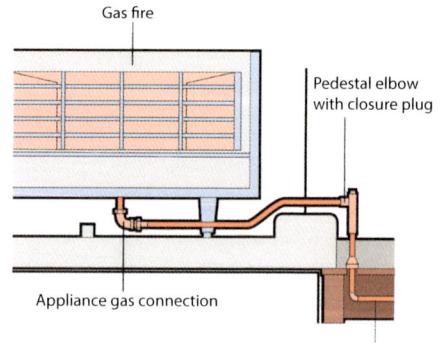

Note: The pedestal elbow is provided as a means of isolation for the gas supply to the appliance.

Figure 37: Unconcealed connection

| BPEC | Module 19 |

Preparing the fire

The fire should firstly be checked to make sure that it is suitable for the operating pressure and fuel type for the proposed installation i.e. natural gas or LPG, and then it should be prepared and stripped down according to manufacturer's requirements.

When installing used appliances, the original packaging may not be available, however, all the information required will be available on the data badge. If there is any doubt as to the suitability of the appliance it should not be used. Note Gas Safety (Installation and Use) Regulations 1998 Reg 26 (3) states no person shall install a used gas appliance without verifying that it is in a safe condition for further use.

Unless otherwise specified in the manufacturer's instructions, a gas fire will always be fitted using a closure plate, regardless of the type of flue system to which it is connected. A gas fire closure plate will normally measure approximately 660mm x 440mm, incorporating an opening for the insertion of the flue spigot and, where necessary, a ventilation or air relief opening. Closure plates must be checked to ensure that they are the correct type for the appliance (refer to manufacturer's instruction).

Any ventilation or air relief opening in a closure plate will be located and sized by the manufacturer, to allow the correct flue flow rate when the appliance is in operation. The aspect and dimensions of any ventilation or air relief openings will need to be maintained and the opening not obstructed. Any modification to a closure plate shall be in accordance with the manufacturer's instructions.

To eliminate the entry of excess air into the flue, the closure plate must be sealed to the fireplace wall or fire surround using an approved adhesive tape or other sealing material, which is suitable for the type of surface to which it is to be affixed (see Figure 38). The tape shall be capable of maintaining its seal throughout the range of temperature to which it will be subjected.

Only tape or other sealing material capable of maintaining its seal (e.g. adhesive strength) at least to a temperature of 100°C should be used. In this regard, it should be noted that proprietary tapes are available, which have been developed for this application. Where necessary, tapes or sealant should have sufficient flexibility to seal along uneven surfaces. When there is any doubt as to the suitability of surface, such as rough stone fireplaces, it may be necessary to use adhesive primer, or in extreme cases, build and seal a frame into the builder's opening.

Silicone sealants and other non removable methods should not be employed, as removal of the plate for servicing is essential.

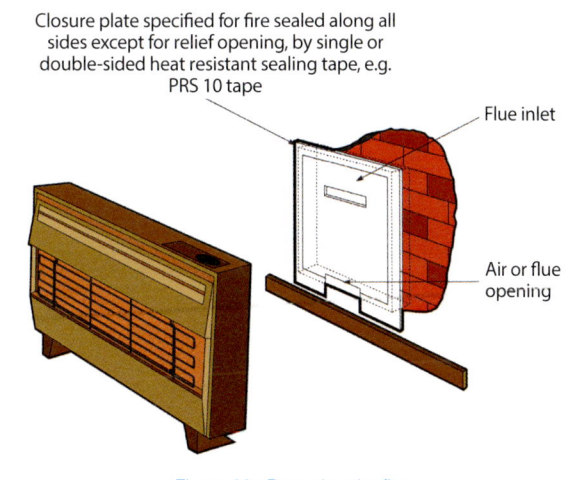

Closure plate specified for fire sealed along all sides except for relief opening, by single or double-sided heat resistant sealing tape, e.g. PRS 10 tape

- Flue inlet
- Air or flue opening

Figure 38: Preparing the fire

April 2017 © BPEC

| BPEC | Domestic Space Heaters, Gas Fires and Wall Heaters (HTR1) |

Spigot restrictor

A spigot restrictor may be required to be fitted (see Figure 39). The purpose of the spigot restrictor is to reduce the flue pull on flue systems of usually over 4m height, resulting in the fire operating more efficiently. Guidance on the use of the spigot restrictor must be sought from the manufacturer's instructions.

A cooler plate may be required to be fitted to the closure plate on pre-cast flue block flue systems. The purpose of the cooler plate is to minimise the temperature which may otherwise occur on the finished surface of the wall. The cooler plate is shown in Figure 40.

Figure 39: Spigot restrictor

Where a closure plate is inadequate to fill the fireplace opening completely, or where required for aesthetic reasons, an infill panel or surround may be used with an opening to which a closure plate can be secured.

The infill panel or surround should be made from a suitable fire resisting material, e.g. calcium silicate, vermiculite or glass reinforced plaster. Boards made from fibre board, particle board, strand or composite veneered boards such as ply wood or block board are not considered suitable.

Where a fire surround is to be fitted, it shall be compatible with the intended appliance (e.g. notice plate). Any superimposed surround and hearth shall be effectively sealed to the wall and floor to prevent air entrainment, which could adversely affect the performance of the flue.

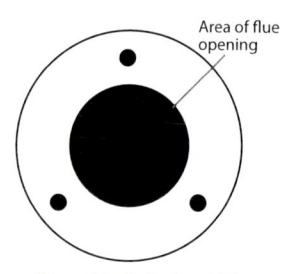

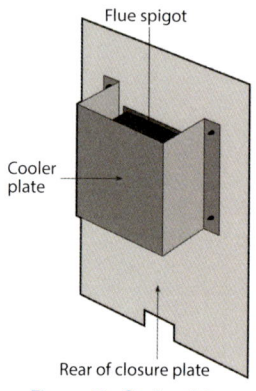

Figure 40: Cooler plate

When installing a gas fire surround the following points should be considered:

- The compatibility between the surround and the fire should be confirmed at the planning stage.
- Fire surrounds are available, which have been tested and found satisfactory for use with gas fires.
- The methods of securing and sealing a surround and hearth to a floor and wall will be given in the fire surround manufacturer's instructions.
- The flue spigot should project a minimum of 15mm past the closure plate as shown in Figure 41.

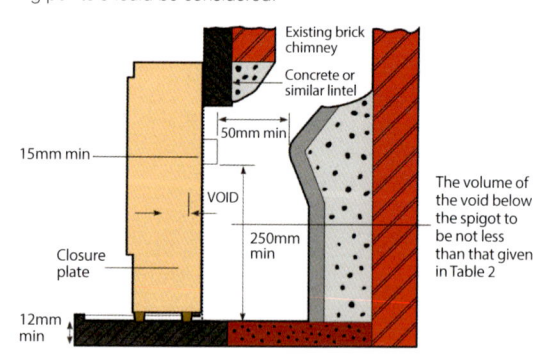

The volume of the void below the spigot to be not less than that given in Table 2

Figure 41: Catchment requirements

- There should be a gap of at least 50mm between the end of the appliance spigot and any surface, including the rear wall of the flue or chairbrick, as shown in Figure 41.

© BPEC   April 2017

Where a gas fire is brought forward from the fireplace opening, e.g. due to the low forward projection of a mantel shelf above a fireplace, a flue spigot extension should be used. The length of a spigot may be increased by use of a spigot extension (supplied by the manufacturer) up to either 150mm from the back of the appliance, or such other length as may be specified in the manufacturer's instructions.

Installing the fire

Once the preliminary checks/preparatory work on the fire itself has been completed, the fire can be installed. The following order may be adopted and should ensure a safe installation:

- Check closure plate for correct size and relief aperture.
- If correct the closure plate should then be taped to the wall using an appropriate sealing tape specifically manufactured for that purpose (PRS 10).
- The fire should either be fixed to the wall where it is to be wall mounted or should be positioned on a hearth. In either case, manufacturer's instructions should be followed.
- With hearth installations it is usual practice to secure purpose designed plastic pads under the appliance feet to prevent the fire moving away from the fireplace opening (the appliance may also require securing at the top to the surround.) With either hearth mounting or wall mounting the appliance must be level.
- Carry out a tightness test prior to breaking into the gas supply.
- Check and fit, if required, the supplied flue spigot restrictor.
- Connect the gas supply using where practical a means of isolation.
- Carry out a tightness test on completion of all gas connections.
- Purge the entire installation.

You are now ready to commission the appliance.

Additional requirements of inset live fuel effect (ILFE) gas fires

The preliminary checks and preparatory work are relatively similar to the radiant convector fire. Specific additional actions that need to be taken are:

- Check to ensure that the catchment space is compatible with the fire. In some cases with traditional solid fuel flue systems, the chairbrick may need to be removed; sweep flue where applicable.
- Check to ensure that the flue opening size is compatible with the ILFE fire to be installed in terms of a correct seal being made between fire and surround/wall surface.
- Once the fire is fitted, check that the fire seal has been correctly made.
- Permanent ventilation may be required.

Figure 42 shows the general methods of installation for ILFE gas fires.

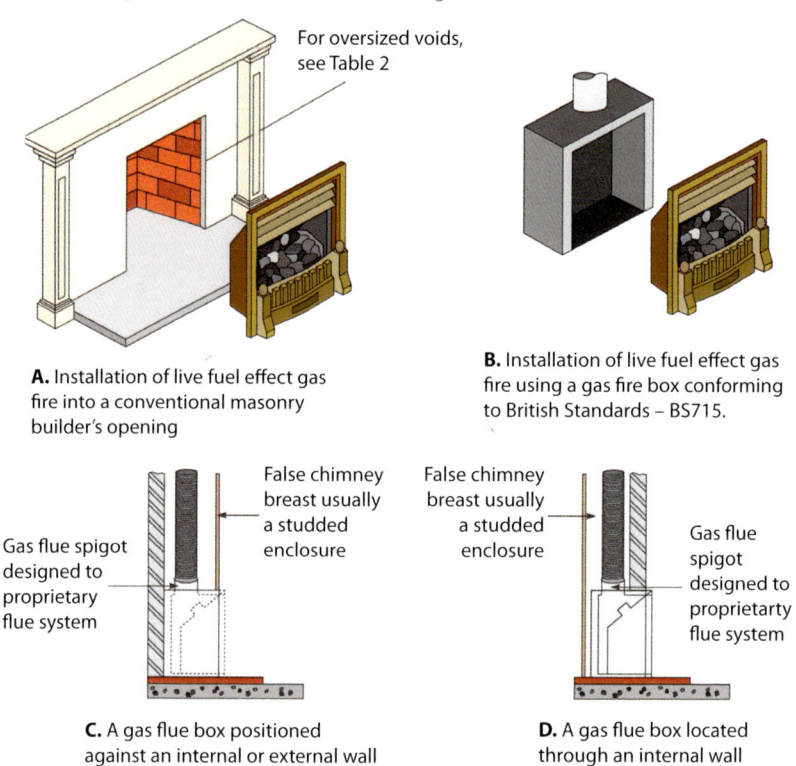

A. Installation of live fuel effect gas fire into a conventional masonry builder's opening

For oversized voids, see Table 2

B. Installation of live fuel effect gas fire using a gas fire box conforming to British Standards – BS715.

Gas flue spigot designed to proprietary flue system

False chimney breast usually a studded enclosure

False chimney breast usually a studded enclosure

Gas flue spigot designed to proprietarty flue system

C. A gas flue box positioned against an internal or external wall

D. A gas flue box located through an internal wall

Figure 42: General types of installation methods

Note 1: The gas flue box manufacturer's installation requirements may require an air gap clearance from the outside of the box to any combustible material. That would include a wall of timber stud and plasterboard construction.

Note 2: The gas appliance manufacturer's installation instructions may, as a condition of approval, require additional insulation material to be placed around the outer surface of the flue box.

Note 3: If the gas supply to the appliance is to be made through the wall of the gas flue box, it shall be sealed at the point of entry with a suitable non setting sealant.

Additional requirements of decorative fuel effect gas fires

Great care needs to be taken with the siting of the appliance and its relative location with the flue system. In particular, detailed checks should be carried out on the flue system materials, including any associated canopies or terminals, hearths etc.

Permanent ventilation will usually be required with this type of appliance, of at least 100cm^2 up to 20kW input.

The remaining installation process is relatively similar to those previously discussed.

Additional requirements of fanned draught open flued gas fires

With this type of appliance the following should be considered:
- The fire should be sited so that the flue length is within tolerances specified by the appliance manufacturer and does not use more flue bends than specified.
- The appliance terminal must be sited in an acceptable position.
- If the appliance incorporates a fan box built into the outside wall (skirting flue system etc.), this must be sealed in accordance with manufacturer's requirements.
- The flue system must be cut and jointed following manufacturer's procedures.
- The electricity supply to the gas fire components should be made in line with manufacturer's guidance and the IET Regulations 17th edition.
- A flue terminal guard may be required as the flue will often be sited under two metres from ground or balcony level.

With this type of appliance/installation consideration should be given to the following:
- The flue terminal should be positioned to allow the free passage of air across its external face, as well as conforming to the flue system manufacturer's specifications concerning the minimum acceptable distance from the terminal to ground level obstructions and ventilation openings, and with the requirements of BS 5440-1: 2008.
- It should be noted that all fanned draught flue systems are required by the Gas Safety (Installation and Use) Regulations 1998 to shut down the appliance in the event of failure of the draught, e.g. fan failure.

Additional requirements of room sealed natural draught wall heaters

Key additional features with this type of appliance include:
- The flue should be installed in a position recommended by the appliance manufacturer, regarding openings into the building etc. The terminal shall not be sited within one metre of LPG supply cylinders.
- Ensuring that the appliance flue/air duct is adequately cut (if required), made to length and jointed and sealed with approved flue tape. A typical flue/air duct is shown in Figure 43.
- The hole through the wall is cut to meet installation requirements, allowing a 25mm air gap all round the flue and the internal external surfaces are sealed into the flue/air duct using a sand/cement mortar mix.
- The appliance is mounted following manufacturer's instructions.
- A flue terminal guard must be fitted where the flue terminal is sited below 2m from the outside/ground or balcony level.

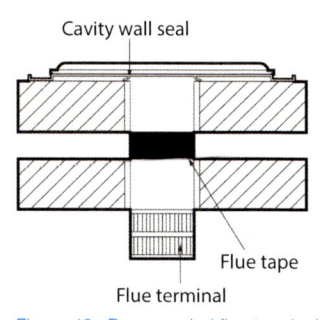

Figure 43: Room sealed flue terminal

The flue guard must be installed so that it is not less than 50mm from any part of the terminal. The guard should have no sharp edges, nor shall any opening be greater than 16mm.

The remaining installation procedures are common with those previously identified.

Before we move on to commissioning, we will review the special requirements of flues discharging through timber framed properties.

Timber framed properties

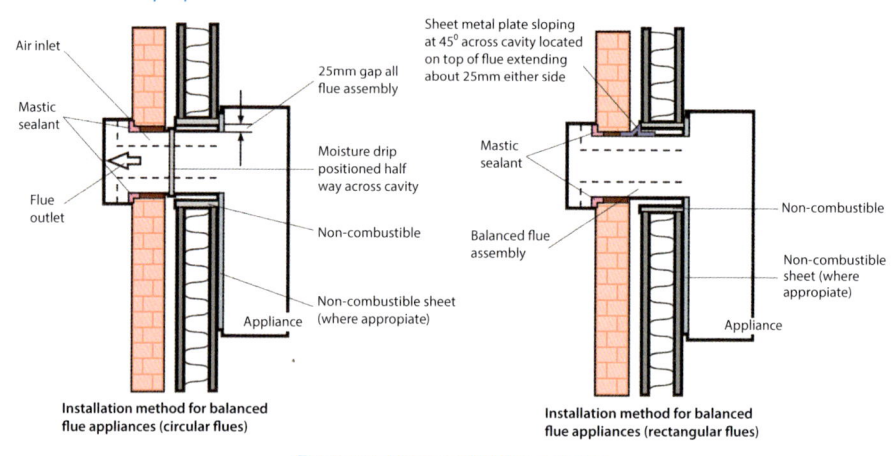

Figure 44: Room sealed flue systems

As shown in Figure 44, room sealed appliance terminal ducts passing through combustible walls should be surrounded by a non-combustible sleeve with a 25mm air gap between the sleeve and the duct. The sleeve itself should project no more than 10mm into the cavity, unless it is designed to do so and incorporates a drip feature. If it does protrude further, it may collect dampness on the timber sheath and result in rotting of the timberwork. The sleeve must, however, project to at least the depth of the timber sheathing/breather paper so that they are protected.

The hole in the vapour barrier should be cut 10mm smaller than the sleeve so that it can be forced carefully through it to minimise damage to the barrier. If the appliance does not incorporate a rope seal between the appliance and the wall, the 25mm gap will need to be sealed. This can be achieved by using a sheet of non-combustible material.

Combustible outer leafs need to be protected with non-combustible metal end plates, extending 25mm beyond the terminal flange.

Care needs to be taken with the flue, which has effectively bridged the cavity and may allow moisture to rot the inner leaf timbers and insulating materials:

- **Circular flues** that do not incorporate a drip collar require either a bead of mastic moulding around the flue, or a non-corrosive wire wrapped round the flue with the twisted ends pointing downwards.
- **Rectangular flues** require a cavity tray to be installed above the flue, sloping from the inner to outer leaf.
- **Purpose designed panel.** Where this is provided a damp proof membrane should be incorporated into the panel design.

Open flued systems

When an open flue is to penetrate a timber framed house, a single wall flue pipe should be sleeved with a non-combustible sleeving incorporating a 25mm gap between the sleeve and the flue, which should be packed with non-combustible material. Where a twin wall or insulated flue is used, the gap may be measured from the inner skin of the flue material.

The sleeve should penetrate through the vapour barrier making as little damage as possible. To prevent moisture from crossing the cavity, a damp proof membrane 400mm wide should be dressed up behind the breather paper. This may be carried out by gaining access through the outer leaf. A wall plate may be fitted to the flue to cover the gap; the wall plate should be secured to the flue.

Part 5 – Commissioning of Space Heaters

We shall now complete the installation module by taking a look at the commissioning of space heaters. We shall focus on the following:

- Open flued radiant convector fires
- Additional features of fan assisted appliances

Open flued gas fires

If you have not installed the gas fire you are about to commission, you should first carry out the installation checks as described in Part 4 of this module.

Once the installation checks have been completed, you can go on to commission the appliance. The following procedure may be used:

- Fit the radiants/appliance coal bed.
- Check the electrical supply to the appliance, including fuse ratings, polarity and continuity checks (if fitted), and that any lights work.
- Check the positioning/operation of the spark electrode and the operation of the control tap.
- Connect a pressure gauge to the pressure test point and light the appliance. With the appliance operating on full, check the gas pressure and ensure that it corresponds with manufacturer's data. If a greater pressure drop occurs, check to ensure that all the gas cocks are opened correctly and that the meter pressure is correct. If the fault still exists, detailed checks on the gas pipework may need to be made.
- Turn off the gas fire and disconnect the pressure gauge.
- Re-light the appliance and test the pipework joints and test point within the fire for tightness with a suitable leak detection fluid.

- Where the appliance uses a flame supervision device:
  - Check that the pilot burner assembly components are correctly positioned.
  - Light the pilot and check that the pilot flame correctly envelopes the thermocouple and that the burner flame picture shows correct 'playing' on to the appliance burner.
  - Check the safe operation of the flame supervision device (FSD) following manufacturer's procedures.

Where the manufacturer's instructions do not specify a procedure, the following may be used as a guide:

- Ensure that all primary and secondary controls are set so that the burner will not be turned off during this procedure.
- Ensure all safety checks and procedures have been carried out and it is safe to ignite the appliance.
- Light the appliance and allow the burner to reach its normal working temperature.
- Turn off the appliance shut-off device (appliance isolation valve) and simultaneously start a stop watch.
- Halt the stop watch when the valve is heard to close; recommended fail safe period for space heaters is 180 seconds.
- Immediately check that the valve in the FSD has shut off completely, using the most appropriate method. This can be checked by using a pressure gauge as described in CCN1 or by passing a lit taper over the burner.
- Test the appliance for spillage, with all doors and windows closed and with any extractor or paddle fans are switched on.

Test procedure

The manufacturer will usually have identified a test procedure for this process and will also indicate the position on the appliance where the test should be carried out (this does vary from appliance to appliance, so be careful).

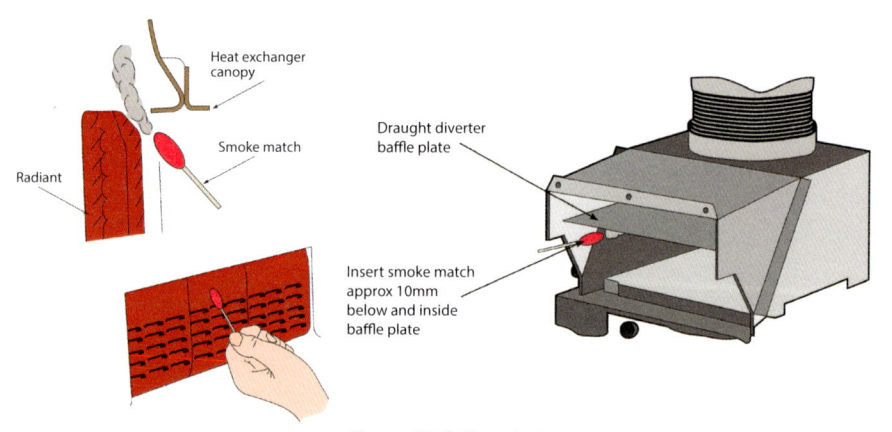

Figure 45: Spillage test

- When carrying out a spillage test, it is advisable to use a smoke match pluming device. This holds the smoke match firmly and will assist in positioning the smoke match at the correct test point location as per manufacturer's instructions, and also protects the operative coming in contact with any hot surface on the appliance.
- Typically the test will include operating the fire on maximum for a period of usually five minutes, to warm the chimney or flue.
- As illustrated in Figure 45, a smoke match should be lit and inserted into a point at the draught diverter or fire canopy, as identified by the manufacturer. The trail of smoke from the match should be drawn into the flue. If the smoke is not being drawn into the flue, spillage of combustion products is indicated.
- If spillage occurs, the test should be repeated after a further 10 minutes of warming the flue. If spillage still occurs, the problem should be investigated further and resolved.

Remember to always follow the appliance manufacturer's instructions with regard to spillage testing.

Where the room contains an extractor or ceiling paddle fan, the test should be carried out with the fan operating at maximum in all directions with all the doors and windows closed. Where the fan is in an adjacent room a second test should be carried out with the connecting door open and the fans on (maximum speed and both directions where applicable):

- Check the safe operation of the gas taps/control devices.
- Re-assemble the appliance if all the checks prove satisfactory.
- You should demonstrate the safe use of appliance to the occupant of the building and leave all the appliance instructions on site for future reference purposes.
- Instruct the user that any live fuel effects must be fitted only as described in the manufacturer's instructions and make reference to any fire-guard requirements of BS 8423.
- Finally, advise the customer that the appliance should be serviced annually.

Additional features of fanned draught appliances

With these types of appliances it is important to check the operation of the appliance fan and safety controls, i.e. air pressure switch. The manufacturer will have produced specific procedures which should be followed.

Advice to be given to the user

The installer shall ensure the user has been provided with the manufacturer's instructions for operating the appliance.

Wherever possible the installer shall demonstrate the correct and safe operation of the appliance including any special features of the appliance e.g. spillage monitoring system.

If the premises in which the gas appliance is installed are owned by the occupier, the occupier shall be advised in writing that, for the continued efficiency and safe operation of the appliance, it is important that adequate and regular maintenance is carried out by a competent person in accordance with the manufacturer's instructions. If the premises are tenanted then the written advice shall be notified to the landlord in accordance with the Gas Safety (Installation and Use) Regulations [1].

Section 3 – Servicing, Maintenance and Repair of Space Heaters

Introduction
In this section we shall be taking a look at:
- Service and maintenance of space heaters.
- Appliance fault finding.
- Typical gas component faults on space heaters.

Part 1 – Service and Maintenance of Space Heaters
A space heater service visit will be broken into three distinct areas, the first being an installation/appliance **preliminary examination**. This will highlight any major problems before work is undertaken upon the appliance itself. Discussions can subsequently be held with the customer to agree and establish a course of remedial action. Remember a user may not wish remedial action to be carried out. Therefore, if a **full** service has been completed, only to have the appliance disconnected, the customer is unlikely to be pleased at having to pay for the service.

Once the preliminary examination has been completed, the **appliance service** can be undertaken. However, be prepared for problems to be unearthed, which must be addressed. A **final** examination will then be completed to ensure the continued safe operation of the appliance.

During the preliminary examination, the gas operative may encounter appliances installed which do not comply with the Current Regulations and Standards, and the customer should be advised to have remedial work undertaken.

An example of this is when a gas fire with no atmospheric sensing device is installed in a bedroom. If the heater was fitted after January 1996 it is an At Risk installation. The gas operative should inform the user of the potential dangers of continued use and encourage them to have the appliance replaced and the unsafe situation procedures followed. If the appliance was installed before 1996, it can be classed as Not Current Standards. However, the recommendation should be to replace it with a model fitted with a atmospheric sensing device (ASD).

What follows is a procedure that may be used for any service visit, though certain tasks may be omitted if not required.

Step 1 – Carry out preliminary checks
- Check that the flue terminal and termination are acceptable and that a guard has been fitted (where required).
- Check the general condition of the appliance, and that the appliance is installed in accordance with the appropriate standards and manufacturer's instructions, including asking the customer if there are any known faults or problems with the appliance:
  - Check the correct distances from and location of the appliance in proximity to other fixtures, fittings and combustible materials.
  - Check the stability of the appliance.
  - Check the suitability of any hearth and/or surround as required.
  - Check visually for signs of spillage on the appliance and/or adjacent decoration.

- Inform the customer of any damage that exists on the appliance and/or surroundings before commencing work.
- Light the appliance and put into full operation and check the flame picture and the operation of the user control devices.
- Check ventilation is adequate where applicable.
- Check appropriate labels are fitted.
- Check that pipework for the appliance connection is suitably sized, correctly installed, suitably protected and the correct materials have been used.
- Test the operation of electrical components on the appliance, e.g. decorative lights, and check there are no signs of damage to the wiring, the fuse rating is correct; carry out polarity and continuity checks.

Note any defects and advise the customer prior to the service taking place

Step 2 – Fire removal and flue system (see Figure 46)
- Isolate the gas and electric supplies as required.
- Remove the fire and any closure plate if fitted, check the catchment area, flue opening and visually inspect the entire flue, including any section in the roof space.
- Check the appliance flue connection to any chimney or flue-liner, annular spaces between flue liner and chimney, that voids entering the base of the chimney are sealed, that any dampers or restrictors have been removed or fixed securely in the open position.
- Clean any dust and deposits within the catchment area as necessary.
- Check flue flow and continuity using a smoke pellet and re-inspect all exposed flue pipes, including any section in the roof space, for leakage (especially ridge connector seals and bolts).
- Check for correct fitting of flue spigot restrictor and that cooling plates, where applicable, are correct for the appliance, and the correct size including the relief opening.
- Check closure plate.
- Re-seal the closure plate with suitable new heat resistant tape (PRS 10).

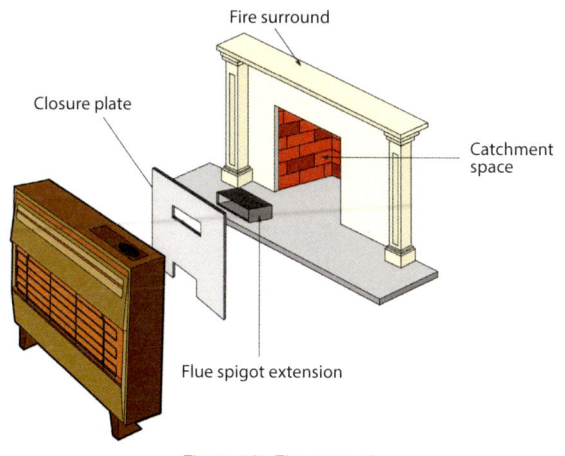

Figure 46: Fire removal

Step 3 – Appliance servicing

- Strip down the appliance, including the removal of radiants, coal bed etc.
- Remove the main burner from the appliance.
- Remove the injectors from the burner and clean (see Figure 47).
- Clean the burner and any associated lint arrestors.
- Check the pilot burner and injector, cleaning as necessary (if fitted).
- Check case for staining or scorching, check case, sight glass and other seals on room sealed or open flued appliances, replace as necessary.

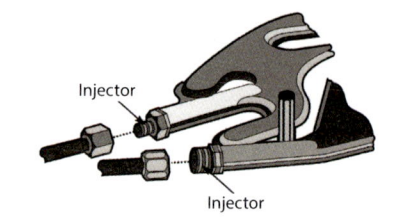

Figure 47: Burner assembly

Step 4 – Appliance flueways

- Clean out the appliance flueways, fire canopy etc. Clean lint deposits etc. from within the fire casing.

Step 5 – Controls

- Clean, adjust or replace ignition components.
- Check operation of gas taps; clean, adjust and lubricate as required.
- Clean the fan (where fitted) and check the condition of the air pressure switch and associated sensing tubes for splits, cracks, kinks, etc.
- Re-assemble components, replacing defective components as necessary.

Step 6 – Re-assemble the fire

- Re-fit the fire.
- Re-connect the gas/electricity supplies.
- Check the appliance gas connections by testing for tightness; check all disturbed joints with leak detector solution.
- Check that the electrical components are sound and the wiring is showing no signs of damage.
- Check any appliance seals.
- Re-fit radiants or 'live fuel' as necessary, in accordance with manufacturer's instructions.

Step 7 – Final checks

- Check the appliance operating pressure, test with a suitable gauge and check the heat input at the meter, adjust if necessary (test disturbed joints and test point with leak detection fluid) on completion.
- Check, with any appropriate fans running, the flame picture and flame stability of all burners, on all settings, ensure live fuel bed and components correctly located.
- Check the safe operation of all the appliance and system controls including gas taps, ignition devices, flame supervision devices, atmospheric sensing devices and other safety devices (test disturbed joints with leak detection fluid).

- Close all doors and windows, test appliance(s) for spillage, carry out individual and combined spillage tests. Where fans are fitted, the test should be carried out with the fan operating at maximum speed in all/both directions where applicable. Where the fan is in an adjacent room a second test must be carried out with the connecting door open and again with the fan operating at maximum speed in both directions.
- Reset the controls to suit customer's requirements.
- Complete all necessary documentation and advise customer of any remedial work required.

Remember to consult the appliance manufacturer's instructions, as these are an important source of specific appliance details.

Part 2 – Appliance Fault Finding

When dealing with faults upon gas appliances, the gas operative is not always given precise details. A typical opening conversation between a gas operative and the customer may begin something like:

Customer:	"We have a problem."
Gas operative:	"What do you mean?"
Customer:	"Something is wrong."
Gas operative:	"What is wrong?"
Customer:	"I don't know, but this thing isn't working properly".

The 'thing' under discussion could be any piece of equipment from a cooker burner to a combination boiler.

Fault finding procedures

Sometimes the gas operative is given more comprehensive instructions than 'attend to faulty appliance', but in solving the problem they are obliged to follow a diagnostic process similar to that which you would use for an 'attend to fire' job. This process comprises five steps, which are:

- Step 1 — Question the user.
- Step 2 — Check the extent and nature of the fault.
- Step 3 — Locate the defective part or parts.
- Step 4 — If possible, repair or replace.
- Step 5 — If not, decide on suitable action.

If these steps are linked together in a logical sequence like this, they provide the basis for any fault diagnosis. Before we look at the steps in detail, we need to decide what is the meaning of a fault.

On a gas appliance we have to respond on a simple down-to-earth and personal level. The definition of a fault must be expanded to include anything, even non-technical problems, which provokes the customer to complain.

The gas operative is faced with effecting a cure for the defect, but must remember that many customers are not technically trained. Therefore, from the technical point of view, we cannot ignore their lack of knowledge or understanding. Most gas operatives know of cases where the customer forgot to 'Reset to Manual' or put credit in the meter. In fact, looking for differences between the normal performance of a component and the customer's expectations of its capabilities forms part of the fault finding process.

Step 1 – Questioning the user

Questioning the user should be carried out systematically, with the use of carefully worded questions. The gas operative must ask the user what he thinks is wrong and allow him to express in his own words what happens. Then ask specific questions to obtain further detail and listen carefully to the answers. Above all, find out whether or not the customer actually knows what the 'normal' function of the component or system should be. Remember, especially with new appliances, the user's expectations may actually be beyond the appliance capability.

Step 2 – Checking the extent and nature of the fault

Step 2 involves several lesser stages. Firstly, the gas operative will have to rely upon observations of the actual behaviour of the appliance in question, knowledge and experience of what comprises normal behaviour and the customer's expectations, obtained during Step 1. Then, by making a comparison between the normal behaviour and the other variants, you will be able to decide which particular 'something' is not right.

No matter how sophisticated the equipment, the effect of the fault can be identified in the same way, by comparing normal behaviour or operation with actual behaviour. The extent of the difference between these two gives us a very useful starting point for correcting the fault. Whether it is a doctor taking a patient's temperature, or a gas operative checking a gas pressure, the aim is the same, to identify any variation from 'normal'.

The ability to recognise the 'norm' can only be gained by reading the manufacturer's instructions and by seeing correct operation in practice. Learning to recognise the normal functions of different appliances takes time, but it is a valuable product of experience, which provides the basis for knowing what is wrong.

When you are making a comparison between what you know should happen and the actual behaviour, you should also make a comparison between the customer's expectations and the normal behaviour. This is because the 'fault' may be no more than the result of a misread User's Instruction.

Step 3 – Locate the defective part or parts

Having diagnosed the fault, locating the defective part or parts may be tackled. As mentioned earlier, this also includes overcoming the customer's misunderstandings or misuse. In such cases, the user of the appliance could be looked upon as being the 'Defective Part'! It does not sound very complimentary, but a tactful demonstration of the correct methods of operation will normally overcome the problem.

In the majority of cases, this stage requires knowledge of the function of the appliance and its components.

If there is no ignition when a fire is turned on, then one or more components or the links between them could be at fault.

It has been shown that with experience, the use of fault flow diagnosis charts or algorithms improves fault finding on more complex appliances, and it is not long before the average user becomes familiar with the chart format.

Step 4 – If possible, repair or replace

Having decided what is causing the fault, and after locating the defective part or parts, the gas operative must either repair the fault or replace the component. If the repair or replacement can be carried out on the initial visit, with the permission of the user, then do so.

However, if the repair will be time consuming, or a part is to be ordered, then the appliance must be left in a safe condition. The gas operative should not be tempted to carry out temporary measures to bring the appliance into operation that may constitute a danger. For example, if a flame safety device is in need of repair it must not be disabled, by-passed or bridged, even on a temporary basis.

Once the repair or replacement has been made, the appliance must be thoroughly checked to ensure it is operating in a satisfactory and safe manner. Repairs must not be made which alter the design of the appliance; for example, a faulty regulator, fitted by the manufacturer, must not be made inoperative by the gas operative.

Step 5 – If not able to rectify, decide on suitable action

Rectification of the fault may not be possible for many reasons, which may include the repair is too expensive, the parts required are no longer available or the customer wishes a second opinion. When this situation occurs, the gas installer must ensure that any appliance that has been worked on is left in a safe condition, even if it means isolating it from the gas supply.

The actions to be taken will depend upon the fault that is present with the appliance and, therefore, the unsafe situations procedure must be adhered to.

Finally, there will always be those jobs, that make these five steps seem unnecessary, but in fact they will all still be there, the brain just runs them together to save time and effort. That can usually be put down to the proper application of experience, for as practice increases, common causes and signs of faults are memorised and the diagnostic process takes hardly any time at all. However, not every problem can be so easily resolved.

Part 3 – Typical Gas Component Faults on Space Heaters

The section focuses on the diagnosis of typical faults associated with space heaters. The section will focus on:

- Unsatisfactory ignition of burners/defective flame supervision devices.
- Unstable flame picture.
- Incorrectly positioned fuel on firebed.
- Signs of spillage.
- Stiff gas control tap.
- Inoperable air pressure switches.

Unsatisfactory ignition of burners

Table 5 lists typical faults associated with unsatisfactory ignition of burners.

Table 5: Pilot ignition (not fitted to all appliances)

Fault	Reason for fault	Suggested remedy
Pilot does not light.	i) Gas service cock closed. ii) Air in pipe. iii) Pilot injector blocked. iv) No Ignition spark.	Open service cock. Purge line. Clean or change. Check electrode, lead and ignitor.
Poor pilot flame.	i) Pilot injector dirty. ii) Wrong injector. iii) Pilot head blocked. iv) Faulty pilot tube. v) Pilot injector loose.	Clean or change. Change for correct diameter. Clean. Clean or replace. Tighten.
Pilot will not stay alight.	i) Pilot flame poor. ii) Thermocouple not working. iii) Thermoelectric valve faulty. iv) Gas pressure low/variable. v) Terminal wrongly positioned. vi) Badly assembled flue. vii) Pressure switch faulty. viii) Plug loose on PCB. ix) PCB faulty.	See above. Check connection, clean and tighten as necessary. Replace as necessary. Check at inlet to appliance. Re-position. Re-fit check seal and check operation. Replace. Secure. Replace.

Main burner ignition

There may be problems with the actual main burner lighting procedure, where the main burner does not light smoothly or lights with a 'bang'. This can be caused by the following results (see Table 6):

- The ignition electrode is not correctly positioned or is not operating correctly, or
- The pilot assembly is partially blocked or incorrectly positioned, resulting in the pilot flame not adequately playing on the main burner. In terms of this fault, the pilot burner assembly should be cleaned and/or re-positioned.

Table 6: Main burner ignition may be affected by a number of possible faults

Fault	Reason for fault	Suggested remedy
Main burner does not light correctly.	i) Gas service cock not open fully. ii) Gas pressure low. iii) Main burner does not light. iv) Main burner does not light.	Open fully. Check with the appliance running. Check ignition electrode, lead etc. Check PCB, control devices on appliances which are fan assisted.

Unstable flame picture

With space heaters an unstable flame picture is usually caused by:

a) **An inadequate supply of combustion air.** Air inlets (including radiants) which are choked with lint, or a blocked heat exchanger or flueways will result in an unstable flame picture.

The solution to this problem is to:

- Ensure that adequate permanent ventilation is provided.
- Clean any choked lint arrestors, burners or heater flueways.

b) **Incorrectly set gas rate.** The main problem here tends to be with over-gassing of the appliance. This can be caused by installation of the wrong sized injectors or incorrect control of the gas rate.

The symptoms of over-gassing are similar to a lack of air supply, where the flames become longer and softer.

The solution in this case could be to check if the injectors are of the wrong size or correctly set the appliance gas consumption rate.

Incorrectly positioned fuel on fire bed

The positioning of the live fuel effect on a gas fire is in many cases critical. The position of the fuel will be given in the manufacturer's instructions and the operative must not deviate from these recommendations.

The result of an incorrectly positioned fuel on the fire bed can be:

- Flame impingement.
- Incomplete combustion.
- Spillage of combustion products.

In either case the burner will not operate satisfactorily. It is likely that pointed yellow flames will result in sooting of the appliance.

The solution is to clean the appliance if sooting has occurred and position the fuel correctly on the fire bed.

If the user has added extra fuel, coals etc, to the fuel bed, then these must be removed and discarded. If the user of gas refuses to allow this, it could result in the products of combustion spilling into the room, resulting in an Immediately Dangerous (ID) situation. The gas operative must deal with all unsafe situations in accordance with the industry unsafe situations.

Signs of flue spillage

Spillage of products of combustion is of great concern to the gas operative; spillage is associated with poor flue performance or blockages within appliances. If products of combustion are allowed to spill into the room, the atmosphere will quickly become vitiated. If appliances are installed which draw air for combustion from the room, then incomplete combustion may result and there is a risk that carbon monoxide will enter the room or internal space in which the appliance is fitted.

Some indications that products of combustion are spilling into a room or internal space from an appliance include:

- Staining around a draught diverter on open flued appliances or flue seals on room sealed appliances.
- Excessive condensation within a room.
- Evidence of appliance overheating, for example, burnt appliance finish on open flued appliances.
- Complaint of sore eyes, headaches or tiredness when the gas appliance is operating.
- Complaint of a smell from the gas appliance when it is operating – remember this could also indicate a gas escape from the appliance.

Any of these indicators should ring alarm bells with the gas operative to indicate there is a potential problem with the flue system or the appliance. The indicators of spillage will be discussed individually below.

Staining around the appliance

Spillage is the passage of products of combustion through areas other than the appliance flue. Typically, where spillage occurs, appliance surfaces, above pilot windows and on wall surfaces around draught diverter inlets will show signs of discolouration. This is because the products of combustion contain water vapour that will condense upon contact with cooler appliance surfaces.

Where incomplete combustion is taking place, in addition to spillage of combustion products, sooty marks will be seen at points around the appliance. The gas operative must therefore be aware of any staining around appliances and take appropriate actions to identify the cause and rectify the fault or make the appliance safe.

Excessive condensation within a room

When open flued and room sealed appliances are spilling combustion products into a room, some of the water vapour contained within the products may condense upon the inside of external windows and mirrors. This will be more obvious in the winter months, as the windows will be colder. This visual sign may give the gas operative an indication of a fault even before entering the property.

However, this is only an indication and other causes may contribute to this problem, and so the operative must ensure an appliance is spilling before any action is taken. Flueless appliances, such as single point water heaters, may cause windows to suffer with condensation if they are fitted in small rooms with no ventilation or are kept running for extended periods of time.

Evidence of appliance overheating

If an appliance is designed to operate with the products of combustion exiting through a flue, the temperature of the appliance casing will be relatively low. If the products of combustion are not escaping in the usual way, but spilling back through the appliance, the temperature of the appliance case will rise. This rise in temperature may cause damage to the appliance case, e.g. staining and scorching.

If the operative observes a heat damaged case then spillage may be suspected, and the cause of the damage must be verified. If spillage of combustion products is identified, the gas operative must take the appropriate action to either rectify the fault or make safe the installation, including isolation from the gas supply if necessary.

User complaints

The user of a gas appliance may complain of symptoms that can be attributed to carbon monoxide poisoning or smells emanating from combustion products. In all cases the cause must be investigated, also considering CO-migration from another property, especially flats, maisonettes etc.

It should be borne in mind that not all symptoms must be attributed to a faulty gas appliance. If the cause is not evident, then the user may be suffering from some other illness, outside the gas operative's brief.

Common causes of spillage

Spillage of combustion products from open flued appliances will usually be caused by either one or a combination of the following faults:

- Inadequate or damaged flue system.
- Inadequate or lack of permanent ventilation.
- The heat exchanger within the appliance may be blocked or partially blocked.

Spillage of combustion products from room sealed appliances will usually be caused by either one or a combination of the following faults:

- Faulty or damaged appliance case seals, flue seals or broken sight glass.
- Flue outlet close to building re-entry points, e.g. windows and air vents.

Spillage on flueless appliances will always occur, as the appliance has no flue for combustion products to exit. However, signs of incomplete combustion and damage may be evident. These may be caused by usually either one or a combination of the following:

- The appliance has been operated for extended periods of time.
- Excessive gas rate or burner pressure.
- The heat exchanger within the appliance may be blocked or partially blocked.

Where spillage occurs, this must be regarded as an Immediately Dangerous (ID) appliance/installation and immediate remedial action should be taken.

Stiff gas control tap

Identifying the signs of a stiff gas control tap are obviously quite easy to determine. There are two possible solutions to rectify the problem:

- Strip down the control tap and grease the spindle and tap components in line with manufacturer procedures, replace any seals as necessary, or
- In the event that greasing the tap does not work, then it should be replaced.

Remember that the tap should be checked for tightness after undertaking any work.

The procedure for greasing a gas fire control tap is as follows (see Figure 48):

- Turn off the gas supply to the appliance.
- Dismantle the tap, taking care to observe the relationship between the components; there will be a spring inside so beware.
- Clean the barrel and plug, and ensure that all traces of the original grease and dirt are removed from the gas ways.
- Sparingly grease the plug's bearing surfaces, insert into the barrel and turn from side to side a few times.
- Withdraw the plug and check the grease has spread evenly, not blocking any gas ways.
- Remove surplus grease and re-insert the plug and re-assemble.
- Re-establish the gas supply.
- Check for leakage with leak detector or soft soap solution in both on and off positions and check operation of the tap at all settings.

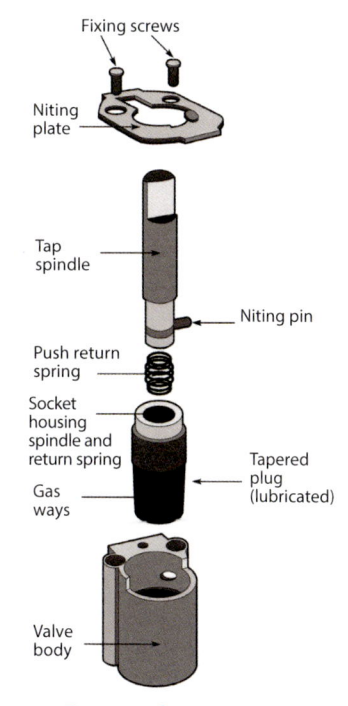

Figure 48: Gas tap assembly

Inoperative air pressure switches

Air pressure switches are usually installed in an appliance which may have relatively complex electronic circuitry.

The manufacturer's fault flow chart should be referred to at all times.

The symptom of air pressure switch failure is usually that the fan runs and the appliance fails to commence its lighting sequence.

The manufacturer may have a procedure developed for checking the operation of the air pressure switch, or alternatively the switch can be checked (if possible) by pulling off one of the input pipes. Fit a suitable input tube to the input port, blow gently into the valve and listen for clicking of the micro-switch. Its operation can also be checked using a multimeter continuity test, which should show a zero reading.

Note: The air pressure switch may be affected by defective appliance seals and by splits, kinks or loose connections associated with air supply tubes.

Practical Tasks

The practical tasks link directly with the performance criteria of the Nationally Accredited Certification Scheme (ACS) assessments for HTR1 – Domestic Space Heaters.

Your tutor will assess your practical training requirements before undertaking the practical tasks and may require you to:

- Complete all the tasks identified, or
- Complete some of the tasks identified (based on previous experience).

You should have access to the appliance manufacturer's instructions. You may also use the knowledge manuals associated with the course.

You will be given the following tasks to be carried out:

- Installation or exchange of either a radiant convector or ILFE gas fire. Specific installation tasks on other appliances may be required.
- Commissioning a gas fire.
- Servicing a gas fire.
- Diagnosing typical faults on a range of gas fires.

To assist you in the process of carrying out the work, you should complete the information required in the following pro-forma.

Note – To complete all the tasks you will be required to work on more than one appliance.

Pre-installed checks

Task 1

Do the fireplace opening/hearth construction and dimensions conform to requirements?   Yes   No

If no, what remedial action is necessary?

Task 2

Does the catchment area conform to requirements?　　　　　　　　Yes　No

If no, what remedial action is necessary?

Task 3

Check the integrity of the flue system and that it discharges to atmosphere by carrying out a flue flow test.
Flue flow test satisfactory?　　　　　　　　　　　　　　　　　　　Yes　No

If no, what remedial action is necessary?

Task 4

Visually check the existing pipework system and note any defects below, and any remedial actions necessary, e.g. pipework fixings, pipe size and materials used etc.

Task 5
Check to ensure that the gas supply has been effectively isolated prior to the work commencing.
Has the gas supply been effectively isolated?   Yes   No

If no, what remedial action is necessary?

Task 6
Carry out a gas tightness test of the existing pipework installation prior to the work commencing.
Does the tightness test indicate that the pipework system is leak free?   Yes   No

If no, what remedial actions are necessary?

Task 7
Visually check the appliance to be installed and identify whether there are any obvious defects.
Is the appliance in suitable condition?   Yes   No

If no, what remedial action is necessary?

Installation (or exchange) of the appliance

Task 8
Connect the flue spigot restrictor to the appliance (if required).

Task 9
Fit and seal the closure plate to the fireplace opening (radiant convector fires only), after satisfactory and successful flue flow test.

Task 10
Site/fix the gas fire (radiant convector fires only).

Task 11
The fire is correctly fitted and sealed to the fireplace opening (ILFE only).

Task 12
The appliance is correctly located, level and stable.

Task 13
Connect the gas pipework to the appliance and carry out tightness test.
Is the reading acceptable?   Yes   No

Task 14
The radiant(s) are correctly positioned (radiant convector only).

Task 15
The coal/log effect is correctly positioned (ILFE only).

Commissioning the appliance

Task 16
The appliance/installation is purged of air. Yes   No

Task 17
The working pressure at the appliance is correct. Yes   No

Task 18
The burner flame picture, stability and ignition is correct. Yes   No

Task 19
The spillage test is carried out. Yes   No

Task 20
The user controls are operating satisfactorily. Yes   No

Task 21
The safety control devices are operating correctly. (FSD etc.) Yes   No

Tasks 16-21 – Note any deficiencies in the commissioning procedure in this box:

Task 22
Subject to the installation being satisfactorily commissioned, explain the safe operation of the appliance.

Servicing an appliance

Task 23

Carry out a full service on a gas fire. The following table is included for your use. Note details of any components which may need replacement.

Component	Serviced/Cleaned YES/NO	Requiring replacement YES/NO	Not fitted to appliance
Burner(s), including injector(s) and lint arrestors			
Primary air port			
Combustion chamber			
Heat exchanger/flueways			
Ignition device			
Control taps/isolation valves			
Flame supervision device and safety devices			
Radiant/fuel effects			

Note further details here:

Fault diagnosis

Task 24

You will be given a number of appliances with specific gas safety faults. Your tutor will advise on the number of faults per given appliance. You should list the faults associated with each appliance below.

Appliance 1 – Faults identified:

Appliance 2 – Faults identified:

Appliance 3 – Faults identified:

Appliance 4 – Faults identified:

Appliance 5 – Faults identified:

Knowledge Questions

Domestic Space Heaters, Gas Fires and Wall Heaters – HTR1

Section 1 – Types of Appliances and their Operating Principles

1. What is the minimum size flue to which a radiant/convector gas fire may be fitted?
   a) 100mm across the axis of the flue.
   b) 125mm across the axis of the flue.
   c) 175mm across the axis of the flue.
   d) 225mm across the axis of the flue.

2. Unless otherwise stated by the appliance manufacturer, a DFE fire has which of the following ventilation requirements?
   a) No ventilation to be provided.
   b) Ventilation of 100cm^2 to be provided.
   c) Ventilation of 5cm^2 per kW (net) of rated input.
   d) Ventilation of 5cm^2 per kW (net) of rated input in excess of 7kW (net).

3. What is the purpose of an atmosphere sensing device fitted to an open flued gas fire?

4. Although less time is desired, the flame supervision device for a gas fire other than DFE when tested should activate within:
   a) 60 seconds.
   b) 120 seconds.
   c) 180 seconds.
   d) 240 second.

5. What is the purpose of a lint arrestor fitted to a gas fire burner?
   a) To give a luminous flame on ILFE fires.
   b) To prevent lint entering the burner and causing incomplete combustion.
   c) To collect lint at the burner ports.
   d) To increase the efficiency of a gas appliance.

6. What is the name of the component fitted to a fan assisted gas fire, which prevents the appliance from operating if the fan fails?

7. What are the differences between a simplex and a duplex burner?
   a) The number of injectors.
   b) Simplex has greater flexibility of output settings.
   c) Duplex burners cannot be fitted with lint arrestors.
   d) Simplex burner has a number of divisions.

8. What are the three components of the pilot assembly in a gas fire using a flame supervision device working on the thermo-electric principle?
   a)
   b)
   c)

9. What must be included into the design of a glass fronted fire?
   a) Radiants.
   b) A live fuel effect burner.
   c) A down draught diverter.
   d) An atmosphere sensing device.

10. What is the possible effect of incorrect positioning of the fuel bed or coals on a live fuel effect gas fire?

Section 2 – Installation and Commissioning of Space Heaters

1. In which of the following locations do the current Gas Safety (Installation and Use) Regulations 1998 prohibit the installation of open flued gas fires?
   a) A kitchen.
   b) A bathroom.
   c) A lounge.
   d) A garage.

2. Gas fires with a net input below 12.7kW which are to be installed in a bedroom must be:
   a) Fitted with a down draught diverter.
   b) Fitted with an atmosphere sensing device.
   c) Fitted with a flame supervision device.
   d) Supplied with ventilation of 5cm^2 per kW (net) of rated input.

3. When installing a gas fire, unless otherwise stated by the manufacturer, the burner must be situated at least:
   a) 200mm from a combustible side wall.
   b) 300mm from a combustible side wall.
   c) 400mm from a combustible side wall.
   d) 500mm from a combustible side wall.

4. A flueless heater is to be installed in a conservatory measuring 3.0m x 2.5m x 2.4m. Calculate the maximum rated input of heater which may be installed:
   a) 0.81kW.
   b) 1.62kW.
   c) 8.1kW.
   d) 16.2kW.

5. When a radiant/convector gas fire is to be installed onto a new pre-cast flue, what is the minimum cross sectional area of the flue?
   a) 12,000mm^2.
   b) 13,500mm^2.
   c) 15,000mm^2.
   d) 16,500mm^2.

6. A catchment space with an existing traditional unlined flue system measures 0.2m high x 0.2m wide 0.25m deep. What is the volume of the void and is it suitable for the installation of a gas fire?
   a) 1 dm^3 and no.
   b) 10 dm^3 and no.
   c) 100 dm^3 and yes.
   d) 10 dm^3 and yes.

7. When is it not necessary to fit a flue terminal to a flue system?
   a) When an ILFE fire is fitted.
   b) When a radiant/convector fire is fitted.
   c) When the flue has a diameter less than 170mm.
   d) When the flue has a diameter more than 170mm.

8. When installing a wall mounted gas fire, unless otherwise stated by the manufacturer, the top of the burner must be situated at least:
   a) 225mm from the carpet.
   b) 300mm from the carpet.
   c) 400mm from the carpet.
   d) 500mm from the carpet.

BPEC   Module 19

9. When may a cooler plate be required on a gas fire installation?
    a) When a DFE fire is fitted.
    b) When a fire with a closure plate is installed onto a pre-cast flue.
    c) When a fire with a closure plate is installed onto a chimney over 4m high.
    d) When there is a danger that there could be spillage of combustion products.

10. What are the procedures for carrying out a spillage test on an open flued gas fire?

11. Before installing an open flued radiant gas fire in a chimney previously used for an appliance burning solid fuel, the flue shall be:
    a) Lined.
    b) Be fitted with a terminal.
    c) Tested using a smoke match.
    d) Thoroughly swept in accordance with BS 5440-1.

Section 3 – Service, Maintenance and Repair of Space Heaters

1. Discolouration of the wall paper above a gas fire is likely to be the result of:
    a) Lack of use.
    b) Excessive use.
    c) The use of cheap wall paper.
    d) Spillage of products of combustion.

2. Two visual signs of incomplete combustion on a gas fire are:
    a) A blue flame.
    b) A yellow flame.
    c) The radiants glowing orange.
    d) Soot deposits on the radiants.

3. List the final checks that should be made following the service of a gas fire:

April 2017   © BPEC

Model Answers

Section 1 – Types of Appliances and their Operating Principles

1. b) 125mm across the axis of the flue.
2. b) Ventilation of 100cm^2 to be provided.
3. To monitor the concentration of oxygen within the room in which the appliance is installed and by activating the flame supervision device. Close the gas supply to the burner in the event of the oxygen levels falling too low.
4. c) 180 seconds.
5. b) To prevent lint entering the burner and causing incomplete combustion.
6. **Air pressure switch.**
7. a) The number of injectors.
8. a) Pilot burner.
   b) Ignition electrode.
   c) Thermocouple.
9. c) A down draught diverter.
10. Spillage of products may occur.

Section 2 – Installation and Commissioning of Space Heaters

1. b) A bathroom.
2. b) Fitted with an atmosphere sensing device.
3. d) 500mm from a combustible side wall.
4. a) 0.81kW.
5. d) 16,500mm^2.
6. b) 10dm^3 and **no**.
7. d) When the flue has a diameter **more** than 170mm.
8. a) 225mm from the carpet.
9. b) When a fire with a closure plate is installed on a precast flue.
10. Operate the fire on full for 5 minutes. A lighted smoke match should be inserted to a point within the fire identified by the manufacturer. The trail of smoke from the match should be drawn into the appliance.

    If spillage occurs, the test should be repeated after a further period of 10 minutes' flue warm up. If spillage still occurs, the fault should be investigated and the appliance disconnected.
11. d) Thoroughly swept in accordance with BS 5440-1.

Section 3 – Service, Maintenance and Repair of Space Heaters

1. d) Spillage of products of combustion.
2. b) A yellow flame.
   d) Soot deposits on radiants.

3. Final checks following the service of a gas fire include:

   Check the appliance operating pressure, test with a suitable gauge and check the heat input at the meter, adjust if necessary (test disturbed joints with leak detection fluid), including test nipple.

   Check, with any appropriate fans running, the flame picture and flame stability of all burners, on all settings. Ensure 'live fuel' bed and components correctly located.

   Check the safe operation of all the appliance and system controls including gas taps, ignition devices, flame supervision devices, atmospheric sensing devices and other safety devices (test disturbed joints with leak detection fluid).

   Test appliance for spillage – carry out individual and combined spillage tests. Reset the controls to suit customer's requirements. Complete all necessary documentation and advise customer of any remedial work required.

BPEC	Module 20

Contents

	Page
Introduction	2
Section 1 – Types of Appliances and their Operating Principles	4
Part 1 – Ducted Air Heaters	4
Section 2 – Installation and Commissioning of Ducted Air Heaters	10
Part 1 – Permitted Installation Locations for Appliances	10
Part 2 – Return Air Connection to Air Heaters	11
Part 3 – Plenum Base Ducts	14
Part 4 – Plenums	14
Part 5 – Commissioning of Ducted Air Heaters	16
Section 3 – Service, Maintenance and Repair of Ducted Air Heaters	21
Part 1 – Servicing and Maintenance of Ducted Air Heaters	21
Part 2 – Fault Finding Procedures for a Typical Ducted Air Heater	24
Practical Tasks	32
Knowledge Questions	40
Model Answers	43

April 2017	© BPEC

Introduction

The objective of this module is to enable you to successfully complete assessment across the following range of ducted air heaters:

- Open flue natural draught.
- Open flue fan draught.
- Up flow models.
- Down flow models.
- Horizontal flow models.

You will be required to prove that you can install, disconnect, service, repair, breakdown and commission domestic gas fired ducted air heaters up to 60kW.

Practically, you should be able to ensure the following:

- The compartment construction and ventilation meets current requirements.
- The appliance assembly is complete and is fit for use and purpose.
- The gas supply is isolated prior to work commencing.
- The existing heater is disconnected and removed.
- The replacement heater is positioned in the compartment.
- The plenum base is sized, located and adapted to fit replacement appliance.
- The return air duct is sized, located and adapted to fit replacement appliance.
- A suitable rigid connection is made between the gas point and the appliance.
- The open flue is connected to the appliance.
- The gas supply is re-established.
- The work carried out is gas tight.
- The appliance is correctly located, level and stable.
- The appliance operational gas safety components are dismantled and cleaned, using appropriate cleaning methods and agents (e.g. burners, primary air ports, combustion chambers, ignition devices, thermostats, limit switch and flame supervision).
- The appliance is commissioned as follows:
    - The appliance is purged of air.
    - The working pressure at the appliance is correct.
    - The burner flame picture, stability and ignition are correct.
    - The user controls are operating correctly.
    - The safety control devices are operating correctly.
    - The temperature controls are operating correctly.
    - The plenum/return air ducts are adequately sealed.
    - The flue is correctly clearing products of combustion.

- The connections are gas tight and flues are operating correctly.
- Defects on gas safety components are identified.
- The safe operation and use of the appliance is explained.

Additionally, you should know the following:

- Identification of unsafe conditions.
- Diagnosis of gas safety faults.
- The causes and effects of split heat exchangers.
- Suitable and unsuitable locations/compartments – fire proofing.
- Air filters and their effects on the appliance.
- Requirements where combustion air is supplied by the heaters circulating fan.
- Clearance requirements (proximity of combustible materials) and fire proofing of compartments.
- The operation of mechanical and electrical controls.

Section 1 – Types of Appliances and their Operating Principles: Ducted Air heaters

Introduction
In this module we shall be taking a look at the various types of appliances and the key operating principles of:
- Up flow models.
- Down flow models.
- Horizontal flow models.

Part 1 – Ducted Air Heaters
For the purposes of this training course we shall define ducted air heaters as gas appliances designed to provide heat for space heating.

What types of appliances are available?
Ducted air heaters fall into one of three categories:
- Up flow models.
- Down flow models.
- Horizontal flow models.

These categories can be manufactured as open flued, natural convection or open flued fitted with a flue boost.

However, ducted air heaters can be categorised further:
- Natural draught and fanned draught.
- Traditional control models.
- Modairflow models.

By understanding the operating principles of these appliance types, we should be able to describe how the mechanical and electrical controls operate within the majority of appliances that we may have to install or maintain.

The operation of a traditional control
When the room thermostat calls for heat, it will operate the gas valve, which in turn will switch on the burner.

Once the temperature in the heat exchanger has reached approximately 58°C, the fan thermostat will operate the fan unit, thus distributing warm air via the register. When the temperature in the heat exchanger falls to approximately 38°C, the fan thermostat will switch off the fan unit.

The problem with the simplistic control system is that the on-off switching of the fan unit creates a feeling of coldness to the room occupants during an off period.

The operation of a modairflow control
A time control in the air heater allows the user to pre-select times of heating system operation.

A thermista-stat on the wall allows selection of comfort level; it senses heat requirement and continuously informs the electronic controls in the air heater of the rate of warm air delivery required. The air heater controls automatically adjust the operation of both gas burner and air circulation fan. Figure 1 shows a typical operating sequence of a modairflow control.

BPEC Module 20

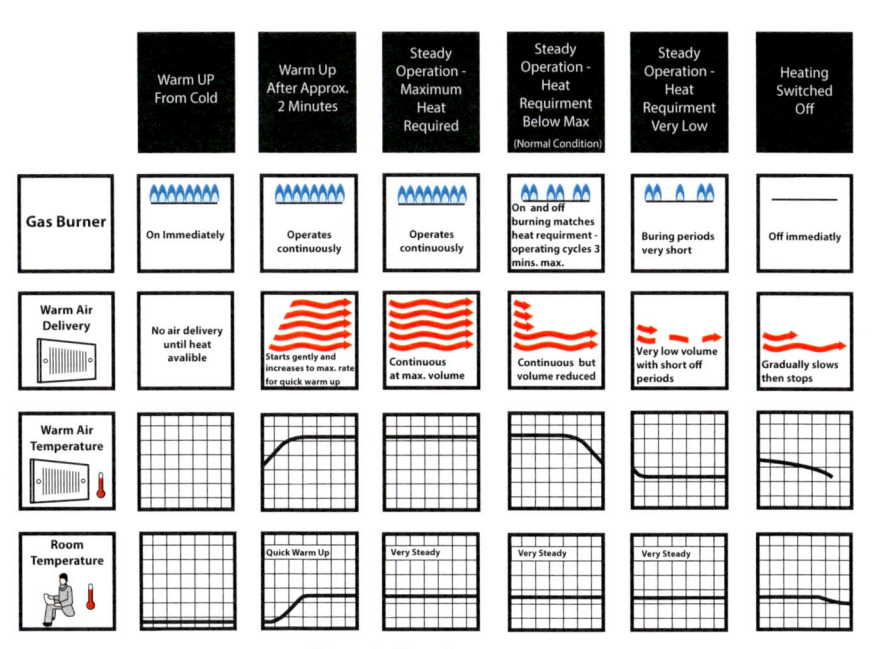

Figure 1: Operating sequence

How does the appliance work?

There are three variations in flow direction:

- **Downflow:**

Where the fan is positioned above the heat exchanger, directing the heat downwards through the unit, with the air distributed from the bottom (see Figure 2).

These are suitable for most dwellings.

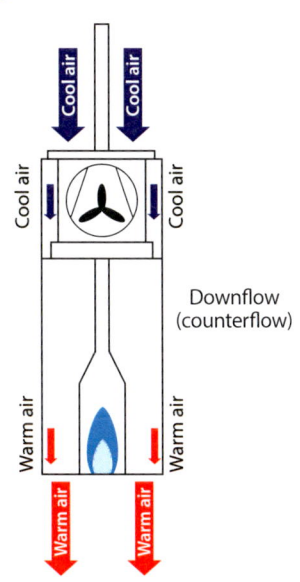

Figure 2: Downflow

April 2017 © BPEC

- **Upflow:**

    Where the fan is positioned below the heat exchanger delivering air upwards for distribution (see Figure 3).

    These are suitable for installations in basement, but can be installed at other levels within a dwelling.

- **Horizontal flow:**

    Has the fan and heat exchanger located side by side and discharges air for distribution horizontally (see Figure 4).

    These are suitable for wall mounting.

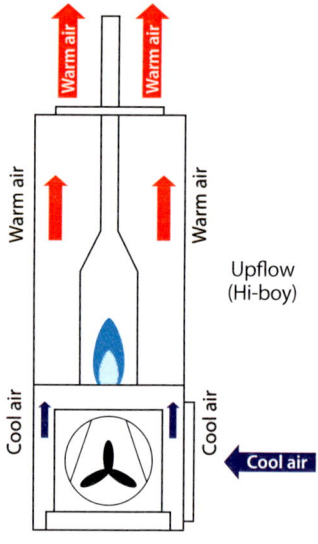

Figure 3: Upflow

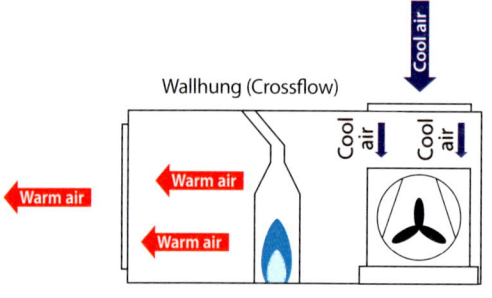

Figure 4: Horizontal flow

The working components

The centrifugal fan has an integral motor with sealed bearings designed to give trouble-free running.

With a basic heater, the fan switch (a bi-metal blade) controls the fan and ensures that it does not blow cold air on starting and that it dissipates warm air before stopping. The fan runs at a single speed.

With a modulating output heater, the airflow sensor (a thermistor) has a similar task to the fan switch, but the fan speed varies automatically. With the system ET (even temperature controls), the thermista stat controls the fan speed as well as the burner.

The heat exchanger – transfers heat from combustion chamber to circulation air without them mixing. It is shaped like a clam and made up of one or more sections. Most are constructed from stainless steel.

The burner – natural gas burners have a single injector, gas and air are mixed before burning. Each heat exchanger clam has its own burner bar.

The flue – takes combustion products from the heater to atmosphere and can be of different types. Mostly open flues are used, where combustion air is drawn in through the front of the heater. The flue products pass through a draught diverter and then to atmosphere via a flue pipe. Fan assisted open flues are also used.

Balanced flues – are used on individual heaters and the flue box induces combustion air and disposes of flue products.

The controls – All heaters use a multi functional gas valve. This allows gas to pass to the burner and is controlled by the limit switch.

The limit switch – performs the same function as a boiler stat and controls the temperature of air distributed to the grilles and registers.

Fan switch control (thermistor) – controls the speed of the fan according to the current temperature, or on basic models shuts the fan off.

Time control – allows the gas valve to open at pre-selected times.

Room stat – This will bring the burner into operation when calling for heat. The gas valve allows gas to permanent pilot, which will ignite the burner when the main gas is supplied.

The thermocouple – is a device to prevent gas being supplied to the burner when the pilot is not alight. Its probe is heated by the pilot, which produces a small electric current of 10-30 Mv, opening the gas valve.

The pilot – can be lit by pushing the gas valve button in (which allows gas to the pilot) and igniting the pilot by the piezo ignition. The button is held in long enough for the thermocouple to operate. Piezo means "pressure electric" and is a crystal which, when pressure is applied, becomes compressed and produces a spark.

Basic control ducted air heaters

These heaters are operated by a 24 volt thermostat which, when calling for heat, brings on the burner at a pre-selected rate via an electrical panel. The fan switch will consequently bring on the fan at a pre-selected speed. Warm air will then be delivered via the system until the thermostat is satisfied; the heater will then shut down.

On short ducted systems this can give fairly large temperature differences, both across rooms and from off and on. Draughts and noises can also be a problem.

Modairflow control ducted air heaters

These heaters are operated by a thermista-stat, which is a heat sensitive resistor sending a continuous signal to the heater. This brings on the burner, which cycles at approximately two minute intervals, with on periods always matching the heat requirement. The fan speed is then matched to the heat output.

This provides a heater with modulating output working almost continuously to match the heat requirement. Continuous output at lower fan speeds mean very stable temperatures, all round comfort and vastly reduced noises and draughts.

The filter contained within the heater can be a passive filter or with modern technology, an extremely efficient electronic air cleaner. Basic air heaters can also have electronic air cleaners fitted.

Open flued natural draught ducted air heaters

An open flued heater incorporates a combination of both mechanical and electrical gas control devices. It uses a permanent pilot as its source of main burner ignition.

Gas is supplied via the service cock (the main point of appliance gas isolation) to the inlet of the multifunctional control valve, which incorporates:

- Constant pressure governor.
- Flame supervision device (in this case working on the thermo electric principle, using a thermocouple).
- Solenoid valve.

A pilot pipe and thermocouple lead connect the multifunctional control valve to the pilot assembly, which is situated adjacent to the main burner. The function of the pilot is to light the main burner. The pilot assembly incorporates:

- Pilot burner (incorporating pilot injector).
- Thermocouple.
- Spark electrode.

The spark electrode is connected via a lead to the piezo unit; its function is to light the pilot burner.

The purpose of the flame supervision section of the multifunctional control valve and its associated thermocouple is to permit a flow of gas to the main burner only when the presence of a pilot flame has been detected. The gas governor section of the control valve allows for adjustment of gas flow through to the main burner. The electric solenoid valve section provides for on/off operation of the main burner.

Limit switch

Both the basic and the modairflow control have a high limit switch, which is a bi-metal strip operating a switch on the 24 volt gas circuit. The limit switch is normally set to close at 200°F by the manufacturer, to shut the gas valve and turn the burner off.

Fan switch/control

The basic air heater has a bi-metal fan switch which closes on temperature rise. The typical setting is 100°F on a difference of 30°F.

The modairflow control has an air flow sensor with heat sensitive resistors, which continuously monitors the temperature around the outside of the heat exchanger, and varies the fan speed accordingly.

Ducted air heater with flue boost fitted

A flue boost fan is used to assist with removal of the products of combustion and the supply of combustion air. The principal additional safety feature is the air flow switch, which must be fitted to all fan assisted appliances. The air flow switch prevents the ducted air heater lighting sequence taking place in the event of the flue boost fan not operating.

Air heater

The basic ducted air heater's (24 Volt) typical operation cycle is as follows:

- Thermostat calls for heat.
- Main burner lights.
- Unit heats up.
- Fan switch operates on reaching temperature.
- Fan starts.
- Burner and fan run until room temperature is reached.
- Burner may be turned on and off by limit switch to keep a constant air temperature.
- Burner goes off.
- Fan over runs to cool unit.
- Switch stops fan at a pre-determined temperature to prevent cold air being blown out of grilles and registers.

Flue boosted appliances may also operate using a permanent pilot light arrangement. The permanent pilot version incorporates a combination of gas-electrical controls including:

- Air flow pressure switch.
- Fan.
- Multifunctional gas control valve.

The manufacturer's flue boost can be fitted to all open flued ducted air heaters. A one speed fan is used, which can be wired in with the gas circuit or with the clock.

We have now covered the various types of ducted air heaters and their operating principles in some detail. This provides important preliminary learning before progressing into the installation and commissioning and service and maintenance sections.

Section 2 – Installation and Commissioning of Ducted Air Heaters

Introduction

In this section we shall focus on the key installation and commissioning aspects of ducted warm air heaters by looking at:

- Permitted installation locations for appliances.
- Appliances installed in cupboards/compartments.
- Flue requirements for ducted air heaters.
- Installation of ducted air heaters.
- Commissioning of ducted air heaters.

Part 1 – Permitted Installation Locations for Appliances

Ducted air heaters cannot be installed in any room

It is usually the appliance flue type which affects the rooms in which ducted air heaters may be installed.

Remember that wherever possible, it is preferable to install a room sealed appliance as the safest option.

Bathrooms/shower rooms

Open flued appliances may not be installed in bathrooms or shower rooms.

Room sealed appliances may be installed. There are however restrictions placed on the actual appliance location (for appliances incorporating electric's) by the IET Wiring Regulations 17th Edition.

Toilets/cloakrooms

It is strongly recommended that only room sealed appliances are installed in these rooms.

Where open flued appliances are installed, air supply for combustion (where required) should be provided direct from the outside air.

Private garages

Up until 31st October 1994, the installation of open flued appliances in private garages was not permitted. A relaxation brought about by the revised Gas Safety (Installation and Use) Regulations 1998 now permits open flued installations in this situation.

Bathrooms/bed sitting rooms (sleeping accommodation)

Appliances over 14kW (gross) heat input must be room sealed. As of 1st January 1996 open flued appliances rated at under 14kW heat input (gross) may be installed. However, the appliance(s) must also have a safety device (atmosphere sensing device) for automatic shut down of the appliance in the event of a build up of products of combustion.

Other siting issues

There are further limitations placed on the siting of ducted air heaters, namely:

- The provision of adequate space, in accordance with the manufacturer's installation instructions:
  - To ensure sufficient air circulation for draught diverter operation.
  - To ensure sufficient air for combustion and cooling purposes.
  - To allow for maintenance and servicing, e.g. removal of the burner tray.
- Protection of the floor or wall on which the appliance is mounted, in line with the manufacturer's installation instructions.
- Any water heater located in a compartment should have at least 75mm clearance from combustible materials or be suitably protected with non-combustible material

Can gas appliances be installed in all other rooms or spaces?

No, there are further restrictions, as shown in appropriate core modules and manufacturers guidance.

Slot fix installations

Appliances must be specifically designed for slot fix of installation and installed in accordance with manufacturer's instructions.

To prevent obstruction of the draught diverter and/or the combustion air inlets, and/or the return inlets, the area above the air heater must be enclosed.

Part 2 – Return Air Connection to Air Heaters

Open flued air heater

Sealed duct from return air grilles to air heater is essential (see Figure 5). This prevents risk of air being drawn from heater compartment and interfering with flue performance. This duct can be of rigid metal construction or of a non-combustible flexible type.

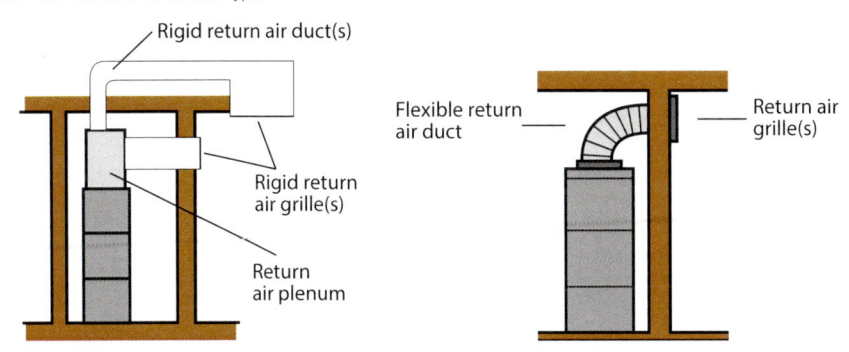

Figure 5: Return air connection

Return air

All return air shall be ducted from outside the compartment to the top of the unit via a return air duct, and mechanically secured. It is recommended that the return air duct is not routed directly from the main living area, but from a convenient central area serving the remainder of the dwelling.

The return air system should be constructed of fire-resistant material. The flue shall not be run through an area serving as a return air path. It is extremely important that the correct size of return air grilles and ducting is used. For heaters, the return air duct size should not be less than 200mm x 200mm (8" x 8"). If a flexible duct is used, the duct diameter should not be less than 250mm (10") dia. The return air grilles should have a free area of not less than 645cm (100").

An adequate and unobstructed return air path is essential from areas not served by a directly ducted return and to which warm air is delivered. All such rooms should be fitted with relief grilles, which have a free area of 88cm² per kW (1"/250 Btu/h) of heat supplied to the room. The only exceptions are kitchens, bathrooms and WCs.

The return air duct should allow for ease of removal for access to the flue.

All ductwork in the room or internal space in which the heater is installed shall be mechanically secured and sealed with ducting tape.

Table 1: Return air grilles and duct sizes necessary for maximum output of heaters

Heater kW rate	Heater (Btu's rate)	Return air grille in	Return air grille mm	Duct in	Duct mm	Flexible duct dia. in	Flexible duct dia. mm
4.4 – 6.5	15 – 22,000	12 x 10	300 x 250	8 x 8	200 x 200	10	250
5.6 – 7.3	19 – 25,000	12 x 12	300 x 300	8 x 8	200 x 200	10	250
7.3 – 8.8	25 – 30,000	16 x 12	400 x 300	10 x 8	250 x 200	12	300
9.7 – 12.6	33 – 43,000	20 x 12	500 x 300	10 x 12	250 x 300	14	350
11.7 – 14.7	40 – 55,000	18 x 12	450 x 450	12 x 12	300 x 300	–	–
14.7 – 19.1	55 – 65,000	22 x 12	560 x 400	12 x 12	300 x 300	–	–
20.5 – 26.4	70 – 90,000	22 x 12	560 x 560	16 x 16	400 x 400	–	–

Note: Other grille sizes with similar free area are permissible.

Size of relief openings

Again this will depend on the amount of heat distributed into the room. However, Table 2 can be used as a guide.

Table 2: Sizing of relief openings

Heat delivered to area served by air relief opening kW	Heat delivered to area served by air relief opening Btu/h	Free area of opening required m²	Free area of opening required in	Grille size to provide required free area mm x mm	Grille size to provide required free area in x in
0.9	3,000	0.008	12	150 x 100	6 x 4
1.5	5,000	0.013	20	200 x 100	8 x 4
2.0	7,000	0.018	28	250 x 100	10 x 4
2.9	10,000	0.026	40	250 x 150	10 x 6

Requirements where combustion air is supplied by the heater's circulating fan

Where the supply of outside air is to be introduced by the heater's circulating fan, a minimum flow of 2.2m^3/h shall be drawn into the return air duct or plenum for every 1kW of net input rating. Provision shall be made for the adjustment of the flow of induced air by means of a lockable damper or a similar control.

For fan assisted provision of outside air, a duct from the ventilated air space or outside wall grille shall be connected to the return air duct or return air plenum.

Where the air supply is ducted from the roof space, a bird guard shall be fitted to the duct inlet. The route for the air supply shall be in the form of a non-closable heat outlet grille located in the same space as the combustion air inlet to the heater. Where the heater is installed within a compartment, the non-closable heat outlet grille shall be located in the same space as the air inlet to the compartment. (See Figure 6 Below)

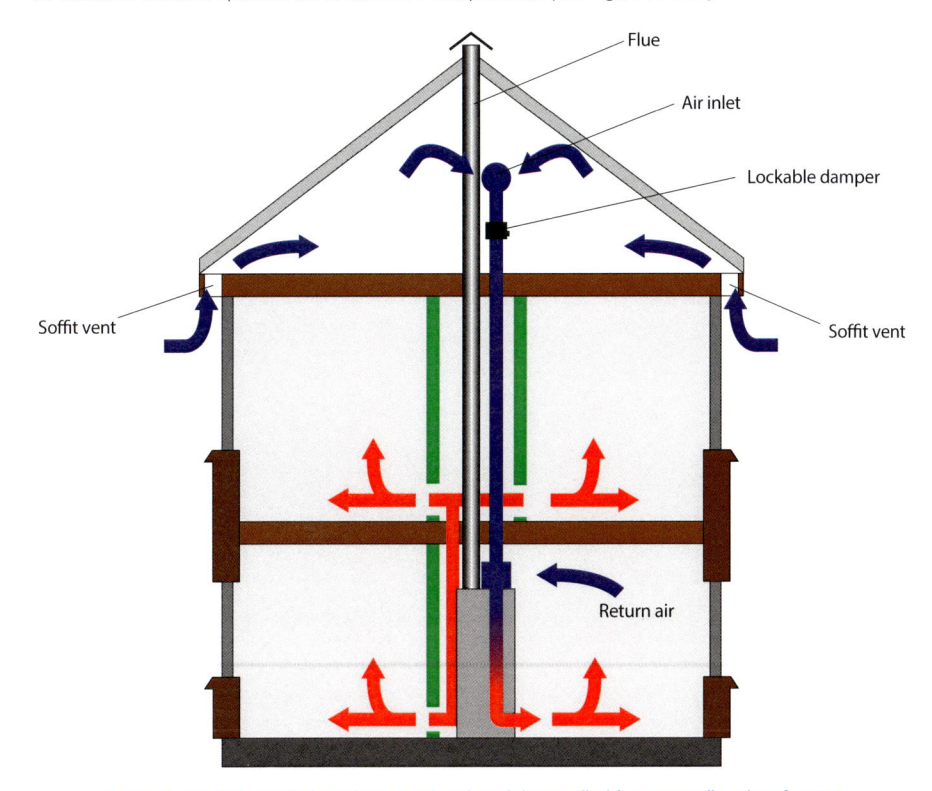

Figure 6: Typical installation where combustion air is supplied from a ventilated roof space

Part 3 – Plenum Base Ducts

It is important that you know the requirements for plenum base ducts.

Overall requirements for plenum ducts:

- The plenum base duct collects the warm air produced from the heater, equalising the air pressure as it passes to the system ducts. It also supports the weight of the heater. The heater must be securely screwed to the plenum on at least two sides, sealing all sides on completion with an approved tape or sealing compound.
- All ducting and blanking plates shall be mechanically secured and sealed.
- Combustible floors must be insulated from air heaters.
- Bay trays appropriate to individual air heaters are available for fitting air heaters directly onto combustible floors.
- When a plenum base duct is used, this provides sufficient insulation, and no other insulation is therefore needed beneath the plenum base duct.

Part 4 – Plenums

Radial ducts

Radial ducts consists of individual ducts branching directly from the plenum and run to perimeter diffusers (see Figure 7).

The branch ducts should not be longer than 6m.

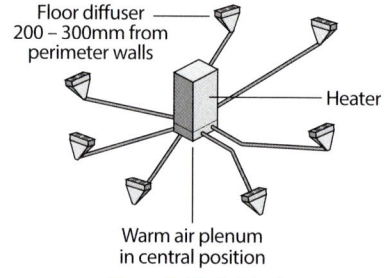

Figure 7: Radial ducts

Extended plenum system

Figure 8 shows an extended plenum system, where the main duct is the same size throughout its length.

Branch ducts are taken off and contacted to the diffusers in duct sizes suitable for the output requirements of each room.

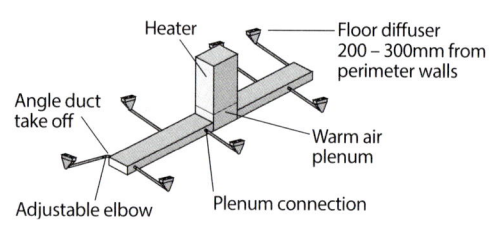

Figure 8: Extended plenum system

Stepped ducts

Stepped ducts (see Figure 9) are usually installed when the warm air unit is positioned at one end of the house. The cross-sectional area of the duct is kept roughly proportional to the volume of air passing through and the main duct is reduced as branches are taken off.

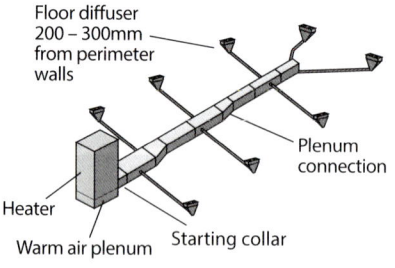

Figure 9: Stepped ducts

Stub ducts

Stub ducts are generally installed in small houses and flats in order to provide heating for a living room and one or two other rooms (see Figure 10).

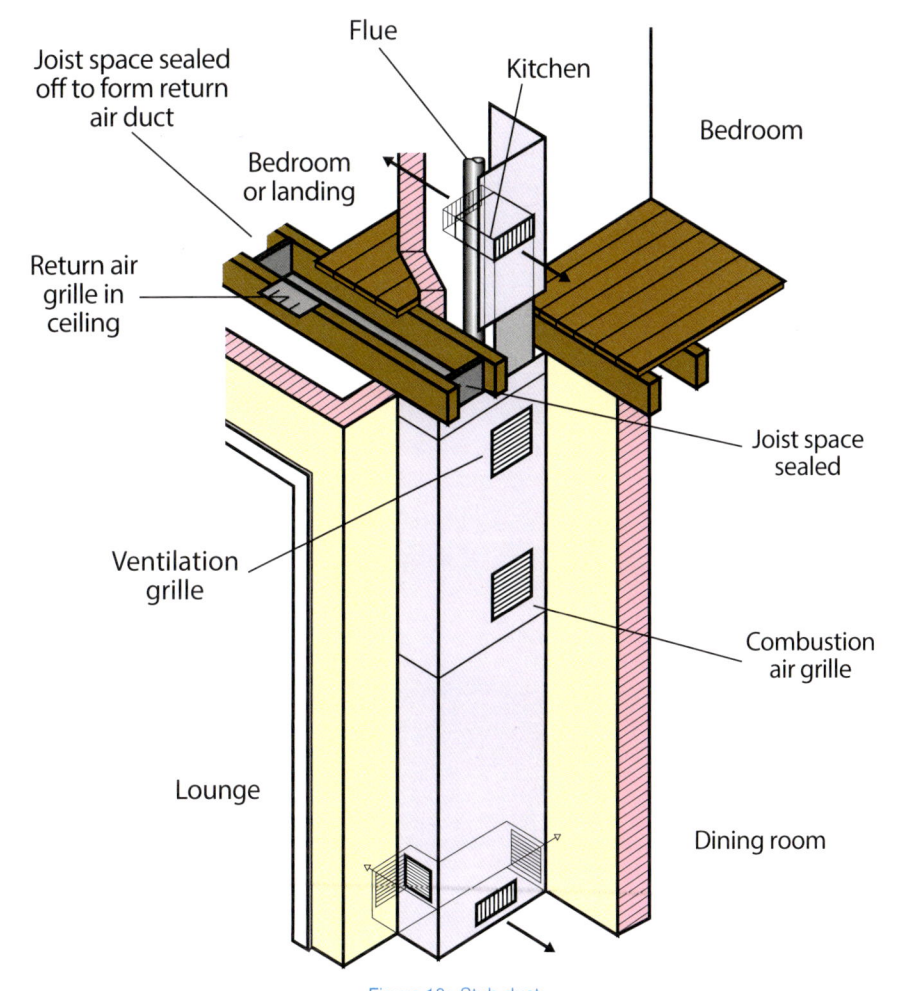

Figure 10: Stub duct

BPEC
Domestic Warm Air (DAH1)

Part 5 – Commissioning of Ducted Air Heaters

The commissioning of gas fired appliances tends to be slightly different for each appliance manufactured. However, by taking a look at the commissioning procedures associated with the J25 air heater, we should have an overview of the commissioning procedures for all types of ducted air heaters:

- Preliminary safety checks.
- Commissioning the J25 air heater.

Before we look at appliance commissioning in detail, remember that if you have not installed the appliance, you need to go through all the relevant checks first to ensure that the installation meets both legislative and manufacturer requirements.

Open flued – Natural draught appliances

The following identifies a common procedure for commissioning an open flued natural draught air heater:

Ensure all preliminary checks have been carried out, including compliance with legislation, gas tightness test and check for adequate ventilation. Check the plenum base duct and the return air duct and return air grille etc; check the effectiveness of the flue system. A typical commissioning procedure is explained after Figure 11.

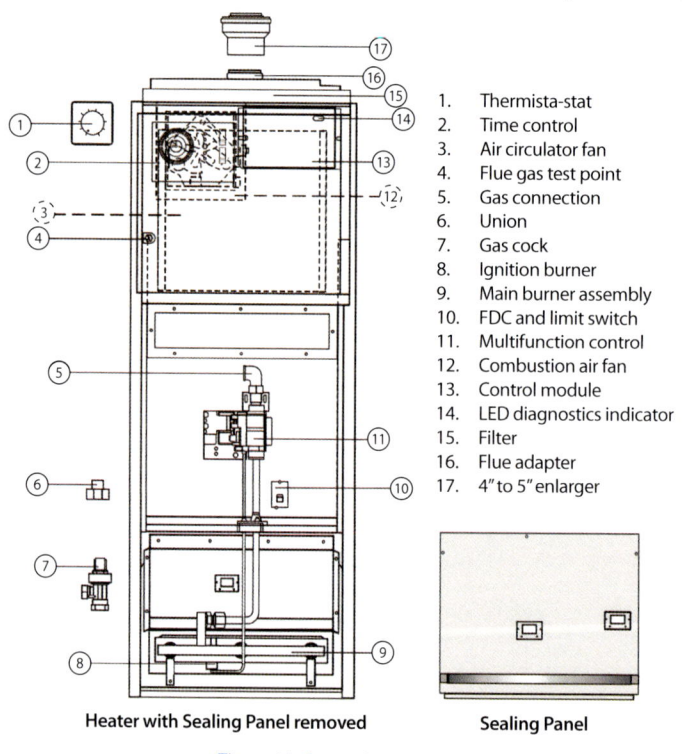

1. Thermista-stat
2. Time control
3. Air circulator fan
4. Flue gas test point
5. Gas connection
6. Union
7. Gas cock
8. Ignition burner
9. Main burner assembly
10. FDC and limit switch
11. Multifunction control
12. Combustion air fan
13. Control module
14. LED diagnostics indicator
15. Filter
16. Flue adapter
17. 4" to 5" enlarger

Heater with Sealing Panel removed   Sealing Panel

Figure 11: Internal components

April 2017

BPEC	Module 20

Commissioning example, as used on Johnson and Starley Ltd J25 air heater

- Ensure that gas and electrical supplies are off, check fuse rating.
- Make sure that the filter, fan and fan compartment are free of obstructions.
- Check that all of the registers or grilles are open and conform to design specifications.
- Check that return air, relief air and ventilation air installation is adequate.
- Set the fan speed with the air filter removed and the fan chamber door open, as follows:

System E-T models: The two switches on the electronic control module marked **rate switch** and **cleanflow**.
Switch: set the fan speed.
Rate switch: Select the max position.
Cleanflow switch: Select position 1 when a **cleanflow** electronic air cleaner is fitted, otherwise select position 0.

Basic models: Set the fan speed selector to the voltage appropriate to the desired heater output, e.g. for maximum fan speed.

- Replace the fan chamber door and filter:
  - Turn the Thermista-stat/room thermostat to the lowest or **off** setting.
  - Remove the cover from the adjustment point on the multifunctional control, release the pressure test point screw and attach a pressure test gauge.
  - Turn on the gas supply to the heater, then test for tightness and purge the whole gas pipe as described in IGE/UP/1B.
  - Push the **start** knob on the multi-functional control fully in and hold it in.
    Repeatedly push and release the piezo button until the pilot is alight. N.B. If the piezo unit should fail to spark, the pilot burner may be lit by applying a lighted taper to the pilot whilst the **start** knob is pushed in.
    Note: Two types of control can be used; Honeywell or SIT. Examples of these are shown in Figures 13 and 14.
  - After 20 seconds release the **start** knob and (Honeywell) let it spring out, or (SIT) turn it ¼ turn anticlockwise to the flame mark. The pilot should remain alight; if it does not, twist the **start** knob clockwise (Honeywell) about ¼ turn, or (SIT) to the off mark, and wait three minutes before repeating (from the previous step).
  - The pilot is factory set and is non-adjustable. Check that the pilot flame envelopes the thermocouple tip (see Figure 12) – if it does not, check that the pilot orifices and aeration port are free of obstruction.
  - When the pilot is alight, switch on the mains electrical supply to the heater. Set the time control to the required Heating On periods and set the selector switch to the Timed position. Adjust the Thermista-stat or room thermostat to maximum. Light the pilot burner.
    Warning: If the pilot light is extinguished, either intentionally or unintentionally, no attempt should be made to relight the gas until at least 3 mins. has elapsed. Ensure electrical supply is **off**, that the time control is in an **off** position and that the switch is in the **off** position.
  - (Honeywell) The main burner will now operate.
  - (SIT) Push the **start** knob in slightly and turn it to the flame symbol; the main burner will now operate.
  - Using a proprietary leak detection fluid, test for gas tightness to the supplies and connections from the multifunctional control to the pilot and main burners. Seal any leakages after turning off the heater.
- Allow the heater to operate for 15 minutes, then adjust the burner pressure to the output required.
  Note: Heaters are factory set to a burner setting pressure giving high rate output, i.e. 7.3kW (25,000 Btu/h) at 17mbar (6.8" wg).

BPEC
Domestic Warm Air (DAH1)

- To adjust the burner pressure, remove the cover from the gas pressure adjusting point and turn the flow rate screw clockwise to increase, anticlockwise to decrease. Fix the pressure set arrow under the appropriate column on the data badge.

- Turn off the heater before removing the pressure test gauge and re-tightening the pressure test point screw. Test the pressure test point for gas tightness, using a proprietary leak detection fluid, and replace the cover on the adjustment point.

- Balance the warm air system as follows: Light the main burner and leave it to operate for at least 15 minutes. System E-T control will give a fan speed corresponding to a temperature rise of 50°C +5°C. Balance the system to give the required volume proportions at the warm air outlets.

- System E-T units only: If the appliance is set to operate at minimum rate and the ducting has been sized accordingly, move the switch on the module marked **rate switch** to the **min** position to reduce fan speed.

- Basic units only: Light the main burner and leave it to operate for at least 15 minutes. With the fan chamber door in place, check that the temperature rise across the heater is 45°-55°C. Adjust the fan speed if necessary; increase speed to reduce temperature rise, decrease speed to increase temperature rise.

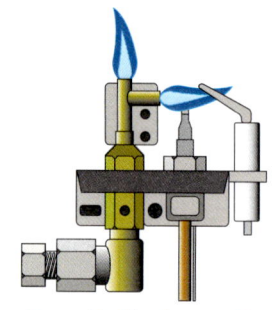

Figure 12: Pilot flame profile

Note: If the system includes ceiling diffusers, it is important that the velocities of air through these (except in very small rooms like bathrooms etc.) are at least 1.5 m/s (300 ft/min). To achieve this, it may be necessary to blank off part of the outlet face.

Automatic controls check – lighting the heater and allowing it to run for a short time checks these controls:

a) System E-T controls:

With the air heating switch set to 1, turn the Thermista-stat control knob slowly clockwise until the main burner ignites. Shortly afterwards the fan will start at a low speed and gradually build up to top speed. When room temperature is under control, the main burner will cycle on and off at approximately one to two minute intervals.

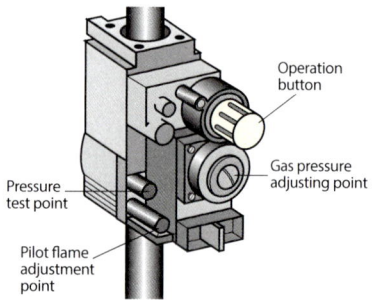

Figure 13: Honeywell control

b) Basic controls:

With the air heating switch set to 1, increase the room thermostat setting slowly until the main burner ignites. Shortly afterwards the fan will start. When room temperature is under control the main burner will switch off, followed shortly afterwards by the fan. After the room temperature has fallen slightly the burner will re-ignite, followed by fan operation.

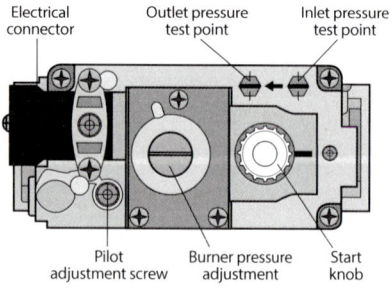

Figure 14: SIT control

© BPEC   18   April 2017

Safety checks

Check the fail safe section of the multifunctional control and flame supervision devices (FSD) by turning off the gas at the gas service cock and checking that the control fails safe (loud click heard from control) within 60 seconds. There are numerous procedures for determining whether these devices have shut down correctly and within the specified time. The factors that determine which procedure to adopt are generally dependent upon the appliance design.

The availability of pressure testing nipples after the FSD will enable the installer to assess whether the device is passing gas.

The accessibility of the burner or pilot burner being controlled (i.e. open or room-sealed flues) will allow the installer to blow out the pilot flame or require the isolation valve to be turned off.

Whether the FSD shut-off can be proved by including the procedure within a test for tightness of the complete gas installation using the test nipple on the gas meter by reading working and then standing pressure when the appliance has shut down.

Test procedure

Where the manufacturer's instructions do not specify a procedure, the following may be used as a guide:

- Ensure that all primary and secondary controls are set so that the burner will not be turned off during this procedure.
- Ensure all safety checks and procedures have been carried out and it is safe to ignite the appliance.
- Light the appliance and allow the heater to reach its normal working temperature.
- Turn off the appliance shut-off device (appliance isolation valve) and simultaneously start a stop watch.
- Halt the stop watch when the valve is heard to close.
- Immediately check that the valve in the FSD has shut off completely, using the most appropriate method as indicated below.

Preferred option

Where the appliance gas control system has a test nipple upstream of the FSD device (normally defined as test point PI), test for tightness and let-by between the appliance isolation valve and the FSD. If the FSD has not shut off completely, a drop in pressure will occur.

Option 2

Where it is possible to complete a tightness test at the meter or other suitable position upstream of the appliance isolation valve, then by turning on the appliance isolation valve the integrity of the FSD is also included. When the appliance FSD is passing gas before shut down, the gauge will be reading working pressure (approximately 21mbar). Once the FSD shuts down, the pressure should rise to standing pressure if the system is sound, due to governor lock-up (approximately 25mbar).

Option 3

Where neither of the above options are available and the appliance is open flued, or the pilot and main burner are readily accessible, then where possible connect a gauge to the burner test nipple and turn on the appliance isolation valve. If any apparent increase in pressure is observed, immediately turn off the isolation valve as this indicates that the FSD has not shut off completely. If no apparent increase in pressure was observed (or no gauge was connected), immediately check with a lighted taper that gas has been interrupted to the main and pilot burner.

Check that the time recorded by the stop watch conforms with the current requirements for gas appliances of heat inputs below 70kW (BS EN 778: 2009).

Important note

It is not sufficient to wait to hear the click of the valve closing onto its seat, as this only indicates that the valve has dropped and not that the gas has been shut off. To ensure this, a pressure gauge must be used and where it is not possible, a taper to check for gas at the burner.

Check the overheat (limit) control by operating the heater with the main burner alight and the fan disconnected – the main burner must extinguish within 2-3 minutes. To disconnect the fan, turn off the electrical supply, remove the fan chamber door and disconnect two red wires at electronics module, numbers 30 and 31 (System E-T) or connections to terminals 16 and 18 on the electrical panel (basic model). Reconnect wires after testing. Check that the fan switch control is set correctly.

Air filters

Air filters which are blocked with dust, because they have not been cleaned thoroughly during the annual service, will cause the heat exchanger to overheat. The normal temperature rise across the heat exchanger from the return air to discharge should be between 45°C and 55°C. Blocked air filters will cause the temperature to rise above 55°C, the heat exchanger to overheat, and the limit switch to shut off the burner. The burner will then cycle until the air filter is cleaned. Dirty air filters can also lead to a build up of dust on the fan blades, causing them to be less effective. The effect of the lack of efficiency of the fan blades can lead to the overheating of the heat exchanger, and the limit switch to cause the burner to cycle.

With heating system on:

- Check for gas tightness within the appliance
- Check that the flue operates effectively with heating system on, all doors closed and extractor fans, if fitted, running. After connection to the flue system, follow the lighting procedure and run the appliance for 20 minutes to preheat the flue. Use the following procedure to test for spillage:
  - Close all doors and windows, check for additional extractor fans etc. If the draught diverter is accessible, introduce smoke, e.g. by means of a puffer or preferably using a smoke match pluming device into the draught diverter adjacent to an exit from the heat exchanger. The trail of smoke from the match should be drawn into the flue. If the smoke is not drawn into the flue, spillage of combustion products is indicated.
  - If access to the draught diverter is not possible or if it is not visible, insert a lighted smoke pellet or part of a pellet on a non-combustible support into, but not in contact with, the heat exchanger. Turn off the appliance. Spillage is indicated by the discharge of smoke from the draught diverter. In a compartment this would be indicated by the presence of smoke within the compartment.
  - In the case of an extractor fan in an adjoining or adjacent room, the spillage test procedure must be carried out with interconnecting doors open and the fan running at maximum speed in all directions.

BPEC   Module 20

Section 3 – Service, Maintenance and Repair of Ducted Air Heaters

Introduction
In this section we shall be taking a look at:
- Service and maintenance of ducted air heaters.
- Typical gas component faults on ducted air heaters.
- Fault finding procedure on typical ducted air heaters.

Part 1 – Servicing and Maintenance of Ducted Air Heaters
The following identifies a general procedure for carrying out service/maintenance of central heating ducted air heaters:

Step 1 – Carry out preliminary checks
- Light the appliance and put into full operation, checking the function of the appliance components.
- Check the general condition of the installation and its conformity with the Gas Safety (Installation and Use) Regulations 1998 and British Standard requirements.
- For open flued installations, check to ensure that sufficient free area of ventilation has been provided.
- Check compartment ventilation requirements and provision of appropriate warning notices.
- Check that the flue is free from obvious defects. Check the effectiveness of the flue.
- Check that the flue terminal is suitable and that the termination location is acceptable with BS 5440-1: 2008.
- Check that the appliance includes an atmosphere sensing device (ASD) where required.
- Check for signs of spillage on the appliance and adjacent decoration.
- Check the plenum base duct for suitability.
- Check that all ducting and blanking plates have been mechanically secured and sealed and are free from leaks.
- Check that the return air is ducted from outside the compartment to the air heater and that it is mechanically secured.
- Check that the correct size of return air ducting has been used.
- Check the size of the return air grille.

Note any defects and advise the customer prior to the service taking place.

Step 2 – Servicing procedures
- Isolate the gas and electrical supplies to the appliance.
- Remove the casing, any control panel and electrical connections to permit the burner and controls assembly to be removed (see Figure 15).

Lift off front panel

Figure 15: Front casing removal

April 2017   21   © BPEC

BPEC
Domestic Warm Air (DAH1)

Step 3 – Burner removal
Remove the main burner and controls assembly from the combustion chamber (see Figure 16). Examine the main burners for cracks, including hairline cracks, at the burner ports and exchange burners if necessary.

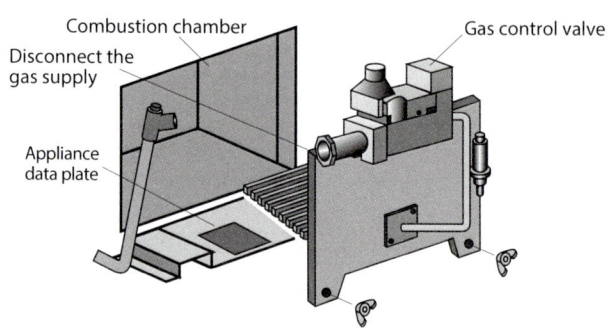

Figure 16: Burner tray removal

Step 4 – Burner components
Clean the lint arrestor. Lint gauze arrestors may be included within the burner, mounted on the burner or included within the heater casing (see Figure 17).

Step 5 – Cleaning the burner assembly
- Brush off any deposits that may have fallen onto the burner head, ensuring that the flame ports are unobstructed. Remove any debris that may have collected on the assembly components. Brushes with metallic bristles should not usually be used for this purpose.

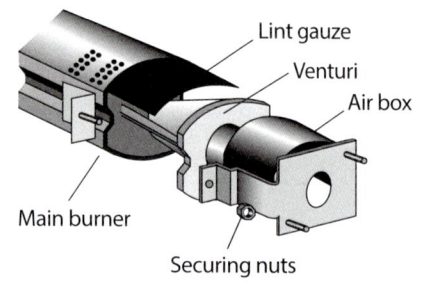

Figure 17: Burner components

- Remove the burner injector(s). Ensure that there is no blockage or damage. Clean or renew as necessary.
- Refit the injector(s) using an approved jointing compound.
- Inspect the pilot, thermocouple and spark electrode; ensure that they are clean and in good condition.

In particular check that:
- The pilot burner is clean and unobstructed. Clean the pilot injector if necessary.
- The spark electrode is clean and undamaged.
- The piezo igniter works.
- The spark lead is in good condition and securely connected.
- The spark gap is correct.
- The thermocouple tip is not burned or cracked.
- The position of the thermocouple relative to the pilot burner is correct, as shown in Figure 18.
- The thermocouple terminal at the gas valve is clean and tight.

- Clean or renew components as necessary.

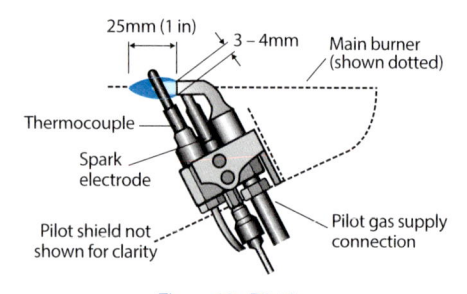

Figure 18: Pilot burner

© BPEC   April 2017

Step 6 – Clean the flueways
Remove the access cover and brush out any deposits on the top of the heat exchanger and baffles (if fitted). Brush through the heat exchanger with an appropriate flue brush, removing all deposits. Remove all debris from the combustion chamber base and check that the flue outlet is unobstructed.

Step 7 – Check heat exchanger
Heat exchangers can develop faults, such as small cracks caused by metal fatigue, corrosion or faulty welding or overheating.

Cracked heat exchangers can be very dangerous on ducted air heaters, as the following can occur:
- Air leaks into combustion chamber, causing an adverse effect on the combustion process.
- The above combined with spillage from an open flue could cause toxic fumes to circulate through the building.
- Products of combustion leaking into the air distribution system could also spread toxic fumes.

Therefore, during service the heat exchanger must be checked carefully:
- Light the main burner.
- Make sure the gas rate is correct for the appliance.
- Check that flame picture is good.
- Switch the fan on and check flame picture; uneven burning indicates a leakage of air into the heat exchanger.

Checking a heat exchanger using the smoke method (BS 5864: 2010 – Annex C.2)
- Light appliance and allow it to reach normal operating temperature
- Turn off the appliance (gas and electricity)
- Close all warm air outlet registers except the one closest to the heater
- Light a suitable smoke pellet and place it into the combustion chamber
- Switch on the circulation fan and check for traces of smoke from the nearest outlet register
- Traces of smoke at the outlet indicates damaged heat exchanger, strip appliance and visually inspect heat exchanger.

Faulty heat exchangers must be replaced.

Step 8
Clean the air filter and make sure that the return air path is not restricted in any way. Remove and clean fan assembly and check air passages through the heater into the base. Check outside of heat exchanger from above.

Step 9
Check the appliance gas connections for gas tightness, including multi-functional valve connections, main burner connections, pilot burner connections and connections to gas service cocks, test points etc.

Step 10
Check that there is no obvious damage to the electrical wiring. Carry out polarity and continuity checks.

Final checks

Light the appliance pilot:

- Check to ensure that the pilot flame correctly envelopes the thermocouple/flame supervision device (FSD).
- Light the main burner and check/re-set the operating pressure to meet system requirements (confirm satisfactory flame picture).
- Carry out a spillage test on open flued appliances.
- Check the operation of the flame supervision device and air pressure switch (if fitted) following manufacturer's procedures.
- Check the operation of the thermostat(s).
- Check that the fan switch and limit switch are set correctly.
- Leave the site in a clean and tidy condition; ensure that the customer understands the safe and efficient operation of the appliance.

Part 2 – Fault Finding Procedure for a Typical Ducted Air Heater
(Johnson and Starley Ltd J25)

Fault finding

Note: Only if a fault occurs after installation of the appliance should preliminary earth continuity, polarity and resistance to earth checks be carried out with a multimeter. On completion of any service/fault-finding task which has required the breaking and remaking of electrical connections, checks of continuity, polarity and resistance to earth must be repeated.

Also, when purging or checking gas supplies, ensure that there is adequate ventilation to the room or cupboard, open doors and windows and ensure all naked lights are extinguished.

System E-T Models only: See page 28 for fault diagnostic chart.

Warning – When carrying out electrical testing, a test meter must be used. Low resistance test devices can cause damage to the electronics module. Before commencing fault finding, turn the Thermista-stat to maximum setting, turn the mains supply on and set the air heating switch to position 1 (continuous). Return the switch to the timed position after completing fault finding checks.

Care must be taken during replacement and handling of electronic assemblies, i.e. electronics module, fan delay/overheat limit control and Thermista-stat. It is not practical to rectify any faults in these assemblies except in the factory, and any attempt to do so may render any guarantee or factory replacement arrangement void.

Note: If a fault occurs concerning the pilot burner, thermocouple or spark electrode, then the complete pilot assembly **must** be replaced.

Before undertaking this part you should understand how a multimeter is used.

It is important that all electrical test instruments are regularly checked, tested and re-calibrated to ensure safety and accuracy.

SYMPTOM	POSSIBLE CAUSE	REMEDY
(a) Pilot will not light.	(i) No gas supply to heater.	Check for gas at inlet pressure test point on multi-functional control.
	(ii) Gas supply pipe not purged.	Purge gas supply pipe to IGE/UP/1B 2nd/Edition.
	(iii) Pilot orifice restricted.	Clean pilot orifice or replace pilot assembly (see note above).
	(iv) Pilot aeration port obstructed.	Clear aeration port or replace pilot assembly (see note above).
	(iv) Piezo system faulty.	Check/replace piezo unit, lead or pilot assembly (see note above).
(b) Pilot lights but goes out on releasing **start** button during initial light-up or after normal operation.	(i) Connection between thermo-couple and multifunctional control not secure.	Check connection is secure.
	(ii) Faulty multifunctional control.	Replace multifunctional control.
	(iii) Faulty thermocouple.	Replace pilot assembly (see note above).
	(iv) Draughts affecting pilot flame.	Eliminate draughts.
	(v) Combustion air contaminated.	Conduct spillage test and rectify.
(c) Main burner operating intermittently with fan running.	(i) Gas rate or burner pressure setting high.	Check gas rate and burner pressure setting.
	(ii) Temperature rise excessive.	Adjust fan speed or gas rate to give 45°-55°C temperature rise.
	(iii) Air filter or return air path restricted.	Check filter is clean and air path is clear.
	(iv) Excessive number of outlets closed.	Open additional outlets.
System E-T control heaters only:		
(d) Incorrect operation of fan or main burner.	Fault related to System E-T control.	Consult diagnostic chart and follow recommended procedure.
Basic control heaters only:		
(e) Pilot alight but main burner not igniting.	(i) Mains electrical supply not connected to heater.	Check mains supply.
	(ii) Controls not calling for heat.	Check that time control (if fitted) and room thermostat are operating correctly.
	(iii) T3.15A fuse failed.	Replace. If failure occurs again, check wiring for short circuits.
	(iv) Loose connection on room thermostat, limit control, gas control lead, time control, or 24V transformer output or relay module.	Check connections for soundness.
	(v) 230V/24V transformer failed.	Check 24V side with meter. If no voltage, replace transformer.

SYMPTOM	POSSIBLE CAUSE	REMEDY
	(vi) Relay module faulty.	Confirm 230V supply on white wire from switch S5.
	(vii) Multifunctional control faulty.	Replace multi-functional control.
	(viii) Limit control faulty.	Disconnect and loop across control and replace if necessary.
	(ix) Room thermostat or external wiring faulty.	Fit temporary loop in heater thermostat socket – if heater fires, external circuit or room thermostat is faulty.
(f) Main burner lights but fan fails to run after approx. 3 min.	(i) Loose electrical connection on fan control.	Check connections for soundness.
	(ii) Fan delay control faulty.	Replace.
	(iii) Faulty fan assembly.	Replace, taking care not to damage impeller.
	(iv) Burner setting pressure incorrect.	Adjust pressure as necessary.
(g) Main burner operating intermittent fan operation.	(i) Gas rate or burner pressure setting incorrect.	Check gas rate and burner with pressure setting.
	(ii) Fan delay control faulty.	Replace.
(h) Fan runs for excessive period or operates intermittently after main burner shuts down.	Fan delay control faulty.	Replace.
(j) Noisy operation.	(i) Gas pressure too high.	Check burner pressure setting.
	(ii) Noisy fan motor.	Replace fan assembly.
	(iii) Fan speed setting too high.	Adjust fan speed to give 45°–55°C temperature rise.
(k) Uneven flame picture with fan on. Fumes leaking into building, room or space.	(i) Cracked heat exchanger.	Replace heat exchanger.
	(ii) Leak in primary flue in fan chamber.	Repair joints or gaskets.

Domestic Air Heaters Unsafe situations

Situation	Category	RIDDOR	Regulation	Notes
Unsealed plenum or duct in appliance compartment effecting the safe operation of the appliance	ID	R	GSIUR	Where and unsealed plenum is encountered which does not effect the safe operation of the appliance it should be regarded as AR.
Open flued WAU in a compartment without a positive Return Air Connection	AR		GSIUR	Where an Open flued WAU in a compartment without a positive Return Air Connection is encountered a return air duct should be fitted (this is usually on older appliances) The responsible person should be advised to have the appliance replaced.

Blocked air filters – possible effects

- Limit switch cycling on and off
- No heat to rooms furthest away from appliance
- Noisy fan
- Fan runs for excessive periods

Split heat exchanger – possible effects

- Uneven flame picture when fan is operating
- Products of combustion leaking into room
- Pilot outage
- Overheat devices operating

BPEC Domestic Warm Air (DAH1)

System E-T operational checks

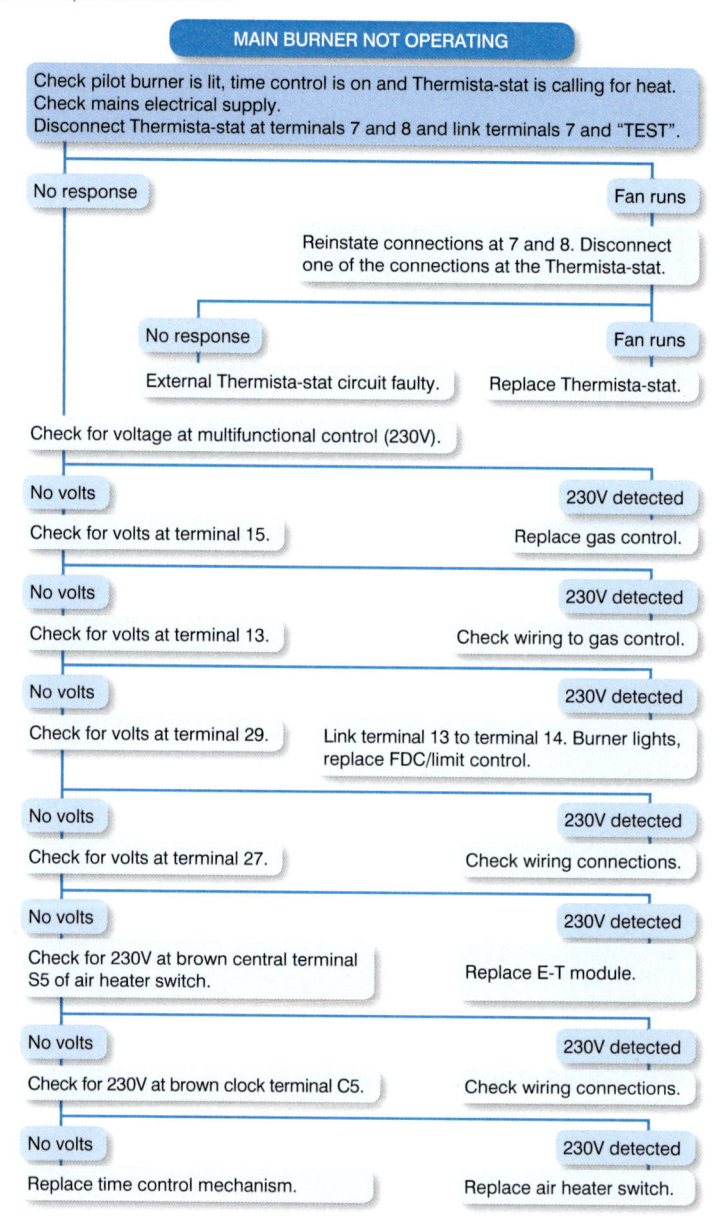

MAIN BURNER NOT OPERATING

Check pilot burner is lit, time control is on and Thermista-stat is calling for heat.
Check mains electrical supply.
Disconnect Thermista-stat at terminals 7 and 8 and link terminals 7 and "TEST".

- **No response** → Reinstate connections at 7 and 8. Disconnect one of the connections at the Thermista-stat.
- **Fan runs** →
  - **No response**: External Thermista-stat circuit faulty.
  - **Fan runs**: Replace Thermista-stat.

Check for voltage at multifunctional control (230V).

- **No volts**: Check for volts at terminal 15.
- **230V detected**: Replace gas control.

- **No volts**: Check for volts at terminal 13.
- **230V detected**: Check wiring to gas control.

- **No volts**: Check for volts at terminal 29.
- **230V detected**: Link terminal 13 to terminal 14. Burner lights, replace FDC/limit control.

- **No volts**: Check for volts at terminal 27.
- **230V detected**: Check wiring connections.

- **No volts**: Check for 230V at brown central terminal S5 of air heater switch.
- **230V detected**: Replace E-T module.

- **No volts**: Check for 230V at brown clock terminal C5.
- **230V detected**: Check wiring connections.

- **No volts**: Replace time control mechanism.
- **230V detected**: Replace air heater switch.

System E-T operational checks *(continued)*

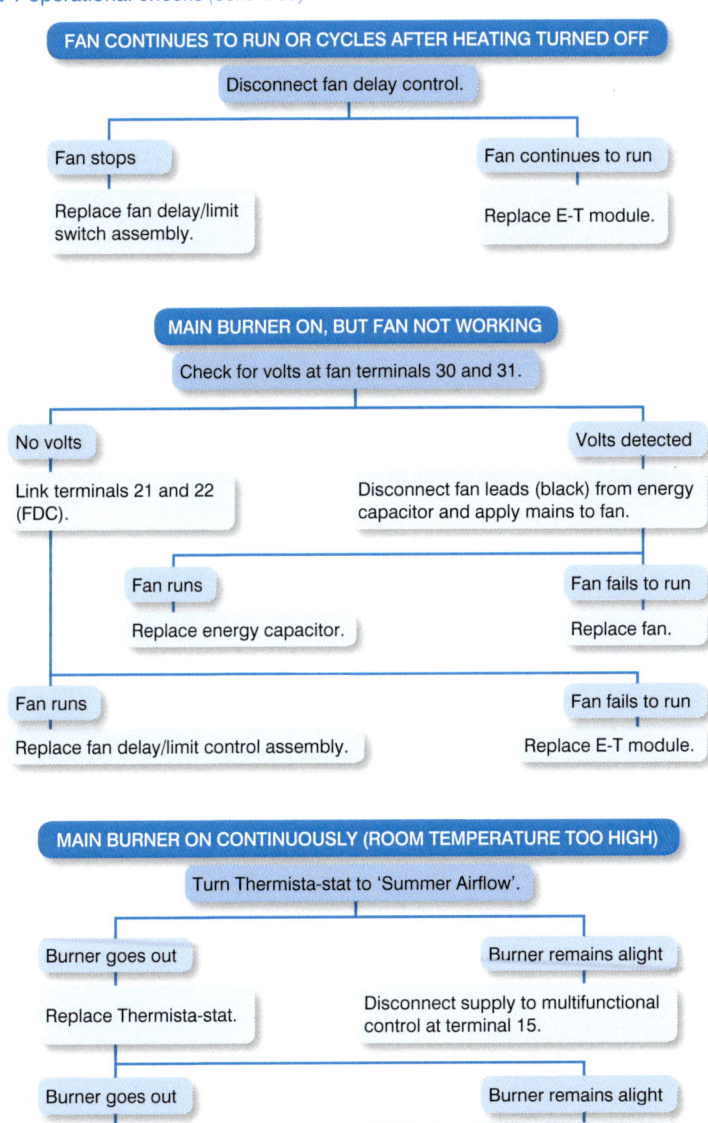

FAN CONTINUES TO RUN OR CYCLES AFTER HEATING TURNED OFF

Disconnect fan delay control.

- **Fan stops** → Replace fan delay/limit switch assembly.
- **Fan continues to run** → Replace E-T module.

MAIN BURNER ON, BUT FAN NOT WORKING

Check for volts at fan terminals 30 and 31.

- **No volts** → Link terminals 21 and 22 (FDC).
  - **Fan runs** → Replace fan delay/limit control assembly.
- **Volts detected** → Disconnect fan leads (black) from energy capacitor and apply mains to fan.
  - **Fan runs** → Replace energy capacitor.
  - **Fan fails to run** → Replace fan.
  - **Fan fails to run** → Replace E-T module.

MAIN BURNER ON CONTINUOUSLY (ROOM TEMPERATURE TOO HIGH)

Turn Thermista-stat to 'Summer Airflow'.

- **Burner goes out** → Replace Thermista-stat.
- **Burner remains alight** → Disconnect supply to multifunctional control at terminal 15.
  - **Burner goes out** → Replace E-T module.
  - **Burner remains alight** → Replace multifunctional control.

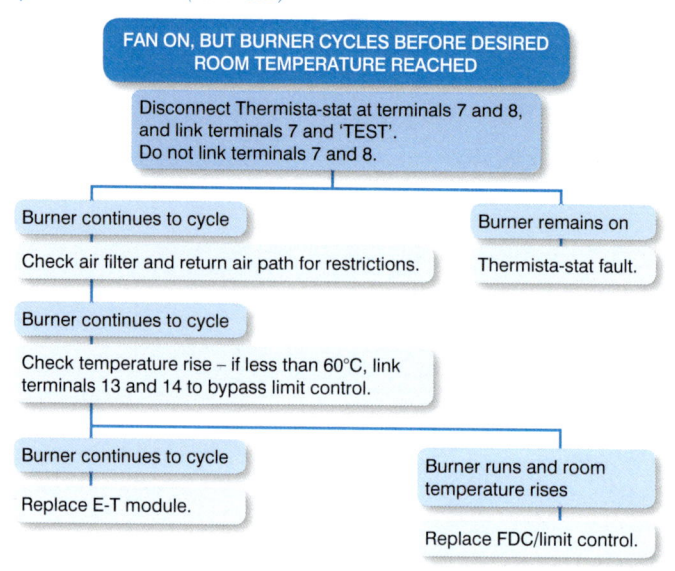

System E-T operational checks *(continued)*

FAN ON, BUT BURNER CYCLES BEFORE DESIRED ROOM TEMPERATURE REACHED

Disconnect Thermista-stat at terminals 7 and 8, and link terminals 7 and 'TEST'.
Do not link terminals 7 and 8.

- **Burner continues to cycle**
  Check air filter and return air path for restrictions.

- **Burner remains on**
  Thermista-stat fault.

- **Burner continues to cycle**
  Check temperature rise – if less than 60°C, link terminals 13 and 14 to bypass limit control.

- **Burner continues to cycle**
  Replace E-T module.

- **Burner runs and room temperature rises**
  Replace FDC/limit control.

System E-T operational checks *(continued)*

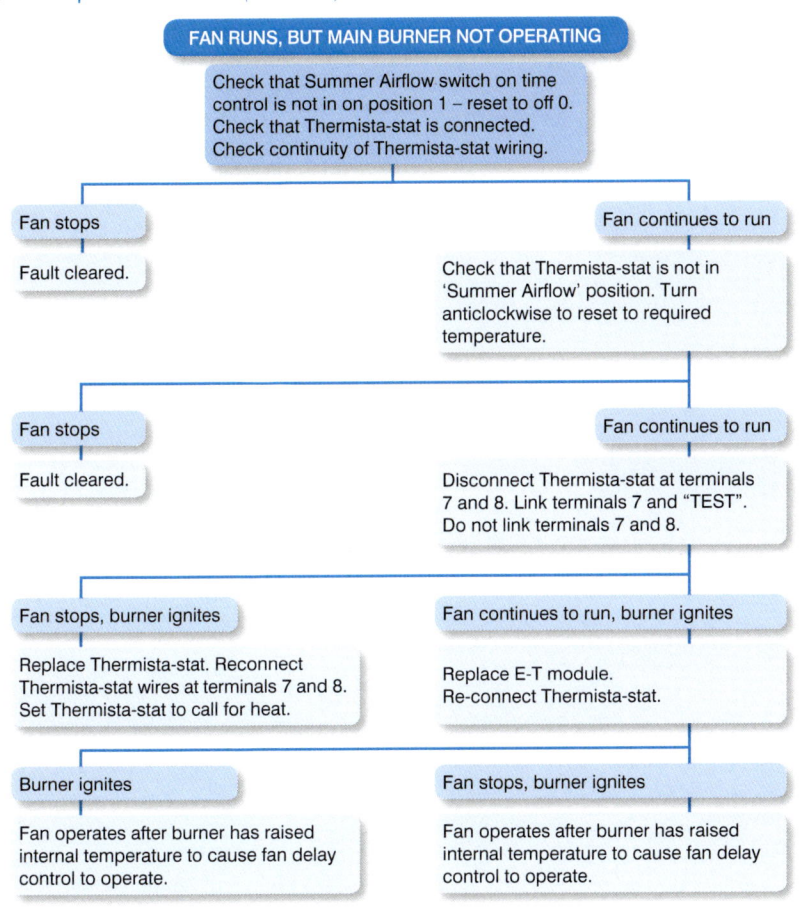

FAN RUNS, BUT MAIN BURNER NOT OPERATING

Check that Summer Airflow switch on time control is not in on position 1 – reset to off 0.
Check that Thermista-stat is connected.
Check continuity of Thermista-stat wiring.

Fan stops
Fault cleared.

Fan continues to run
Check that Thermista-stat is not in 'Summer Airflow' position. Turn anticlockwise to reset to required temperature.

Fan stops
Fault cleared.

Fan continues to run
Disconnect Thermista-stat at terminals 7 and 8. Link terminals 7 and "TEST". Do not link terminals 7 and 8.

Fan stops, burner ignites
Replace Thermista-stat. Reconnect Thermista-stat wires at terminals 7 and 8. Set Thermista-stat to call for heat.

Fan continues to run, burner ignites
Replace E-T module.
Re-connect Thermista-stat.

Burner ignites
Fan operates after burner has raised internal temperature to cause fan delay control to operate.

Fan stops, burner ignites
Fan operates after burner has raised internal temperature to cause fan delay control to operate.

Special note – The System E-T model is fitted with a diagnostic light-emitting diode (LED) visible through a hole in the model cover. If the LED is flashing, this means:

- The fan is not connected, or
- The energy capacitor is not connected, or
- There is a short circuit in the fan supply.

Practical Tasks

The practical tasks link directly with the performance criteria of the Nationally Accredited Certification assessments (ACS) for DAH1 – Ducted Air Heaters.

Your tutor will assess your practical training requirements before undertaking the practical tasks and may require you to:

- Complete all the activities identified, or
- Complete some of the activities identified (based on previous experience).

You should have access to the appliance manufacturer's instructions. You may also use the knowledge manuals associated with the course.

You will be given the following activities to be carried out:

- Installation of an open flued ducted air heater. The flue systems will be pre-installed. Specific installation tasks on other appliances may also be required.
- Commissioning an open flued ducted air heater.
- Servicing an open flued ducted air heater.
- Diagnosing typical faults on a range of gas ducted air heaters.

To assist you in the process of carrying out the work, you should complete the information required in the following pro-forma.

Note – To complete all activities you will be required to work on more than one appliance.

Pre-installation/exchange checks

Task 1

Is the proposed appliance location in a permissible position?   Yes   No

If no, identify the problem:

BPEC   Module 20

Task 2
Visually check the existing pipework system and note any defects below, and any remedial actions necessary, e.g. pipework fixings, pipe size, materials etc.

Task 3
Check to ensure that the gas supply has been effectively isolated prior to the work commencing.
Has the gas supply been effectively isolated?   Yes   No

If no, what remedial action is necessary?

Task 4
Carry out a gas tightness test of the existing pipework installation prior to the work commencing.
Does the tightness test indicate that the pipework system is leak free or within permissible tolerances?
                                                                      Yes   No

If no, what remedial actions are necessary?

April 2017   © BPEC

Task 5
Visually check the entire flue system to confirm that it conforms with manufacturer/British Standard requirements.
Is the flue system acceptable?　　　　　　　　　　　　　　　　Yes　　No

If no, what remedial action is necessary?

Task 6
Visually check the appliance to be installed and identify whether there are any obvious defects.
Is the appliance in a suitable condition?　　　　　　　　　　　　Yes　　No

If no, what remedial action is necessary?

Task 7
Check that the plenum base duct is sized correctly for the appliance to be installed/exchanged.
Is the plenum base duct suitable?　　　　　　　　　　　　　　　Yes　　No

If no, what remedial action is necessary?

Task 8
Check that all ducting and blanking plates are mechanically sealed and free of leaks.
Are the ducting and blanking plate seals acceptable?   Yes   No

If no, what remedial action is necessary?

Task 9
Check that the return air duct is sized correctly for the appliance to be installed/exchanged.
Is the return air duct suitable?   Yes   No

If no, what remedial action is necessary?

Installation of the appliance
Task 10
Connect the appliance to the flue system following manufacturer's installation procedures.

Task 11
Connect the gas pipework to the appliance.

Task 12
Carry out a gas tightness test on the installation.
Is the reading acceptable?   Yes   No

| BPEC | Domestic Warm Air (DAH1) |

Task 13
On an open flued air heater check that the flue connection has been made satisfactorily. Carry out a flue flow test on the appliance.

Is the flue system satisfactory? Yes No

If no, what remedial actions are necessary?

Commissioning the appliance

Task 1
Have all preliminary checks been made? Yes No

Task 2
Are the filter, fan and fan compartment free of obstructions? Yes No

Task 3
Are the return air, relief air and ventilation air installations adequate? Yes No

Task 4
Is the fan speed set correctly? Yes No

Task 5
Is the application/installation purged of air? Yes No

Task 6
Is the working pressure at the appliance correct? Yes No

Task 7
Are the burner flame picture, stability and ignition correct? Yes No

Task 8
Is a spillage test on an open flued appliance confirming that the flue system is operating correctly? Yes No

Task 9
Are the user controls operating correctly? Yes No

BPEC   Module 20

Task 10
Are the safety (flame supervision) devices operating correctly?   Yes   No

Task 11
Are the temperature controls operating correctly?   Yes   No

Task 12
Is the plenum adequately sealed to ducted air heater?   Yes   No

Task 13
Is the return air duct positively sealed to the ducted air heater?   Yes   No

Task 14
Are all ducting and blanking plates mechanically sealed and free from leaks?   Yes   No

Tasks 1-14 – Note any deficiencies identified during the commissioning procedure in this box:

Task 15
Subject to the installation being satisfactorily commissioned, explain the safe operation of the appliance to the customer leaving all installation and user instructions, benchmark log book on site.

Servicing an appliance
Task 16 Carry out preliminary checks

Operation of appliance	Satisfactory	Unsatisfactory
The installation	Satisfactory	Unsatisfactory
Ventilation	Satisfactory	Unsatisfactory
Warning notices	Satisfactory	Unsatisfactory
Flue and flue terminal	Satisfactory	Unsatisfactory
Plenum duct base	Satisfactory	Unsatisfactory
Blanking plates and ducting seals	Satisfactory	Unsatisfactory
Return air duct	Satisfactory	Unsatisfactory
Size of return air duct	Satisfactory	Unsatisfactory
Size of return air grille	Satisfactory	Unsatisfactory
Atmospheric sensing device fitted	Yes	No
Signs of spillage	Yes	No

April 2017   © BPEC

| BPEC | Domestic Warm Air (DAH1) |

Task 17

Carry out a full service on a gas air heater. The following table is included for your use. Note any components in the box below which may need replacement.

Component	Serviced/Cleaned Yes/No	Requiring replacement Yes/No	Not fitted to appliance
Burner(s)/injector(s)			
Primary air port			
Combustion chamber			
Heat exchanger			
Ignition device			
Thermista-stat			
Overheat limit switch			
Fan switch/control			
Flame supervision device			
Fan			
Air filter			

Note defects identified here:

Fault diagnosis

Task 18

You will be given a number of appliances with specific gas safety faults. Your tutor will advise on the number of faults per appliance. You should list the faults associated with each appliance below.

Appliance 1 – Faults identified:

Appliance 2 – Faults identified:

Appliance 3 – Faults identified:

Appliance 4 – Faults identified:

Appliance 5 – Faults identified:

Knowledge Questions

Domestic Warm Air – DAH1

Section 1 – Types of Appliances and their Operating Principles

1. What are the three different types of ducted air heater?
   a)
   b)
   c)

2. What are the names of the three separate control devices of a standard multi-functional control valve fitted to a ducted air heater?
   a)
   b)
   c)

3. What is the purpose of the following components which may be fitted to air heaters?
   a) Fan switch/controls
   b) Limit switch

4. What temperature does the manufacturer normally set the limit switch at?

5. What is the purpose of a lint arrestor fitted to an air heater burner?

6. What type of ducted air heater is most suitable for wall mounting?

7. On a modairflow control system, is it true that the air heater controls automatically adjust the operation of both the gas burner and the air circulation fan?

8. What are the names of the two components in the pilot assembly of a fan assisted appliance using a flame supervision device working on the flame rectification principle?
   a)
   b)

BPEC   Module 20

Section 2 – Installation and Commissioning of Ducted Air Heaters

1. Can an open flued air heater be installed in a bathroom?

2. Is a sealed duct from return air grilles to open flued air heaters essential to prevent air being drawn into the heater and interfering with the performance of the flue?

3. What are the four key requirements which must be met when installing an air heater in a compartment?
    a)
    b)
    c)
    d)

4. What is the normal temperature rise across the heat exchanger from the return air to discharge?

5. What effect does an air filter blocked with dust have on the heat exchanger?

6. Will a blocked air filter affect the limit switch and cause the burner to cycle?

7. When a plenum base duct is used, is there is a need to provide insulation if the air heater is situated on a combustible floor?

8. Should all ductwork in the room or internal space in which the air heater is installed be mechanically secured and sealed with ducting tape?

9. Do appliances for slot fix installations need to be specially designed:
    a) To prevent obstruction of the draught diverter?
    b) To prevent obstruction of the return inlets?
    c) To prevent a build up of dust in the appliance?
    d) To enclose the area above the heater?
    e) To prevent heat damage to the floor?
    f) To ensure that the combustion air inlets are not obstructed?
    g) To prevent noise when the appliance case touches the wall?

10. What is the minimum clearance distance between a ducted air heater and the wall of a compartment?

BPEC   Domestic Warm Air (DAH1)

Section 3 – Service, Maintenance and Repair of Ducted Air Heaters

1. Which three things can occur when the heat exchanger on a ducted air heater develops a crack?
   a)
   b)
   c)

2. An open flued air heater which you have been asked to look at has been described by the customer as making a loud 'bang-like explosive noise' when it lights up. What are two possible causes for this?
   a)
   b)

3. You have been asked to look at an air heater which the customer says is continually going off and coming on again. What are five likely causes of the problem?
   a)
   b)
   c)
   d)
   e)

4. Yellow flames are being discharged from an open flued gas air heater burner which has not been serviced for three years. What is the most likely cause of the problem?

5. You have been called to a ducted air heater on which the main burner operates intermittently with the fan running. What are four likely causes of the problem?
   a)
   b)
   c)
   d)

6. You have been called to a ducted air heater on which the pilot will not light. What are five likely causes of the problem?
   a)
   b)
   c)
   d)
   e)

7. A pilot light on a ducted air heater lights but goes out on releasing start button during light-up. What are the three possible causes?
   a)
   b)
   c)

© BPEC   April 2017

Model Answers

Section 1 – Types of Appliances and their Operating Principles

1. a) Downflow.
   b) Upflow.
   c) Horizontal flow.

2. a) Constant pressure governor.
   b) Flame supervision device.
   c) Solenoid valve.

3. a) The fan switch turns the fan on when the heater reaches the set operating temperature and when it reaches a low set point.
   b) The limit switch (or thermistor control) turns the gas valve on or off to maintain the correct operating temperature.

4. 82°C.

5. To prevent lint from entering the main burner via the air supply.

6. Horizontal flow.

7. Yes.

8. a) Pilot burner.
   b) Ignition/conductance/rectification electrode.

Section 2 – Installation and Commissioning of Ducted Air Heaters

1. No.

2. Yes.

3. You should have chosen four of the following:
   a) Be fixed, rigid structures with internal surfaces that comply with any special requirements of the appliance manufacturer. Should have a minimum clearance of 75mm at the sides and rear and 75mm at the front (450mm for service access).
   b) Allow access for inspection.
   c) Allow access for maintenance.
   d) Utilise a warning notice advising against:
      – It being used for the purposes of storage.
      – Blocking or restricting of any air vents or grilles into the compartment.
   e) Be ventilated in accordance with the requirements of BS 5440 Flues and ventilation.

4. 45°C to 55°C.

5. Cause the heat exchanger to overheat.

6. Yes.

7. No.

8. Yes.
9. a) Yes.
   b) Yes.
   c) No.
   d) Yes.
   e) No.
   f) Yes.
   g) No.
10. 75mm.

Section 3 – Service, Maintenance and Repair of Ducted Air Heaters

1. a) Air can leak into the combustion chamber and affect combustion.
   b) Poor combustion combined with spillage from an open flue could cause toxic fumes to circulate the building.
   c) Products of combustion could leak into the air distribution system.

2. a) Poor size of pilot flame – either requiring adjustment or with a partially blocked injector.
   b) The pilot burner is not correctly positioned in relation to the main burner.

3. a) Defective limit switch.
   b) Blocked air filter.
   c) Defective fan.
   d) Down draught.
   e) Gas pressure too high.

4. Burner choked/blocked with lint.

5. a) Gas rate on burner pressure too high.
   b) Air filter or return air path restricted.
   c) Excessive temperature rise.
   d) Excessive number of outlets closed.

6. a) No gas supply to heater.
   b) Gas supply pipe not purged.
   c) Pilot orifice restricted.
   d) Pilot aeration port obstructed.
   e) Piezo system fault.

7. You should have chosen three of the following:
   a) Connection between thermocouple and multifunctional control not secure.
   b) Faulty multi functional control.
   c) Faulty thermocouple.
   d) Draught affecting pilot flame.
   e) Contaminated combustion air.